Bayswater

Teacher's Manual 3

Für Klasse 7 an Realschulen, Regelschulen, Mittelschulen
und Sekundarschulen

Verlag Moritz Diesterweg

Frankfurt am Main

Bayswater

Teacher's Manual 3
für Klasse 7 an Realschulen, Regelschulen, Mittelschulen und Sekundarschulen

Herausgegeben von: Christoph Edelhoff
Erarbeitet von: Dr. Ursula Karbe
unter Berücksichtigung von Ideen von Gisela Schultz-Steinbach

Weitere Zusatzmaterialien zum Schülerbuch (3-425-03103-1)
- Practicebook zum Schülerbuch (Best.-Nr. 3-425-03113-9)
- Kassette zum Schülerbuch (Best.-Nr. 3-425-08712-6), identischer Inhalt wie CD
- CD zum Schülerbuch (Best.-Nr. 3-425-08703-7), identischer Inhalt wie Kassette
- Folien (Best.-Nr. 3-425-03133-3)
- Practicebook mit Multimedia Language Trainer (Best.-Nr. 3-425-03153-8)

ISBN 3-425-09103-4

© 2001 Verlag Moritz Diesterweg GmbH & Co, Frankfurt am Main

Redaktion und Satz: p.u.n.k.t.genau Caroline Byrt, Speyer
Illustrationen: Friederike Großekettler, Hameln; Steffen Gumpert, Hildesheim
Umschlaggestaltung: Boros, Wuppertal
Druck: fgb · freiburger graphische betriebe
                       www.fgb.de

Inhaltsverzeichnis

Zeichenerklärung:

CD	Copymaster	S	Schüler/in/nen
		S1	erste/r Schüler/in
		L	Lehrer/in
Spiel	Folie/Transparency	**Differenzierung:**	
			Zusatzaufgabe
Portfolio			

Einleitung

Bayswater ist ein modernes Unterrichtswerk, das den Anforderungen der aktuellen Lehrpläne bzw. Rahmenrichtlinien entspricht, grundlegenden didaktisch-methodischen Prinzipien gerecht wird und neueste Erkenntnisse der Spracherwerbsforschung sowie der Fachdidaktik berücksichtigt:

- Die Befähigung der Schülerinnen und Schüler zu fremdsprachlicher Kommunikation steht im Mittelpunkt. Dabei orientiert sich das Werk an der Lebenswelt heutiger Schülerinnen und Schüler, deren Erfahrungen insbesondere durch multikulturelles Miteinander und internationalisierte Medien geprägt sind. Vorkenntnisse und bereits erworbene Fähigkeiten der Schülerinnen und Schüler werden systematisch einbezogen, so dass diese den Lernprozess aktiv mitgestalten können.
- **Bayswater** bietet authentischen Sprachgebrauch. Mit unterschiedlichsten Textsorten aus wichtigen Lebensbereichen und vielseitigen Aufgaben werden Schülerinnen und Schüler zu einem Transfer der Themen und Probleme auf die eigene Lebenssituation, zum „Probehandeln" angeregt. Dabei verstehen sie weit mehr Sprachmaterial, als sie produktiv beim Sprechen und Schreiben anwenden sollen.
- Zentrales Anliegen ist die fremdsprachliche Umsetzung von Redeabsichten. Diesem Ziel sind die lexikalische und grammatische Progression untergeordnet; grammatische Strukturen haben lediglich dienende Funktion für das Verstehen und Ausdrücken von Inhalten. Der Wortschatz wird thematisch und situativ eingeführt, ihm gebührt größere Aufmerksamkeit als der Grammatik, da Wörter die Grundlage jeder Äußerung darstellen. Viele Übungen vernetzen neues Vokabular mit bereits bekanntem zu Wortfeldern, mit gezielten Übungen zur Erschließung neuer Texte wird lexikalisches Vorwissen aktiviert, um den Wortschatz auf sicherem Fundament weiter auszubauen.
  Im Lehrwerk wird zwischen Gesamtwortschatz und Lernwortschatz unterschieden: Letzterer erscheint in den Wortlisten zu den *Themes* (*Words*, TB ab Seite 137) wie auch im *Dictionary English-German* (TB ab Seite 168) fett gedruckt. Das deutsch-englische Wörterverzeichnis (TB ab Seite 193) unterstützt Schülerinnen und Schüler bei der Lösung produktiver Aufgaben.
- Die sichere Aneignung der Redemittel wird durch ein Spiralcurriculum unterstützt, indem alle wichtigen Pensen nach ihrer Einführung in späteren Kapiteln mehrmals wiederkehren und eine konzentrische Erweiterung erfahren. Auch Strukturen aus vorangegangenen Lernjahren werden im *lif*-Teil wiederholt und gefestigt (*Remember: ...*).
- **Bayswater** ist interkulturellem Lernen verpflichtet. Vielfältige Einblicke in den Alltag und die Traditionen eines ebenfalls stark multikulturellen europäischen Nachbarstaates regen Schülerinnen und Schüler zu Vergleichen mit ihrer eigenen Umwelt an und lassen sie Verständnis für landestypische Besonderheiten entwickeln. Darüber hinaus werden ausländische Mitschülerinnen und Mitschüler und Nachbarn mit ihren unterschiedlichen kulturellen Erfahrungen verstärkt in den Unterricht einbezogen, da sie den Schülerinnen und Schülern die „Normalität des Fremden" und Ungewohnten sehr anschaulich und überzeugend nahe bringen können.
- Mit **Bayswater** wird ganzheitliches Lernen gewährleistet. Ein Lernen, an dem Verstand und Gefühl ebenso beteiligt sind wie alle Sinne, kann Schülerinnen und Schüler mit ihren unterschiedlichen Fähigkeiten, Bedürfnissen und Interessen ebenso ansprechen wie es den Anforderungen des Sprachaneignungsprozesses gerecht zu werden vermag. Die bewusste Arbeit erstreckt sich dabei vorrangig auf das Bewältigen von Redeabsichten, das Bewusstwerden des eigenen Lern- und Arbeitsstils sowie das Wahrnehmen der sprachlichen Umgebung der Kinder außerhalb der Schule, da im eigenen Entdecken eine hohe motivierende Kraft liegt.
  Vielseitige, abwechslungsreiche Übungen und Aufgaben mit einer hohen Wiederholungsfrequenz von Äußerungen sorgen für einen flüssigen Sprachgebrauch, der für reale Kommunikationssituationen unbedingt erforderlich ist.
  Durch humorvolle, aber auch ernsthafte und nachdenklich stimmende Themen und Texte werden bei den Lernenden vielfältige Emotionen ausgelöst, damit sie Sprache erleben und nicht nur erlernen.
  Die praktische Komponente des Lernens schließt die Arbeit der Hände beim Gestalten von Postern, Zeichnungen usw. wie auch die Bewegung des Körpers ein. Diese Elemente haben nicht allein eine beträchtliche behaltensfördernde Wirkung, sondern bieten auch allen Beteiligten eine Chance, sich in den Unterricht einzubringen.

- Da zu Beginn der Klasse 7 häufig Schülerinnen und Schüler aus verschiedenen Schulen mit sehr unterschiedlichem Leistungsprofil zusammenkommen, gebührt differenzierendem Arbeiten große Aufmerksamkeit, wofür *Textbook* und *Teacher's Manual* zahlreiche Anregungen enthalten. Für die innere Differenzierung bieten die A- und B-Teile der einzelnen *Themes*, die Zusatzaufgaben (mit einer Sonne versehen) sowie die *Optionals* vielerlei Möglichkeiten und Anreize. Um allen Leistungsniveaus wie auch Lerntypen gerecht zu werden, bietet **Bayswater** Material an, das visuell, auditiv und praktisch orientierte Lerner gleichermaßen motiviert und dem Grundsatz des ganzheitlichen Lernens entspricht.

Die Konzeption von Bayswater

Thematischer Aufbau

Jedes der acht *Themes* behandelt in den A- und B-Teilen jeweils verschiedene Aspekte eines übergeordneten Themas. So geht es zum Beispiel unter dem Thema *No man is an island* um persönliche Probleme und Sorgen, aber auch um das Schicksal Robinson Crusoes, um Einsamkeit und Kinder geschiedener Eltern; unter dem Thema *Going public* erfahren die Kinder etwas über den *Notting Hill Carnival* als ein großes Fest, sie lernen zugleich London und seine Sehenswürdigkeiten intensiver kennen. Damit werden die Themen *Celebrations* und *Around London* aus **Bayswater 2** wieder aufgegriffen und erweitert.

Da die A- und B-Teile nicht bestimmten didaktischen Funktionen zugeordnet sind, ist es völlig unproblematisch, sich je nach Klassensituation und Interessen der Lerngruppe auf bestimmte Teile daraus zu konzentrieren.

Schauplatz und Figuren

Die Handlung ist im Stadtteil Bayswater in der Nähe von Kensington Gardens und Hyde Park, also weitgehend im Zentrum Londons angesiedelt. Weitere touristische Attraktionen Londons und Schottlands rücken in den Mittelpunkt der Betrachtungen. Ein spezieller Fokus wird auf Indien gelegt, das in der Vergangenheit ein wichtiges Land des Commonwealth war. Heute leben zahlreiche Familien indischer Herkunft in Großbritannien, sie sind zu einem festen Bestandteil der Bevölkerung und des kulturellen Lebens geworden.

In der zentralen *constellation of characters* sind weibliche und männliche Rollen ausgewogen verteilt und verschiedene ethnische Gruppen berücksichtigt. Die Figuren bewegen sich in einem soziokulturellen Kontext, der durch typische Phänomene moderner westlicher Gesellschaften gekennzeichnet ist, wie etwa allein erziehende Elternteile neben Kernfamilien usw.

Schülerorientierte Aufgaben

Die konsequente Schülerorientierung wird in **Bayswater** durch die Wahl der Themen sowie die mündlichen und für das Portfolio schriftlich zu verfassenden Texte über die eigene Erlebniswelt erreicht. Einzel-, aber auch Partner- und Gruppenarbeit erfordern interaktives kommunikatives Handeln sowie das Einfügen in eine Gemeinschaft, das Akzeptieren anderer Auffassungen oder die Übernahme von Verantwortung für die Lernergebnisse einer Gruppe. Die Arbeitsanweisungen für Partner-, Gruppen- und Projektarbeit sind durch Symbole, Illustrationen oder Sprechblasen veranschaulicht. Der selbstständigen Arbeit der Schülerinnen und Schüler wird weiter Raum gegeben, denn sie müssen die Bedeutsamkeit des Lernens für sich erkennen, indem sie Möglichkeiten erhalten, ihren Lernprozess aktiv mitzugestalten, Inhalte auszuwählen und zu bearbeiten und dabei Erfolg zu haben. Vorschläge enthalten die didaktisch-methodischen Hinweise zu den einzelnen *Themes*.

Für Phasen differenzierender Arbeit, in denen die Lernenden still arbeiten müssen, empfiehlt sich die Anlage einer *Treasure box*, in der auf Karteikarten, in kleinen Heften oder auf laminierten Blättern fortlaufend Texte unterschiedlicher Textsorten, aber auch Aufgaben und Redemittel gesammelt werden, die zur Wiederholung und Festigung genutzt werden können.

Entwicklung der vier Fertigkeiten

Das Material von **Bayswater** entwickelt kontinuierlich und ausgewogen alle vier Fertigkeiten: Hörverstehen, Sprechen, Lesen und Schreiben.

- Zu jedem Kapitel gibt es Hörverstehensaufgaben im *Textbook* und im *Practicebook* – zum Teil mit, zum Teil ohne schriftliche Textvorlage, den Gegebenheiten realer Kommunikation entsprechend.
- Dem Sprechen ist eine breite Palette von Aufgaben gewidmet. Es nimmt eine zentrale Stellung im Fremdsprachenunterricht ein, da diese Fertigkeit alle anderen positiv beeinflusst. Zahlreiche Sprechanlässe ergeben sich bei der Auswertung von Texten, aber auch durch Rollenspiele und andere Sprachspiele. Die Folien bieten zusätzliche Sprechanlässe.
- Das Lesen dient vornehmlich der Informationsentnahme, der Vorbereitung auf nicht sprachliche Tätigkeiten wie Kochen und Backen sowie der Unterhaltung. So ist vor allem bei humorvollen Texten auf eine umfangreiche Textauswertung zu verzichten und *Reading for fun* zu praktizieren. Dies sollte auch durch den Einsatz kleiner Lektüren unterstützt werden, die von den Kindern frei gewählt werden und nicht Gegenstand des Unterrichts sind.
  Um Schülerinnen und Schülern den Umgang mit längeren Texten zu ermöglichen, werden sukzessive das *skimming* (globales Leseverstehen) und das *scanning* (selektives Leseverstehen) entwickelt, um allmählich vom intensiven (Wort-für-Wort-)Lesen wegzukommen. Das laute Lesen hat in den meisten Fällen nur eine Mittlerfunktion zur Entwicklung des Sprechens und ist daher sparsam einzusetzen.
- Fähigkeiten und Fertigkeiten auf dem Gebiet des Schreibens werden über verschiedene Wege weiter ausgebaut. Vorbereitende Aufgaben leiten die Lerner beispielsweise dazu an, Wörter zu gruppieren, Wortfelder bzw. Assoziogramme zusammenzustellen und Stichwörter zu sammeln. Die Textproduktion umfasst eine Vielzahl verschiedener Textsorten. So fertigen die Schülerinnen und Schüler unter anderem Postkarten, Briefe, Texte in der Ich-Form, Gedichte, Berichte, Collagen und Reportagen an. Die Schreibübungen enthalten Hilfen durch Beispiele oder sprachliche Vorgaben, die auch schwächeren Schülerinnen und Schülern die Möglichkeit eröffnen, sich schriftlich zu äußern.

Lern- und Arbeitstechniken

Die in **Bayswater 1** und **2** begonnene Vermittlung von Lern- und Arbeitstechniken wird mit Band 3 weitergeführt. Dazu gehören die Sozialformen der Partner- und Gruppenarbeit, das Notieren, Sammeln, Ergänzen und Verknüpfen sprachlicher Elemente, der Umgang mit dem Wörterbuch und anderen Nachschlagewerken sowie das Nutzen von Visualisierungshilfen. Tipps und Erläuterungen dazu finden sich im Übungsbereich und im Anhang des *Textbook*. Ein besonderer Schwerpunkt liegt in Band 3 auf einer systematischen Weiterführung der Projektarbeit mit schülergerechter Schritt-für-Schritt-Anleitung.

Besonderheiten des Werks

Differenzierung

Sonnenübungen sind zusätzliche Übungen, die ein weitergehendes Lernangebot für leistungsstarke Schülerinnen und Schüler bieten. Dabei wird sichergestellt, dass keine zusätzlichen aktiven Vokabeln eingeführt werden. Häufig handelt es sich um kreative Übungen oder eigene Textproduktionen.

Das Portfolio-Konzept

Die Vorschläge des Europarats zu einem *European Language Portfolio* gaben den Anlass, ein Portfolio-Konzept in **Bayswater** zu integrieren, das sich im Englischunterricht leicht umsetzen lässt. Grundidee des Portfolio ist es, das autonome Lernen zu fördern. Zwei Aspekte tragen in **Bayswater** wesentlich dazu bei:

1. Individuelle Dokumentation der Lernfortschritte

Die im *Textbook* und *Practicebook* verankerten Portfolio-Aufgaben lassen im Verlauf des Schuljahres eine Sammlung von Schülerarbeiten entstehen, die individuelle Lernfortschritte dokumentiert. Der Begriff „Portfolio" meint nichts anderes als eine Sammelmappe, in der die Lerner sowohl kreative Produkte wie Zeichnungen und beschriftete Collagen als auch auf Englisch verfasste Texte über sich selbst aufbewahren. Das Sammeln solcher Produkte kann die Motivation entscheidend fördern und trägt zur Entwicklung und Pflege eines persönlichen Lernstils bei.

2. Selbsteinschätzung der Lerner

Ein wichtiger Bestandteil der Lernerautonomie ist die Reflexion des eigenen Lernens. Die Fragen „Was habe ich gelernt?" und „Wie habe ich gelernt?" sind wichtig für die Entwicklung eines eigenen Lernstils. Gegenstände dieser Selbstreflexion sind die vier Fertigkeiten Hörverstehen, Sprechen, Schreiben, Lesen sowie das Lernen von Wortschatz und grammatischen Strukturen. Im *Practicebook* befinden sich Portfolio-Selbsteinschätzungsbögen, mit denen die Lerner ihre persönlichen Stärken und Schwächen erkennen können. Nach *Theme 4* wird eine Zwischen-, im Anschluss an *Theme 8* eine Abschlussbewertung der Leistungen in den einzelnen Fähigkeitsbereichen vorgenommen.

Einige Hinweise zur Umsetzung des Portfolio-Konzepts im Englischunterricht

Das *English Portfolio* kann ein einfacher Schnellhefter/Ordner oder auch eine Sammelmappe sein, wie sie für den Kunstunterricht üblich ist. Es bleibt Lehrenden und Lernenden offen, wie sie diese Mappe gestalten: Sie kann beklebt, bemalt oder mit einem Deckblatt *(My English Portfolio; Name; School, Class)* versehen werden. In ihrem Portfolio können die Schülerinnen und Schüler selbstverständlich auch englischsprachige Produkte sammeln, die nicht aus dem Unterricht hervorgegangen sind (z. B. Briefe von Brieffreund/innen, E-Mails, Realien aus dem Urlaub usw.).
Das Portfolio ist als Angebot, nicht als verpflichtender Bestandteil des Lernprozesses konzipiert. Es ist absichtlich sehr offen angelegt, die Lerner selbst wählen aus, was sie in ihr Portfolio aufnehmen. Keinesfalls sollte die Sammelmappe der Leistungsmessung dienen, wenngleich sich ihre Inhalte durchaus mit Testinhalten kombinieren lassen. Wichtig ist ein ernsthafter Umgang mit dem Portfolio, wozu auch die kontinuierliche Weiterführung des Konzepts im nachfolgenden Schuljahr und bei eventuellem Lehrerwechsel gehört.
Verschiedene Bundesländer führen bereits ein vom Europarat akkreditiertes Sprachenportfolio (mit Gütesiegel) ein, das aus einem Sprachenpass, einer Sprachenbiographie und einem Dossier (eben der oben beschriebenen Sammelmappe) besteht. Es soll künftig über Erst- und Zweitsprache, gelernte Fremdsprachen und deren Niveau Auskunft geben sowie dokumentieren, zu welchen Leistungen ein Lerner fähig ist. Mit diesen drei Bestandteilen wird das Sprachenportfolio künftig bei Bewerbungen im In- und Ausland ein sehr aussagekräftiges Instrument sein, sehr viel aussagekräftiger als Zeugnisnoten.

Folgende Elemente in **Bayswater 3** eignen sich für das Portfolio:
Theme 1: TB: B6, B7; PB: A11
Theme 2: TB: A4, A8, B5
Theme 3: TB: A8, B3b), B4, B5; PB: B5
Theme 4: TB: A4b, A9, B2b), B5, B7; PB: B4
Theme 5: TB: A4c, A5, B9; PB: A5
Theme 6: TB: A8, A10c), B8; PB: B4
Theme 7: TB: A3, A7, B5; PB: B4
Theme 8: TB: A5a), B4b), B6.

Landeskunde

In der Rubrik *People and places* im *Textbook* erhalten Schülerinnen und Schüler in englischer Sprache Informationen über Großbritannien (speziell Schottland), London und Indien. In den vergangenen Jahrhunderten gab es zahlreiche Einwanderungsströme von Indien nach Großbritannien, so dass in London heute die größte indische Gemeinde in Europa mit über 400 000 Menschen lebt.
Ein Ziel in Verbindung mit der Erarbeitung landeskundlicher Kenntnisse stellt die Erweiterung der Allgemeinbildung der Schülerinnen und Schüler dar; sie sollen jedoch auch Bezüge zu ihren eigenen Lebensgewohnheiten und dem eigenen Land herstellen, um tatsächlich interkulturelles Lernen, das zwischen verschiedenen Kulturen vermittelt, zu ermöglichen. In Texten und Bildern können die Kinder eine Fülle landeskundlicher Details entdecken und sich so mit der Zielkultur und dem konkreten Schauplatz vertraut machen. Geografische Details können den Karten Londons (vordere innere Umschlagseite), Schottlands (TB Seite 100) und der Britischen Inseln (hintere innere Umschlagseite) entnommen werden.

Die Werkteile von Bayswater

1. Das Schülerbuch (Textbook ➔ TB)

1.1 Aufbau
Bayswater 3 besteht aus acht Lerneinheiten *(Themes)* mit je zwei thematischen Unterkapiteln (A, B), acht *Optionals* sowie dem Anhang. Die *Themes* sind so angelegt, dass sie zur Auswahl ermutigen. Keineswegs müssen jeder Text oder jede Übung gleichermaßen bearbeitet werden. Vorschläge für sinnvolle Übungsabfolgen einschließlich Erweiterungsmöglichkeiten finden sich in den Übersichten vor jedem *Theme* in diesem *Teacher's Manual.*

1.2 Introduction: Back to Bayswater
Auch zu Beginn des dritten Lernjahrs wird in einer *warming-up*-Phase das Wissen aus den ersten beiden Lernjahren reaktiviert.

1.3 Language in focus (lif)
Dieser Teil bietet zu jedem *Theme* des *Textbook* drei wichtige Elemente:
Unter der Überschrift *Say it in English* sind die neuen Redemittel des *Theme* zusammengestellt. Da diese Zusammenstellung eine äußerst hilfreiche Erleichterung bei produktiven Aufgaben darstellt, ist zu empfehlen, dass die Lerner diese Übersichten in einen Hefter oder ein Ringbuch übernehmen, die im Laufe der Lernjahre ergänzt werden.
Beispiel:
Bayswater 1: um Erlaubnis bitten: *Can I have an ice-cream? Can we go to the park?*
Bayswater 2: fragen, ob man etwas darf: *Can I wear these jeans?*
Bayswater 3: um Erlaubnis bitten: *May we listen to music in our room?*
Wenn Lerner diese Übersichten über mehrere Jahre führen, werden die bereits bekannten Redemittel bei Neueinträgen immanent wiederholt. Mit wenig Mehraufwand lassen sich solche Übersichten auch noch im Nachhinein erstellen, um eine solide Ausgangsbasis für Klasse 7 zu schaffen.

Im zweiten Element der *lif*-Teile, den *Word fields*, wird neuer Wortschatz nach Wortfeldern geordnet. Dies unterstützt die Verknüpfung von Wörtern wie auch das Einprägen. Da die Wortfelder nicht vollständig ausgefüllt sind, haben Schülerinnen und Schüler die Möglichkeit, die Felder in ihre Hefte zu übernehmen und selbst ausführlich zu gestalten. Die Bildhaftigkeit wie auch die Motorik des Schreibens begünstigen das Lernen und Behalten.

Der *Grammar*-Teil ist schülerfreundlich und anschaulich gestaltet. Dazu tragen Übersichten, Skizzen und farbige Kontrastierungen bei. Neue grammatische Strukturen werden ausführlich auf Deutsch erklärt und mit Beispielen erläutert, bereits bekannte grammatische Strukturen werden in mit *Remember* gekennzeichneten und blau unterlegten Kästen wiederholt und gefestigt.

1.4 Words
In den Wortlisten nach Kapiteln sind alle Wörter in der Reihenfolge ihres Auftretens in den *Themes* aufgelistet. Diese Listen sind dreispaltig: Links stehen die englischen Wörter mit Lautschrift, die mittlere Spalte enthält die deutschen Entsprechungen, und in der rechten Spalte finden sich Visualisierungen, Hinweise auf sprachliche Unregelmäßigkeiten und Beispielsätze. Der Lernwortschatz ist fett gedruckt. Darüber hinaus enthalten die *Words* Tipps zum Vokabellernen.

1.5 Die Dictionaries
Zwei alphabetische Wortlisten enthalten den Lernwortschatz aus den Bänden 1 und 2 sowie den gesamten Wortschatz aus **Bayswater 3**. Im englisch-deutschen Verzeichnis ist der Unterschied zwischen Lern- und Gesamtwortschatz wie auch im chronologischen Vokabular typografisch gekennzeichnet, außerdem ist das jeweils erste Auftreten mit Band, Kapitel sowie Kapitelteil angegeben. In die Liste wurden auch die Wörter aus den Arbeitsanweisungen aufgenommen. Der deutsch-englische Teil dient vorrangig dem Nachschlagen bei kommunikativen Aufgaben.

1.6 Names
Diese Liste enthält alle Vor-, Familien-, Orts-, Länder- und sonstige Namen der Bände 1–3.

1.7 Irregular verbs
Für alle ab **Bayswater 1** eingeführten Verben können hier der Infinitiv, das *simple past* und das *past participle* mit Lautschrift und deutscher Entsprechung des Infinitivs nachgeschlagen werden.

1.7 Glossary
Das grammatische Glossar dient als Orientierungshilfe und umfasst die lateinische bzw. deutsche Bezeichnung einer grammatischen Erscheinung, die englische Entsprechung, einige Beispiele und Hinweise auf die entsprechenden *lif*-Teile.

2 Das Arbeitsbuch (Practicebook ➜ PB)
Als integrierter Bestandteil von **Bayswater** folgt das *Practicebook* in seiner formalen Gliederung dem *Textbook* und entspricht dessen didaktisch-methodischen Prinzipien. Es enthält weitere Höraufgaben und ergänzt das Angebot des *Textbook* vor allem im Bereich der Schreibfertigkeit. Das *Practicebook* eignet sich zum Einsatz in der Klasse wie für häusliches Arbeiten.

3 Die Tonträger
Die von Muttersprachlern gesprochenen Tonaufnahmen auf CD bzw. Kassette sind integraler Bestandteil der *Themes* und beinhalten Lesetexte, Hörverstehensaufgaben sowie Lieder.

4 Die Folien
Die sechzehn *transparencies* bieten Möglichkeiten für alternative Unterrichtseinstiege, Erweiterungen, Visualisierungshilfen und Transferübungen. Hinweise zum Einsatzort der Folien finden sich in diesem *Teacher's Manual*.

5 Das Lehrerhandbuch (Teacher's Manual ➜ TM)
Das vorliegende *Teacher's Manual* enthält Übersichten und Unterrichtsvorschläge mit Lösungen, einen Jahresplan, Kopiervorlagen *(Copymasters)*, einen *Work plan* für den offenen Unterricht und Vorschläge für Lernerfolgskontrollen *(Tests)*. In einer Übersicht vor jedem *Theme*-Teil stellen die grau unterlegten Felder das Pflichtpensum dar, die weißen die Kür. Ergänzende Vorschläge und Aufgaben stehen im laufenden Text jeweils als Erweiterung in einem weißen Kasten.

5.1 Übersichten und Unterrichtsvorschläge mit didaktisch-methodischen Hinweisen
Zur Unterstützung beim Einsatz des Materials geben Übersichten vor jedem *Theme* einen „Kurzweg" und einen „Langweg" durch die einzelnen Lerneinheiten vor. Der grau gekennzeichnete Weg enthält die Bausteine von Texten und Übungen, mit denen die Anforderungen des Lehrplans erfüllt werden. Aus der Darstellung des Langweges lässt sich erkennen, an welchen Stellen des Unterrichts weitere Texte und Aufgaben eingesetzt werden können. TB steht jeweils für eine Einheit aus dem *Textbook*, PB bezeichnet eine Einheit aus dem *Practicebook*.
Im Anschluss an diese Übersichten zeigen die Unterrichtsvorschläge Möglichkeiten der praktischen Umsetzung des Materials auf. Darüber hinaus enthält das *Teacher's Manual* Lösungen, Hörtexte und Erweiterungsvorschläge und Anregungen für Spiele und praktische Aktivitäten sowie vertiefende landeskundliche Informationen. Auch die Angaben zum Einsatz weiterer Begleitmaterialien wie der Folien finden sich in diesem praktischen „Wegweiser".

5.2 Jahresplan
Im Anhang (TM Seite 106–111) befindet sich ein Stoffverteilungsplan für die acht *Themes* des Lehrwerks plus Zusatzmaterialien, konzipiert für 33 Wochen eines Schuljahres. Außerdem muss Zeit für das Schreiben und Besprechen von Klassenarbeiten eingeplant werden.

5.3 Kopiervorlagen (Copymaster ➜ CM)
Einsatzmöglichkeiten der *Copymasters* werden in den didaktisch-methodischen Hinweisen aufgezeigt.

5.4 Work plan

Kopiervorlage mit Muster für den Einsatz von Teilen des Lehrwerks im offenen Unterricht.

5.5 Vorschläge für Lernerfolgskontrollen

Die Tests zu den einzelnen *Themes* beinhalten den Stoff, der eine solide Grundlage für sprachliche Handlungskompetenz darstellt. Sie bestehen aus Aufgaben, die kurzzeitige Lernziele überprüfen, solchen, die auf bereits erworbenes Wissen zurückgreifen und Zuwachs ermitteln, und solchen, die frei gestalteten Charakter haben. Jeder Test beginnt mit einer Hörverstehensaufgabe. Die Lehrkraft liest diese vor und kann durch langsames Sprechen und Wiederholungen erreichen, dass alle Kinder auf die Lösungen kommen. Es folgen Übungen zu Wortschatz und Grammatik sowie thematischen und landeskundlichen Inhalten des *Theme*.

Die Tests bieten Lernenden wie Unterrichtenden eine Gelegenheit, das Leistungsniveau der verschiedenen Fertigkeiten festzustellen. In **Bayswater 3** werden pro *Theme* zwei Testvorschläge für die unterschiedlichen Leistungsniveaus angeboten. Aus diesem Angebot lassen sich Tests auch so zusammenstellen, dass sie dem Leistungsprofil der jeweiligen Lerngruppe gerecht werden. Bei leistungsschwächeren Lerngruppen sollten zwischen den hier vorgeschlagenen Leistungsüberprüfungen Kurztests durchgeführt werden, die dank der Kleinschrittigkeit sogar als motivierend empfunden werden. Zu jeder Lernerfolgskontrolle gibt es ein Deckblatt mit dem Text der Hörverstehensaufgabe, den Lösungen und einer Sammlung von Vorschlägen für weitere Aufgaben, die sich für differenzierende Überprüfungen oder Kurztests eignen.

Auf Bewertungsvorgaben wurde bewusst verzichtet, um den unterschiedlichen Gepflogenheiten der Unterrichtenden und der besonderen Situation der Klasse Raum zu lassen.

Bayswater im offenen Unterricht

Aufgrund seiner offenen Struktur ist **Bayswater** besonders für offene Formen des Unterrichts wie (Wochen-)Planarbeit und Freiarbeit geeignet. Dabei kann die Auswahl der Teile eines *Theme* bis zu einem gewissen Grad den Lernern überlassen werden. Wie viele Vorgaben und Hilfestellungen notwendig sind, hängt davon ab, wie erfahren die Lerngruppe mit eigenverantwortlichen Lern- und Arbeitsformen ist.

Der selbstständige Umgang mit dem Buch wird in **Bayswater** mithilfe des übersichtlichen Verweissystems geschult. Die Referenzteile von **Bayswater**, *Language in focus*, *Words* und *Dictionaries*, sind auf Lernerautonomie hin angelegt. Unterstützung und Anregungen finden die Lerner auch in den Lerntipps in der Randspalte und im Grammatik- und Vokabelanhang. Um den Kindern *study skills* zu vermitteln, werden sie konsequent zur Arbeit mit vorhandenen Hilfsmitteln angeleitet, so dass grundsätzlich keine Vokabelfragen mehr von der Lehrkraft beantwortet werden müssen. *Copymaster 20* und *21* bieten eine Kopiervorlage zur Planarbeit – *Copymaster 20* blanko, *Copymaster 21* exemplarisch ausgefüllt. Dieser *Work plan* kann auf die jeweiligen Erfordernisse angepasst werden.

Für eine weitgehende Selbstkontrolle der Schülerinnen und Schüler sollten möglichst für alle geschlossenen Aufgabenstellungen Lösungsblätter bereitgestellt werden, z. B. indem man die entsprechende Seite im *Practicebook* korrekt ausfüllt und kopiert. Auch die Bewertung der selbst korrigierten Aufgaben kann den Lernern überlassen werden, indem man etwa vorgibt, wie viele der richtigen Lösungen in einer Übung welcher Einstufung entsprechen.

Die Figuren

Vera Gulbenkian (14)

Vera lebt mit ihren Eltern in Bayswater. Ihr Vater ist arbeitslos und kocht zu Hause, ihre Mutter ist berufstätig. Vera spielt gern Fußball und dies oft besser als mancher Junge. Sie sammelt Stofftiere.

David Williams (14)

David, Gillians Cousin, wohnt mit seiner Familie in Hendon. Seine Eltern besitzen einen Supermarkt, in dem David oft aushilft. Er hat einen Hund namens Kenny, er liest gern Comics und mag Wales und das Wandern in den Bergen besonders gern.

Gillian Collins (14)

Sie lebt mit ihrer Mutter ebenfalls in Bayswater. Gillian ist Davids Cousine. Ihre Hobbys sind Musik und Tanz, außerdem mag sie das Theater.

Susan Johnson (13)

Susan lebt in Bayswater und hat eine jüngere Schwester, Rita, und einen älteren Bruder, Jack. Sie liebt Tiere und besitzt selbst einen Hund, einen Hamster und einen Goldfisch. Susan fürchtet sich vor Geistern.

Karim Khan (14)

Karims Familie kommt ursprünglich aus Bombay (Mumbai), Indien. Er lebt mit seinen Eltern und seiner Schwester Sheree in Bayswater. Er mag Computerspiele, er singt gern und spielt Gitarre. Außerdem ist er ein guter Koch und stellt dieses Hobby auch gern in den Dienst seiner Freunde.

Charlie Macintosh (13)

Charlies Familie kommt von den Westindischen Inseln (Barbados). Jetzt lebt die Familie in Hendon. Charlie hat eine jüngere Schwester, Sharon, und eine ältere, Josephine. Er spielt gern Fußball und reitet gern. Außerdem versucht er sich an Zaubertricks.

Das Umfeld

Das Geschehen in **Bayswater** spielt sich vor allem in zwei Stadtteilen ab, die durch starke Gegensätze gekennzeichnet sind und sich von daher in vielerlei Hinsicht auch ergänzen: Hendon und Bayswater.

Hendon ist ein für englische Ballungsgebiete typischer Vorort im Norden Londons mit kleinstädtischem Charakter. Durch die gute Verkehrsanbindung zum Stadtzentrum entstanden neben Wohngebieten mit Reihenhäusern, kleinen Geschäften, einer *High Street* und Grünanlagen viele Neubausiedlungen mit funktionaler Architektur und großen Einkaufszentren. Die Darstellung dieses Schauplatzes regt deutsche Schülerinnen und Schüler oftmals zu Vergleichen mit ihrem eigenen Lebensumfeld an.

Dagegen ist Bayswater ein pulsierendes, multikulturelles Stadtviertel mit eigenem Zentrum im Westen Londons. Hier, in einem Umkreis von zwei Kilometern um die U-Bahnstation *Bayswater*, wohnen mehrere hunderttausend Menschen, die zusammen einen Mikrokosmos der englischsprachigen Welt darstellen. Alteingesessene Londoner, aber auch Einwanderer vom indischen Subkontinent, von den Westindischen Inseln, aus Australien, Neuseeland und der ganzen Welt haben sich hier niedergelassen. Hinzu kommen zahlreiche Touristen und Besucher, denn Bayswater ist auch blühendes Hotel- und Einkaufsviertel.

Bayswater ist durch starke Kontraste geprägt. Inmitten der eleganten georgianischen Wohngegend findet man enge Straßen und Gassen mit fast dörflichem Charakter. So haben sich in Bayswater verschiedene Welten entwickelt: Neben eher konservativen Antiquitätenläden und Gasthäusern findet man lebendige, exotische Restaurants, Ateliers und Boutiquen.

Mitten in Bayswater befindet sich *Queensway*, eine belebte Einkaufsstraße, die Londoner und Touristen gleichermaßen anzieht. Am einen Ende der Straße steht *Whiteleys*. 1885 als das erste Kaufhaus Großbritanniens eröffnet, ist *Whiteleys* heute ein modernes Einkaufszentrum, wo neben vielen modischen Ketten und Boutiquen auch Kinos und Restaurants vertreten sind. *Bayswater Road* verläuft als Grenze zwischen Bayswater und den Parks, *Kensington Gardens* und *Hyde Park*. Jeden Sonntag, ob es regnet oder schneit, stellen etwa 300 Künstler ihre Werke an dem Parkgeländer aus.

Weitere Materialien

Lesebegeisterte Schülerinnen und Schüler finden in der Diesterweg-Reihe **first readers** spannendes Lesefutter, mit dem sie ihr Sprachwissen vertiefen können. Der aktuelle Fremdsprachenkatalog ist bei den Schulbuchzentren oder direkt beim Verlag erhältlich.

Das Internet

Unter **www.diesterweg.de** finden sich Hinweise zu aktuellen Websites, die sich für den Einsatz im Unterricht eignen. So lassen sich mithilfe eines neuen Mediums Inhalte des Lehrwerks vertiefen und erweitern.

Introduction: Back to Bayswater

- **TB: Über Lehrwerkfiguren und Ereignisse sprechen**
- **PB: Englischkenntnisse und Fertigkeiten im Gebrauch der Fremdsprache dokumentieren**

Als Einstieg in das neue Lernjahr werden Wortschatz und Redemittel aus dem vergangenen Jahr wiederholt und gefestigt, um den neuen Stoff auf einer soliden Grundlage aufbauen zu können. In den ersten zwei bis drei Stunden wird ohne TB gearbeitet; es kommen verschiedene andere Medien zum Einsatz wie *Copymaster*, Folie, Gesprächskarten und PB in Verbindung mit spielerischen Elementen.

Vorschläge zur Reaktivierung von Wortschatz und Redemitteln

- *What can you tell us about yourself?*
  Gespräch zwischen L und S, um eine fremdsprachige Atmosphäre zu schaffen; L wirft S1 ein geknotetes Tuch zu und stellt eine Frage zur Person, z. B. *What's your name? How old are you? Where are you from? What's your hobby? Do you like swimming?* Nach einer ersten kurzen L-S-Runde befragen sich S gegenseitig. Besonders sinnvoll ist diese Fragerunde, wenn die Klasse neu zusammengesetzt wurde oder zumindest einzelne S neu in der Klasse sind.   *Tuch*
- L schreibt Oberbegriffe an die Tafel, z. B. *people – animals – holidays – clothes – food – things in the house – buildings – family – hobbies – noun – verb – adjective – ...* L nennt einen Oberbegriff *(food)*, S nennen einen Unterbegriff dazu *(carrot)*. Der/Die S, der/die den ersten Unterbegriff genannt hat, nennt nun den nächsten Oberbegriff. Nach kurzer Einführungsrunde wird das Spiel in Gruppen weitergeführt, um alle S aktiv zu beteiligen.   *Tafel*
- Jede/r S füllt in Stillarbeit eine *identity card (Copymaster 1)* aus, jedoch ohne den Vor- und Nachnamen einzutragen. Die Karten werden eingesammelt und gemischt, danach zieht jede/r S ein Kärtchen und formuliert die Angaben zu vollständigen Äußerungen: *He or she lives in ... His or her address is ... He or she is one metre ... tall. His or her eyes are ... He or she is ... years old and his or her hobbies are ... He or she doesn't like ... He or she has got ... brother(s)/sister(s) and a pet. It's a ...* Danach gibt sich die/der beschriebene S mit *That's me!* zu erkennen.
- S begeben sich auf Wörtersafari: Während eines festgelegten Zeitraums (zwei bis vier Wochen) notieren S alle englischen Wörter, die ihnen im Alltag begegnen (Supermarkt, TV, Radio, Zeitschriften, Werbung usw.).
- S sammeln in Partner-/Gruppenarbeit in Form von *mind maps* Wortschatz zu vorgegebenen Wortfeldern: *free time – shopping – animals – food – clothes – school – traffic – music – sports – hobbies – ...* S wählen ein Thema aus, Themen können auch doppelt bearbeitet werden, in dem Fall tauschen sich die Gruppen anschließend aus und ergänzen Wörter. L achtet darauf, dass jedes Thema mindestens einmal vergeben wird. Die *mind maps* können zudem illustriert werden und werden abschließend allen S zugänglich gemacht, z. B. indem sie im Klassenzimmer, in der *English Corner,* ausgehängt werden.
- *Pantomime:* S überlegen sich zu jeder Stunde drei Wörter, die sie pantomimisch darstellen und die die anderen S erraten, jede Stunde sind ein/e oder zwei S an der Reihe. Auf diese Weise wird mit der Zeit eine beträchtliche Anzahl an Wörtern wiederholt und sicher eingeprägt.
- *From word to word:* Dieses Spiel, bei dem der letzte Buchstabe des einen Wortes der erste des nächsten Wortes ist, kann mündlich (Unterrichtsgespräch) oder schriftlich (an der Tafel oder in Einzelarbeit) durchgeführt werden. Beispiel: *pen – new – way – young – ...*   *Tafel*
- Kreative Elemente kommen ins Spiel, wenn S eine *word snake* oder eine *word snail* gestalten (Wörter werden in Schlangen- bzw. Schneckenform angeordnet) oder andere Figuren mit ihren Wörtern füllen. (Die schönsten Arbeiten werden ausgestellt, damit die Anstrengungen der S auch entsprechend gewürdigt werden.)
- *How many words can you make out of the word I–N–F–O–R–M–A–T–I–O–N?* (*I, a, an, at, on, for, form, to, it, not, tin, fat, ...*). S arbeiten in Einzel- oder Partnerarbeit und stellen sich anschließend untereinander weitere Rätsel.
- *Chain games –* eine ausgezeichnete Möglichkeit, das Gedächtnis zu trainieren:
  – Sehr einfache Variante: S1 sagt ein Wort mit A *(apple)*, S2 wiederholt das Wort und fügt ein Wort mit B an *(apple and banana)*. Usw.
  – Etwas schwieriger: L legt mit S zuvor ein Thema/Wortfeld fest.

– Weitere Erschwernis, wenn die Vorgabe grammatischer Natur ist, z. B. *simple past: Last week I went to the cinema. – Last week I went to the cinema and saw an interesting film. – Last week I went to the cinema, saw an interesting film and bought a T-shirt. – ...*
– Noch mehr Konzentration erfordert es, wenn sich S auch die Sprecher merken müssen: *I played football yesterday. – (Myriam) played football yesterday, and I went swimming. – (Myriam) played football yesterday, (Patrick) went swimming, and I cleaned my room. – ...*

Die Portfolio-Seiten im PB (S. 4–7) knüpfen an die Möglichkeiten der Selbstevaluation aus **Bayswater 2** an. S erhalten ein individuelles Leistungsprofil, das ihre Stärken und Schwächen aufzeigt und ihre Lernzuwächse sichtbar macht. Die Aufgaben sind so konzipiert, dass für ihre Bearbeitung keine speziellen **Bayswater**-Kenntnisse notwendig sind: Der zu diesem Zeitpunkt – also nach zwei Jahren Englischunterricht – erreichte lehrwerksunabhängige Leistungsstand wird dokumentiert.

PB Portfolio 1   Schreiben   *PB, S. 4*
S verfassen die vier Texte und lesen sie anschließend vor. So erhält L einen Eindruck von der Schreibfähigkeit der S. Durch das Anfertigen der *identity cards* (siehe oben) wurde Teilaufgabe 1 bereits vorbereitet.

PB Portfolio 2/1   Hören   Charlie meets a girl who ...   *PB, S. 4*
Der Hörtext lautet: *Outside Hendon Central underground station*

Girl:	Hey, excuse me. Do you know Mr Arthur Trimble's pet shop? It must be here, in Hendon.
Charlie:	A pet shop? Arthur Trimble's ...? Oh yes, of course. Sure, I know it.
Girl:	Is it far from here?
Charlie:	Oh, not too far. About 15 minutes' walk.
Girl:	Oh, okay.
Charlie:	You go to the end of this road – Queens Road; all the way to the end. There's a big road there – Brent Street. You turn left. Uh, yes, left.
Girl:	So, down to the end, then left?
Charlie:	Yes, then it's the first, second, third, fourth, fifth on the right. That's Finchley Lane, another big road.
Girl:	Left, then fifth on the right.
Charlie:	Then second left, and ... first right.
Girl:	Wow. So, left, fifth on the right, second on the left, first on the right.
Charlie:	Yep. That's Garrick Way. You can ask there again. Everyone knows Trimble's Pet Shop. It's ...

S hören den Text von der CD und verfolgen dabei mit dem Bleistift den Weg zur Zoohandlung. Mündlich geben S den Weg wieder, den die beiden gewählt haben.
Lösungen: *Queens Road – Brent Street – Finchley Lane – Garrick Way. Mr Arthur Trimble's pet shop is in Garrick Way.*

PB Portfolio 3   Lesen und verstehen   *PB, S. 6*
S lesen die Geschichte in Einzelarbeit. Die Auswertungsaufgaben unter a) können z. T. mündlich vorbesprochen werden *(What is the story about?/There is an old lady in the story. What do you know about her?)*, dann bearbeiten S die Aufgaben schriftlich. Die Ergebnisse werden anschließend mündlich in der Klasse kontrolliert, alternativ händigt L ein Lösungsblatt für die selbstständige Kontrolle der Ergebnisse an S aus.
Mögliche Lösungen:
a) *The story is about a football match and a lost dog./Vera–Charlie–Susan–Gillian–Karim–Gillian–an old lady/Hendon United: Vera, Charlie, David/Bayswater Allstars: Susan, Gillian, Karim./The old lady walks around the park every day with her cocker spaniel Flopper, but today she was talking to a friend for five minutes, and when she looked again, Flopper wasn't there. Now she's crying.*
b) *7–3–6–5–2–8–9–4–1*
c) *football match, Hendon United, Bayswater Allstars, game, shot, pass, ball, run, stop, catch, goal, team, play, 2:2, throw*

PB Portfolio 2/2   Hören   Radio Junior Europe (RJE) interviews ...   *PB, S. 5*
Der Hörtext lautet: *Radio Junior Europe interviews young people for a talent contest*

Steve:	*We have some people here who want to enter the Radio Junior Europe talent contest. They've all sent me a photo but I need to find out more about them. So it's over to our first guest. Let's hear who it is.*
Nadine:	*Yes, hello, Steve. Yes, my name is Nadine Engel. I'm German and I come from Leipzig. Oh, yes, and I'm 13. I always sing my own songs.*
Steve:	*You mean you write them? That's great. But do you have time for any other hobbies?*
Nadine:	*Well, yes. I like listening to all kinds of music but my main hobby is song-writing. Oh, and reading. I like reading – when I have time.*
Steve:	*Well, good luck, Nadine. I've noted down all your information. And our next guest, please?*
Artur:	*There are four of us. My sisters, Maria and Irina, and my brother, Stanislav. And me, Artur Mikulski. We are from Poznàn in Poland. And we are a folk dancing group.*
Steve:	*Well, nice to have you here, Artur. Are you the oldest?*
Artur:	*The oldest twin. Maria is 14, Irina is 9 and Stanislav, well, we are twins. We are 12 but I am 10 minutes older.*
Steve:	*And what do you all do when you're not dancing?*
Artur:	*We listen to folk music and then there's swimming and, of course, dancing. And the girls like painting. I collect stamps, too.*
Steve:	*And I wish all four of you luck, too. And who's on the line now?*
Gwynedd:	*Gwynedd, Gwynedd Evans. I'm 14, from Llangollen in Wales and I play the saxophone. I love classical music. And when I have time I like to go riding. I have a lovely pony.*
Steve:	*Thank you very much, Gwynedd. You've answered all my questions. And now to our last guest. Hello, who am I talking to?*
Erdal:	*You're talking to Erdal Esin.*
Steve:	*Hello, Erdal. Tell me about your hobbies and your favourite music.*
Erdal:	*I play the drums, solo, you know. And my favourite music is heavy metal and all kinds of rock. And my hobby is football.*
Steve:	*Thank you very much. Oh, and where are you from? That's important.*
Erdal:	*Oh, sorry. I forgot. I'm Turkish. I live in Istanbul. And I'm 13 years old.*
Steve:	*Well, thank you all very much for these quick interviews. Best of luck to you all and may the best man – or woman – win!*

S absolvieren die Aufgaben in der vorgegebenen Form. Damit L erkennen kann, ob die Fehler gefunden wurden, formulieren S noch einmal zusammenhängend, was sie über die verschiedenen Interviewpartner wissen, z. B.: *The first interview partner is ... He/She is 13 and comes from ... He/She lives in ... His/Her special talent is ...*
Lösungen: *first: Nadine – 11 → 13; second: Maria, Irina, Stanislav, Artur – patchwork → painting; third: Gwynedd – reading → riding; fourth: Erdal – Ankara → Istanbul*

PB Portfolio 4   Sprechen   *PB, S. 7*
Copymaster 2 enthält zu vier Themen je eine A- und eine B-Karte mit Redeanweisungen. Das Thema *You and I* wurde ausgespart, da es bereits zu Beginn dieser Unterrichtsphase Thema war (vgl. TM S. 13).
Für leistungsschwache S hält L Karten mit vorformulierten Fragen und möglichen Antworten bereit.

TB Back to Bayswater   **Lesen/Sprechen/Schreiben**   *TB, S. 10–12*
Erinnerung an die Figuren des TB **Bayswater 2**
- S schlagen die Seiten 10–12 im TB auf und erzählen, was ihnen zu den Illustrationen einfällt. L greift je nach Leistungsniveau der S korrigierend ein.
- Gedächtnistraining: Jede/r S wählt eine der Figuren aus und liest ihren Steckbrief (30–60 Sekunden). Bei geschlossenem TB nennt ein/e S über seine/ihre Figur so viele Fakten wie möglich. Die anderen S kontrollieren bei geöffnetem TB und stellen ggf. ergänzende Fragen.
- S finden sich in Gruppen zusammen und gestalten die Stunde als Quiz, bei dem es unterschiedliche Aufgabentypen gibt. Die Aufträge werden von den Gruppen auf unter-

schiedlich farbige Karten geschrieben (vier Farben), die vier Kategorien zugeordnet sind:
– Vokabelfragen, z. B.: *What's the English word for* Ponyrennen/Straßenmusikanten ...?
– Fragen zu den Zeichnungen aus **Bayswater 2** im TB, z. B.: *What's the butler's name in the picture of the special birthday?/Why does Gillian look frightened in one picture?*
– über die Zeichnungen hinausgehende Fragen zu **Bayswater 2**, z. B.: *Tell us what you know about the black dog/the boy and the girl in the park/Gillian's mother/Holland Park School/Charlie's new neighbour?*
– Lehrwerksunabhängige Aufgaben, die Wortschatz und Strukturen wiederholen, z. B.: *Count from 10 to 25./Count from 50 to 35./Sing a song./Name five irregular verbs and their past tense forms./Jump up and down ten times./Draw a cat/a dog and describe it./...*
Je nach Komplexität der Aufgaben werden ein oder mehrere Punkte vergeben, die auf den Aufgabenkarten mit notiert werden. Ein Würfel pro Gruppe wird mit den vier Farben beklebt. Die zwei verbleibenden Felder werden nicht beklebt, die gewürfelte Punktzahl ergänzt als Glückswurf die bisher erarbeiteten Punkte. L fungiert als Helfer und Berater, u. U. auch als Schiedsrichter bei Zweifelsfällen.

> **Erweiterung:**
> Folie 1 *Who is who?* dient der Zusammenfassung der Kenntnisse über die Lehrwerkscharaktere und trainiert das Gedächtnis. Die Folienhinweise enthalten Aufgaben für das monologische und dialogische Sprechen, ein Ratespiel, um S zum Fragenstellen zu veranlassen, sowie eine Transferaufgabe zum Vergleich der S aus der *Hendon School* und der *Holland Park School* mit S der eigenen Klasse.

Für Neunutzer der Bayswater-Reihe:

S schauen sich das Inhaltsverzeichnis des TB und die Übersicht über die verwendeten Symbole an, schlagen die verschiedenen Teile des TB auf und suchen mithilfe der Verweise in den *Themes* die entsprechenden Übungen im *lif*-Teil und im PB, um das Lehrwerk kennen zu lernen und selbstständig mit dem Lehrwerk arbeiten zu können.
L gibt Tipps, wo Hinweise für das Lernen zu finden sind (z. B. TB S. 161, 165, 167), und führt mit S ein Gespräch darüber, wie sie lernen oder bisher gelernt haben und sich mit der Fremdsprache beschäftigt haben.

Grundsatz: Lernen durch Lehren (Das Lehren lernen)

Im Anschluss an den Einstieg in das TB ist zu prüfen, ob nicht manche Lehraufgaben längerfristig an S übertragen werden können, um
• sie stärker in die Planung und Mitgestaltung des Unterrichts einzubeziehen
• eine höhere Verantwortung für das Lernen in der Klasse – nicht nur für den eigenen Lernprozess – zu entwickeln.
Folgende Lehraufgaben bieten sich für wechselnde S-Gruppen an:
• S formulieren vor der Arbeit an einem Text vorbereitende Fragen, die sie an die Klasse richten, um bei der Klasse eine Erwartungshaltung an den Text zu entwickeln *(pre-reading activity)*. Nach dem Lesen des Textes beantwortet die Klasse die Fragen unter S-Regie.
• das Einführen von Wortschatz mithilfe verschiedenster Verfahren (*mind map*, pantomimisch, Kollokationen usw.).
• die Übernahme von Lesephasen.
• die Besprechung von Hausaufgaben (mit Tafelanschrieb, Wendungen der Unterrichtssprache, ggf. Fehlerkorrektur).
• kleine Wortschatzkontrollen in spielerischer Form zu Beginn einer Stunde.

Damit solche zunächst kurzen Phasen gelingen, sind bestimmte Verhaltensweisen zu trainieren, die den Umgang der S miteinander betreffen: Die Teilaufgaben sind in der Gruppe gleich zu verteilen, S müssen sich gut vorbereiten, laut und deutlich sprechen, ihre Klassenkameraden freundlich und höflich behandeln und sie loben bzw. ihnen bei Fehlern helfen. Wenn die Lehrkraft ein solches Ansinnen zum ersten Mal vorbringt, werden S vermutlich erstaunt sein, sich aber bald in ihre neue Rolle finden und Spaß haben, wenn sie feststellen, dass sie die ihnen gestellten Aufgaben meistern.

Medium	Nummer	Seite	Titel	Fertigkeit	Zusatzinfo
Folie 2			Things to eat and drink	Sprechen	Wortschatz: *food + drinks*
TB/CD	A1	14	Eating out	Hören/Sprechen	Entscheidung für den Besuch eines Restaurants
TB	A2	14	Decisions, decisions	Hören/Lesen	
PB	A1	8	Much, many, lots of	Schreiben/Sprechen	*much* und *many* (**R**)
PB	A2	8f.	How much? How many?	Schreiben/Sprechen	*much* und *many* (**R**)
TB	A3	15	Menus	Lesen/Sprechen	Wortschatz: *dishes*
PB	A3	9	Alphabet soup	Schreiben	*scrambled words*
TB/CD	A4	16	Ready to order?	Hören/Sprechen	Speisen bestellen
PB/CD	A4	10	Gillian and Vera in the restaurant	Hören/Sprechen	Speisen bestellen
TB	A5	16	In a restaurant	Lesen/Schreiben/Sprechen	Speisen bestellen
PB	A5	10	Lunch at the Shakespeare restaurant	Schreiben/Sprechen	
TB	A6	17	That's yours, isn't it?	Sprechen/Lesen	*question tags*
TB	lif 1	110	Bestätigungsfragen		
TB/CD	A7	17	Mum's sunglasses	Hören/Lesen/Schreiben	*question tags*
copy 3			Question tags, question tags	Schreiben/Sprechen	*question tags*
PB	A6	11	He was, wasn't he?	Schreiben	*question tags*
PB	A7	11f.	That's right, isn't it?	Schreiben/Sprechen	*question tags*
TB/CD	A8	18	Eating out in foreign restaurants	Hören/Sprechen/Lesen	Hör-/Leseverstehen; Textverständnis
PB	A8	12	True or false?	Schreiben/Sprechen	Textverständnis
TB	lif 2	110f.	Indirekte Rede I		
TB	A9	19	Have you ever …?	Sprechen	*present perfect*
PB	A9	12f.	A terrible day out at the zoo	Schreiben	*present perfect* mit *just*
PB	A10	14	Have you ever …? No, I've never … but I once …	Sprechen	Kontrastierung *present perfect/simple past*
TB/CD	A10	19	Food, glorious food	Hören/Singen	
PB	A11	14	Funny food	Hören/Schreiben	Gedicht

Die grau unterlegten Felder stellen das Pflichtpensum dar, die weißen die Kür.

Theme 1: Eating out

Teil A: • Ein Restaurant auswählen
             Eine Speisekarte lesen und Essen bestellen
             Jemanden zum Essen einladen
             Berichten, was man schon getan hat

Als Einstieg werden bereits bekannte Wörter und Strukturen zu *food and drinks* aktiviert.
Mögliche Varianten:

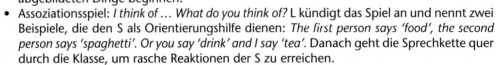

- Folie 2 wiederholt *Things to eat and drink*. Ohne Einführung kann das Gespräch über die abgebildeten Dinge beginnen.
- Assoziationsspiel: *I think of … What do you think of?* L kündigt das Spiel an und nennt zwei Beispiele, die den S als Orientierungshilfe dienen: *The first person says 'food', the second person says 'spaghetti'. Or you say 'drink' and I say 'tea'.* Danach geht die Sprechkette quer durch die Klasse, um rasche Reaktionen der S zu erreichen.
- S sammeln in Partnerarbeit Wortschatz zu dem Wortfeld *food and drinks*. Im nächsten Schritt ordnen sie die Wörter in einem Wortraster an. L gibt ein Beispiel an der Tafel vor: *Tafel*

```
        C
T O A S T
E       R
A       R I C E
        O
        T
```

L nennt ein Anfangswort, dann haben die Paare zwei Minuten Zeit, um ein Wortraster zu erstellen. Beim Stoppsignal zählen sie ihre Wörter, die drei besten Paare schreiben ihre Raster an die Tafel.   *Tafel*

TB A1 Eating out   **Hören/Sprechen**   *TB, S. 14*
- L schreibt vor dem Hören als Stütze folgende Restaurants an die Tafel: *Tafel*

Indian restaurant	*Greek restaurant*
Burger bar	*Shakespeare restaurant*
Chinese snackbar	*Dino's Italian restaurant*

- Zweimaliges Anhören des Textes bei geschlossenem TB: Beim ersten Hören konzentrieren S sich darauf, welche der sechs Restaurants nicht genannt werden (*Chinese snackbar* und *Greek restaurant*), beim zweiten Hören darauf, in welcher Reihenfolge die genannten Restaurants vorkommen (*Burger bar–Dino's Italian restaurant–Indian restaurant–Shakespeare restaurant*).

TB A2 Decisions, decisions   **Hören/Lesen/Schreiben**   *TB, S. 14*
a) Erneutes Anhören der CD bei geöffnetem TB, S machen Notizen zu den Speisen, die sie in den verschiedenen Restaurants essen können. Leistungsschwache Lerngruppen nehmen das geöffnete TB zur Hilfe.
   Lösungen: *Burger Bar: burgers and cola; Dino's: different salads, pasta dishes; Indian restaurant: curries; Shakespeare restaurant: a lot of different things*

b) Lesen des Textes, Sammeln der Beispiele mit *much/many/a lot of* an der Tafel, S schreiben   *Tafel*
mit. Bevor S die Listen um weitere Substantive ergänzen, wiederholen sie die Regel zu *much/many* (bekannt seit **Bayswater 2**, *Theme 4*), um fehlerhafte Einträge zu vermeiden.

Erweiterung:
S legen in ihrem Heft eine Rubrik ‚Redeabsichten' an und sammeln dort sprachliche Mittel. Hier wäre dies ‚Unbestimmte Mengen angeben'. Anfangs erarbeitet L gemeinsam mit S die Einträge, später tragen S selbstständig ein. Damit entsteht über die Jahre ein hilfreiches Nachschlagewerk. Die Ordnung der Strukturen nach Redeabsichten wirkt der Grammatikorientierung entgegen, die S für die Bewältigung produktiver Aufgaben keine Hilfe ist. Alternativ gestalten S ein Lernposter, das im Unterrichtsraum aufgehängt wird und an die Verwendung von *much* und *many* erinnert.

PB A1   Much, many, lots of   Schreiben/Sprechen   *PB, S. 8*
Die Sätze der Übung sind dem Text *Eating out* entnommen. S versuchen ohne Hilfe des TB
die richtige Auswahl zu treffen. Diese wird mündlich mit dem Nachbarn/der Nachbarin,
ggf. mithilfe des TB, anschließend frontal überprüft.

PB A2   How much? How many?   Schreiben/Sprechen   *PB, S. 8f.*
a) Nach dem schriftlichen Ergänzen der Fragen beantworten S die Fragen in Partnerarbeit.
   Lösungen: *many, much, much, much, many*

b) Lösungen: *Yes, but there isn't much milk./Yes, there are lots./Yes, there was lots./Yes, but
   there wasn't much./Yes, there was lots./Yes, but there weren't many.*

TB A3   Menus   Lesen/Sprechen   *TB, S. 15*
a) S lesen zunächst jede/r für sich die Speisekarte und überlegen, welche Speisen sie bereits
   probiert und wie sie geschmeckt haben. Dafür werden an der Tafel Adjektive gesammelt: *Tafel*
   hot, good, tasty, spicy, exotic, … (siehe auch *lif* S. 109). Anschließend tauschen S sich mit   *TB, S. 109*
   dem Partner/der Partnerin aus und verwenden dabei *present perfect* und *simple past*,
   z. B.: *Which of these dishes have you tried?/Have you (ever) tried melon salad? – Yes,
   I have./No, I haven't. – Did you like it? – Yes, I did./No, I didn't. But have you tried apple pie?
   – Oh yes, it was delicious.* Einige Paare präsentieren ihre Dialoge vor der Klasse.

b) Unbekannte Gerichte werden paarweise im Wörterbuch nachgeschlagen.

c) Partnerarbeit: S geben einander Auskunft darüber, wie sie ihre £10 ausgeben würden:
   I would order … as a starter, … as the main dish and … as a dessert.
   L schreibt weitere Redemittel an die Tafel, mit denen S ihre Gespräche fortsetzen: *Tafel*
   What do you like better – fish or meat?
   Would you like soup or salad as a starter?
   Which of the snacks on the menu would you like?
   What is your favourite main dish?
   Are you a friend of vegetarian dishes?
   Do you like desserts?
   Which dessert would you like?

> Erweiterung:
> S schließen die Bücher und zählen auf die Frage *What have you ever had at a burger bar/
> an Italian restaurant/… ?* in 30 Sekunden möglichst viele Speisen auf: *I've had … at the
> burger bar/at the Italian restaurant/…*

PB A3   Alphabet soup   Schreiben   *PB, S. 9*
a) S schreiben die Wörter um den Teller herum.
   Lösungen: *tuna, prawn, carrot, onion, apple, potato, tomato, lamb, chicken, orange*

b) S übernehmen die Tabelle in ihr Heft. Die Liste muss ständig erweitert werden und kann
   auch durch die Spalte *spice (salt, pepper, ginger)* ergänzt werden.

TB A4   Ready to order?   Hören/Sprechen   *TB, S. 16*
Der Hörtext lautet:
Mrs Collins: Have you decided yet, Gillian?
*Gillian: I'm not sure. The steak sounds good. Oh – no. I'm going to order the roast lamb and
              mint sauce.*
Mrs Collins: On a warm day like this?
Gillian: Yes, I'm hungry, and I love roast potatoes. What are you having, Vera?
Vera: I'm having the North Indian vegetable curry.
Gillian: You see? Vegetable curry is just as hot on a day like this.
Vera: Well, Indians eat curry all the time, and it's even hotter in India.
Gillian: The curry or the weather?
Mrs Collins: Here's the waiter. Have you decided what you want?

Waiter:	Are you ready to order?
Mrs Collins:	I think so. Gillian?
Gillian:	I'd like a prawn cocktail to start with and then the roast lamb and mint sauce.
Waiter:	Certainly.
Vera:	And I'd like the North Indian vegetable curry.
Waiter:	Would you like a starter?
Vera:	Hmm. What is the Soup of the Day today?
Waiter:	It's carrot and orange soup.
Vera:	Carrot and orange? Lovely. Yes, I'll have that, please.
Mrs Collins:	I'll have the chicken salad. Oh, and the fresh melon salad to start with.
Waiter:	Certainly. And what would you like to drink?
Mrs Collins:	A glass of white wine for me, and what would you two like?
Gillian:	Fresh orange juice, please.
Vera:	The same for me, please.
Waiter:	Certainly. Thank you.

a) • S lesen die Fragen vor dem Hören, um zielgerichtet hören zu können.
   • S hören den Text von der CD.
   • S hören den Text ein zweites Mal, L stoppt die CD in Abschnitten, damit S Notizen machen können.
   Lösungen: *She wanted to order the steak./She was hungry and she loves roast potatoes./ Gillian chose prawn cocktail./Vera ordered the North Indian vegetable curry./Mrs Collins ordered the chicken salad and the fresh melon salad./Mrs Collins ordered the wine./The Soup of the Day was carrot and orange soup.*

b) Lösung: *hot* bedeutet heiß an Temperatur, aber auch scharf. Beispiel: *It's very hot today. – The curry is very hot. I like hot dishes.*

Erweiterung:
S gestalten nach dem Vorbild von TB S. 15 die Speisekarte eines Restaurants für englische Gäste (mit typisch deutscher oder internationaler Küche). Die Speisekarten werden anschließend in Partner- oder Gruppenarbeit für Kommunikationssituationen im Restaurant, für Gespräche zwischen Bedienung und Gästen genutzt.

PB A4   Gillian and Vera in the restaurant   **Hören/Schreiben**   *PB, S. 10*
Weitere Auswertung des HV-Texts aus dem TB
• Erneutes ein- oder zweimaliges Anhören des Gesprächs und Korrigieren der Vorlage.
   Lösungen: my daughter → Gillian; vegeburger → steak, orange sauce → mint sauce; hot → warm; roast lamb → roast potatoes; South Indian → North Indian; evening → day; most of the time → all the time; chosen → decided; What would you like? → Are you ready to oder?
• Nachstellen des Gesprächs, L bespricht mit S mögliche Variationen der Äußerungen: *Have you decided yet?/What would you like to eat?/What are you having? – I'm not sure./ I don't know./I think I'll take …/I think I'll have …*

TB A5   In a restaurant   **Lesen/Schreiben**   *TB, S. 16*
a) S ordnen die Äußerungen mündlich. Um dies für lernlangsamere S nachvollziehbar zu machen, beschriften S Folienstreifen und legen sie geordnet auf den OHP.   *Folienstreifen*

b) S ergänzen die Sprechblasen gedanklich und schreiben das Gespräch ins Heft. (Hilfe bietet auch *lif* S. 108.)   *TB, S. 108*

c) Zusatzaufgabe: Gestalten einer Szene im Restaurant in Partnerarbeit. Hierbei kommen die selbst gestalteten Speisekarten (siehe Erweiterung oben) ebenso zum Einsatz wie einige Requisiten: Serviette für die Bedienung, Notizblock für die Bestellung und Rechnung.

> Erweiterung:
> L erweitert mit S ihre Liste der Redemittel, damit sie flexibler im Ausdruck werden.
> - Um die Speisekarte bitten: *Waiter/Waitress, the menu, please.* Höflicher: *Could/May I/we have the menu, please?*
> - Bedienung möchte Bestellung aufnehmen: *Are you ready to order?/What would you like to have?*
> - Bedienung bedauert, dass ein Gericht nicht mehr vorrätig ist: *Sorry, ... is out.*

PB A5 Lunch at the Shakespeare restaurant   Schreiben/Sprechen   *PB, S. 10*
a) Ergänzen der Äußerungen des Gastes mithilfe von TB S. 15.

b) Ausführen des Gesprächs mit verteilten Rollen (u. U. mit *role play cards*, die deutsche oder englische Vorgaben oder auch nur stark reduzierte Stichpunkte enthalten).

> Erweiterung:
> Um sich selbst einmal sprechen zu hören, nehmen S zu Hause ein solches Gespräch auf und spielen es vor der Klasse ab. Die gemeinsame Auswertung des Inhalts, der sprachlichen Korrektheit, der Verständlichkeit und Flüssigkeit des Sprachgebrauchs einschließlich einer lebendigen Gestaltung ist hilfreicher als die alleinige Kritik von L.
> Die Videoaufzeichnung eines nachgestellten Restaurantbesuchs mit drei oder vier S ist eine weitere Möglichkeit und mithilfe einiger Eltern sicherlich auch möglich.

TB A6 That's yours, isn't it?   Sprechen/Lesen   *TB, S. 17*
- Zur Einführung der *question tags* nutzt L ein Gespräch mit S über S in der Klasse. S geben die Äußerungen auf Deutsch wieder.
  (Selim) is the tallest boy in your class, isn't he?
  (Katharina) doesn't look very healthy today, does she?
  (Florian) isn't the tallest pupil in your class, is he? Usw.
  Die Bezeichnung *question tags* wird angeschrieben, positive und negative Aussagen werden in zwei Spalten darunter angeordnet. S finden die jeweilige Gemeinsamkeit selbst heraus.
- Lesen und Übersetzen der Äußerungen im TB.
- *lif 1, S. 110*: S arbeiten das Kapitel still durch und geben den Inhalt mit eigenen Worten   *TB, S. 110*
  wieder. Es folgt der Eintrag ins Heft unter der Rubrik ‚Eine Aussage bestätigen lassen wollen'.

TB A7 Mum's sunglasses   Hören/Sprechen/Lesen/Schreiben   *TB, S. 17*
Nach Einstimmung der S auf die Situation und Erläuterung der Wendung *by mistake* hören S das Gespräch bei geschlossenem TB mit folgender Höraufgabe:
- *What do the sunglasses look like?*
- *Does Gillian like them?*
- *Do they find the sunglasses at the restaurant?*

a) S finden die vollständigen Sätze im Text, lesen sie laut und übersetzen sie. Die Regel wird   *TB, S. 110*
hier noch einmal erfragt und kann nun schon sicher formuliert werden. Evtl. wird *lif 1,*
S. 110, noch einmal herangezogen.

b) S ergänzen die Sätze im Unterricht mündlich, schriftliche Sicherung als Hausaufgabe.
Lösungen: *2. didn't she? 3. isn't it? 4. is it? 5. doesn't she? 6. aren't there? 7. wasn't it? 8. aren't there? 9. does it? 10. don't you?*

> Erweiterung:
> Die unterschiedlichen Strukturen bei den *question tags* können S leicht verwirren, *Copymaster 3* vermittelt mehr Sicherheit. S ergänzen die vorgegebenen Äußerungen und schreiben eigene Fragen mit *question tags*. Der *Copymaster* dient auch als kleine Nachschlagemöglichkeit in Zweifelsfällen.

PB A6   He was, wasn't he?   **Schreiben**   *PB, S. 11*
S lösen die Aufgabe in Einzelarbeit, greifen ggf. ein weiteres Mal auf *lif* 1 zurück.   *TB, S. 110*
Lösungen: *isn't it? were they? are you? do you? wasn't he? don't you? didn't you? doesn't she? does she? aren't they? was he? did you? weren't you? is he?*

PB A7   That's right, isn't it?   **Schreiben/Sprechen**   *PB, S. 11f.*
a) S tragen die Fragen und Antworten in Partnerarbeit ein.
    Lösungen: *isn't she? – Yes, she is./aren't they? – Yes, they are./doesn't she? – No, she doesn't./wasn't it? – No, it wasn't./hasn't she? – Yes, she has./don't you? – No, I don't./don't you? – Yes, I do.*

b) S ergänzen die *question tags*. Wenn L noch Probleme beobachtet, erläutert ein/e S die
    question tags nochmals an der Tafel und zieht schwächere S zur Lösung der Aufgaben   *Tafel*
    heran (siehe Lernen durch Lehren, TM S. 16). Nach Sicherung der Ergebnisse stellen und
    beantworten sich S gegenseitig die Fragen.

TB A8   Eating out in foreign restaurants   **Hören/Sprechen/Lesen**   *TB, S. 18*
• Kurzes einleitendes Unterrichtsgespräch: *Have you ever been to a foreign country?/Have you tried dishes from India/China/...?/Do you know what you ate?*
• Hören der CD bei geschlossenem TB mit folgendem Hörauftrag, der an der Tafel festge-   *Tafel*
  halten wird: *Who is the text about? What do you learn about the new girl at Karim's school?*
• S lesen die Sprechblasen in der Zeichnung und geben die Pointe auf Deutsch wieder.
• S sammeln Informationen über Rosemary aus dem Text und schreiben die Sätze ins Heft,
  denkbar als Hausaufgabe.
  Lösungen: *Rosemary thinks that it is really exciting to try new food in other countries. She tells Karim that she has never been to India. Rosemary decides that she wants to go to India.*

PB A8   True or false?   **Schreiben/Sprechen**   *PB, S. 12*
S verbessern die falschen Sätze zunächst mündlich, anschließend schriftlich im Heft.
Lösungen: *Number 1 is not correct. Karim meets Rosemary in a supermarket./Number 3 is not correct. Rosemary says that her father is an international banker./Number 6 is not correct. Rosemary tells Karim that she has met lots of interesting people on her trips abroad./Number 7 is not correct. She says that her favourite cook book has recipes from all over the world.*

lif 2   Indirekte Rede I   **Sprechen/Lesen/Schreiben**   *TB, S. 110f.*
• L verteilt Karten/Zettel mit Äußerungen der direkten und indirekten Rede, S gehen im   *Karten/Zettel*
  Klassenzimmer umher und suchen ihr Pendant. Beispiele: *"I like Chinese food very much."*
  – She says (that) she likes Chinese food very much."/"I want to go to Canada." – He says (that) he wants to go to Canada. Wenn sich alle Paare gefunden haben, Klassengespräch, durch-
  aus auf Deutsch. L: Was geschieht hier? S: Äußerungen von Personen werden wieder-
  gegeben, es wird darüber berichtet. L: *In English we call this reported speech.*
• Gemeinsames Lesen und Besprechen der Sätze in *lif* 2, S. 111.

TB A9   Have you ever ...?   **Sprechen**   *TB, S. 19*
• S gestalten mithilfe der Sprechblasen kleine Dialoge.
• S berichten, was sie in den Gesprächen erfahren haben, z. B.: *(Tim) says (that) he has been to a Turkish restaurant, but he didn't like it because ... (Lena) says (that) she has eaten at a Chinese restaurant and (that) the food was delicious.*

PB A9   A terrible day out at the zoo   **Schreiben**   *PB, S. 12*
a) S vervollständigen die Tabelle in Einzelarbeit und kontrollieren ihre Ergebnisse selbst mit-
    hilfe der Liste der unregelmäßigen Verben im TB, S. 209/210.   *TB, S. 209f.*
    Anschließend hören S sich gegenseitig regelmäßige und unregelmäßige Verben ab: L teilt
    die Klasse in zwei oder mehrere Gruppen, erste Gruppe nennt einen Infinitiv *(go)*, die
    nächste Gruppe nennt die drei Verbformen und die Übersetzung *(go–went–gone–gehen)*
    und gibt dann der nächsten Gruppe einen Infinitiv vor.

b) Lesen der Sprechblasen auf S. 13 oben in Stillarbeit, die kleine Szene kann für eine Wiederholung des *present perfect* herangezogen werden (vgl. *lif*, TB S. 112). Die Sätze im PB *TB, S. 112* werden dann mithilfe der Zeichnungen unterhalb ergänzt, in leistungsschwachen Lerngruppen werden zunächst die nötigen Infinitive an der Tafel gesammelt. Abschließend *Tafel* Anschreiben der fehlenden Verbformen zum Vergleich.

Mögliche Lösungen: *has just fallen, have just broken, has just eaten, has just taken, has just drunk, has just thrown, has just flown, have just stolen*

Erweiterungen:
- Im Sinne des Lernens durch Lehren kann es für ein oder zwei Gruppen Aufgabe sein, sich der unregelmäßigen Verben anzunehmen und für deren intensives Lernen
  - Anschauungsmaterial zu entwickeln (Poster, auf dem die Verben in bestimmten Gruppen nach gleichen Stammformen geordnet sind, z. B. *sing–sang–sung, drink–drank–drunk*).
  - sich Verb-Spiele zu überlegen und sie mit der Klasse durchzuführen.
  - kleine Kontrollen mit einem situativen Kontext zu entwickeln, in denen unregelmäßige Verben in verschiedenen Zeitformen verwendet werden müssen.

- *Memory* *Kärtchen*
  S beschriften kleine Kärtchen (5 x 5 cm) mit Verbformen (eine Verbform pro Kärtchen, also drei Kärtchen pro Verb) und spielen *Memory* nach den bekannten Regeln, allerdings darf jede/r S nicht nur zweimal, sondern dreimal ziehen, entsprechend der Anzahl der Kärtchen pro Verb. Wenn die Karten verdeckt auf den Tisch gelegt werden, sollte dies in geordneter Form erfolgen (in Reihen), um die Aufgabe nicht unnötig zu erschweren. Sieger ist, wer die meisten *triples* aufdecken konnte.

PB A10   Have you ever ...? No, I've never ...   Sprechen   *PB, S. 14*

- Um S Sicherheit bei der Verwendung der Zeiten zu geben, stellt L *present perfect* und *simple past* im Klassengespräch noch einmal gegenüber:
  L: *(Tim), have you ever been to a rock concert?* S1: *Yes, I have.*
  L: *I'm sure it was great. When was it?* S2: *Last year/summer/...*
- In Partnerarbeit formulieren S beliebige Fragen und Antworten.

Erweiterung:
Fragen und Antworten laufen in einem *chain game* quer durch die Klasse. Beispiel: S1: *Have you ever visited (Berlin)?* S2: *Yes, I have. I was there in (August).* (An eine/n andere/n S gewandt) *Have you ever eaten ice-cream for breakfast?* S3: *No, I haven't, but it sounds like a good idea.* (An eine/n weitere/n S gewandt) *Have you ever seen a film star?* S4: *...*

TB A10   Food, glorious food   Hören/Singen   *TB, S. 19*

- Anhören des Liedes bei geöffnetem TB, Bedeutungserschließung mithilfe der Zeichnungen. Nachdem der Text im Plenum gelesen wurde, kann mitgesungen werden.

PB A11   Funny food   Hören/Schreiben   *PB, S. 14*

- Anhören bei geschlossenem PB; kurze Inhaltsangabe; zweites Hören bei geöffnetem PB.
- Angeregt durch Lied (TB) und Gedicht versuchen sich S im Schreiben kleiner Gedichte (4- oder 6-Zeiler). Diese kreative Phase wird im Plenum vorbereitet:
  - Gemeinsames Sammeln von Reimwörtern für das Wortfeld *food*, z. B. *dish–fish, table–able; soup–group, drink–think/sink/pink, pie–fly, cheese–sneeze*
  - Alliterationen: *spicy spaghetti; fresh fish, old onion, tasty Turkish tomatoes* usw.

Medium	Nummer	Seite	Titel	Fertigkeit	Zusatzinfo
copy 4			A questionnaire about eating and cooking habits	Sprechen/Schreiben	
TB/CD	B1	20	Karim's curry party	Hören/Lesen/Sprechen	indisches Gericht
TB	B2	20	What do they need?	Sprechen	Rezepte
PB	B1	14f.	I need some more …	Schreiben/Sprechen	Wortschatzfestigung
PB	B2	16	Cooking pizza	Sprechen/Schreiben	*some* und *any*
copy 5			Where are these things?	Sprechen/Zeichnen	
TB	PP	21	India	Lesen	Geschichte Indiens
PB	B3	16f.	Britain and India	Lesen/Schreiben	Landeskunde
TB	B3	21	What dishes can you make?	Sprechen/Schreiben	mit Fantasie kochen
TB	B4	22	Sweet carrot halva	Lesen/Erproben	Rezept
PB	B4	17	Gujarati carrot salad	Lesen/Erproben	Rezept
TB	B5	22	Eating habits around the world	Lesen/Sprechen	Landeskunde; Leseverstehen
TB	B6	23	YOUR favourite party meal	Schreiben	Portfolio
PB	B5	18	Party food	Lesen/Schreiben	*scrambled sentences*
TB	B7	23	YOUR cookbook	Lesen/Sprechen/ Schreiben	Projekt
TB	Optional	24	Fish and chips	Lesen	Landeskunde

Die grau unterlegten Felder stellen das Pflichtpensum dar, die weißen die Kür.

Teil B: • Über das Kochen sprechen
 Zutaten auswählen
 Ein Rezept lesen
 Über fremde Gewohnheiten reden

L beginnt mit einem offenen Unterrichtsgespräch über die Ess- und Kochgewohnheiten der S: *Do you like cooking? Who does the cooking in your family? How often a week/a month do YOU make breakfast for your family? Are you good at making cakes/pizzas/spaghetti …? Does your family eat a lot of junk food?* S konzentrieren sich darauf, welche Äußerungen die anderen S machen und geben diese anschließend wieder, z. B.: *(Helena) says (that) she's good at making cakes.* Dabei werden die Strukturen der indirekten Rede immanent gefestigt.

• *Copymaster 4* bietet die Vorlage eines Fragebogens zu Ess- und Kochgewohnheiten. S befragen fünf Kinder in der Klasse. Die Ergebnisse werden mündlich vorgestellt.

TB B1 Karim's curry party   **Hören/Lesen/Sprechen**   *TB, S. 20*
• Anhören des Textes bei geschlossenem TB, (ggf. deutsche) Zusammenfassung, was S verstanden haben. Überprüfen des Grobverständnisses: *What is Karim cooking? (curry, poppadoms and cucumber raita) How many people is he inviting? (six – Vera, Gillian, Susan, Charlie, David, and Rosemary) Who is helping Karim in the kitchen? (Gillian and Vera) Why does Vera suddenly say "Ouch!"? (She's cut her finger.)*

TB B2 What do they need?   **Sprechen**   *TB, S. 20*
• Erneutes Anhören bei geöffnetem TB; S notieren die Zutaten für das Curry-Gericht: *What do you need to make a curry? (tomatoes, onions, oil, curry paste, coconut, carrots)*, die Ergebnisse werden an der Tafel zusammengetragen, Überschrift *Ingredients for a curry.*   *Tafel*
• S bilden mündlich Sätze nach dem Vorbild der Sätze im gelb unterlegten Kasten, schriftliche Sicherung in der Hausaufgabe.
Mögliche Lösungen: *Gillian needs some tomatoes. Gillian needs some onions. Karim needs some oil. There isn't any oil in the bottle. There is some oil in the cupboard. Karim doesn't need much curry paste. Karim has some plasters. There are some plasters in the cupboard above the sink. There aren't any knives in the drawers.*

> Erweiterung:
> Interessierte S erkundigen sich in einem indischen Restaurant nach einem detaillierten Curry-Rezept und notieren es für die Klasse. Alternativ finden sie Curry-Rezepte in einem Kochbuch zu Hause oder im Internet.

> **Zusatzinformationen:** *Curry*
> • *Curry is an Indian meal that was brought to Great Britain by Indian and Pakistani emigrants. Curry comes from the Indian word 'kari', which means* Schmorgericht. *The spice mixture that gives the meal its characteristic flavour is called curry after the name of the dish. A curry doesn't have to be hot, there are mild curries as well. The ingredients can be meat, fish or vegetables cooked with spices.*
> • *A poppadom is a crisp pancake usually fried in oil. You break off pieces and dip them in different spicy sauces.*
> • *Cucumber raita*
>
> | | |
> |---|---|
> | *1 cucumber* | *Wash the cucumber and grate one half of it. Mix* |
> | *450g of yoghurt* | *it with the yoghurt. Add the spices and the lemon* |
> | *a pinch of cayenne pepper* | *juice. Cut the other half of the cucumber into* |
> | *a pinch of cinnamon* | *little pieces and then mix everything with a spoon.* |
> | *a pinch of cardamom* | |
> | *1 teaspoon of fresh lemon juice* | |

PB B1 I need some more …   **Schreiben/Sprechen**   *PB, S. 14*
a) S erstellen die Liste in Einzelarbeit, im Anschluss an die Ergebnissicherung stellt L übergreifende Fragen, z. B.: *What's in the fridge? (butter, eggs, cheese, yoghurt, milk, ketchup) What's in the cupboard? (salt, pepper, biscuits, curry, spaghetti, rice, sugar) …*

Lösungen:

curry paste:	*on the middle shelf of the cupboard*
butter:	*in the fridge*
pepper:	*on the bottom shelf of the cupboard*
biscuits:	*on the bottom shelf of the cupboard*
teaspoons:	*in the drawer*
ketchup:	*in the fridge*
spaghetti:	*on the middle shelf of the cupboard*
eggs:	*in the fridge*
cheese:	*in the fridge*
salt:	*on the bottom shelf of the cupboard*
forks:	*in the drawer*
yoghurt:	*in the fridge*
knives:	*in the drawer*
rice:	*on the top shelf of the cupboard*
milk:	*in the fridge*
sugar:	*on the top shelf of the cupboard*

b) • S erarbeiten in Partnerarbeit mündlich Mini-Dialoge nach dem Muster im PB und präsentieren sie anschließend im Plenum. In leistungsschwachen Lerngruppen werden zunächst drei oder vier Dialoge gemeinsam erarbeitet.

• *Chain game:* S äußern sich zu den Vorräten zu Hause, z. B.: S1: *In our fridge there is/are ...* S2: *In (Annika's) fridge there is/are ..., and in our fridge there is/are ...* S3: *In (Annika's) fridge there is/are ..., in (Tim's) fridge there is/are ..., but in our fridge there is/are ...* Das Spiel kann erweitert werden, indem S auch Dinge nennen, die sie nicht im Kühlschrank haben: *In our fridge there isn't/aren't any ...*

PB B2 Cooking pizza   **Sprechen/Schreiben**   *PB, S. 16*

• Zur Vorbereitung übersetzen S einige Sätze ins Englische, um die Unterschiede zwischen *some* und *any* und ihren Zusammensetzungen zu wiederholen.
Ich brauche etwas Zucker. (Aussage) → *I need some sugar.*
Ich kann keinen Zucker finden. (Verneinung) → *I can't find any sugar.*
Hast du Kaffee zu Hause? (Frage) → *Have you got any coffee at home?*
Möchtest du Kaffee? (Frage als Angebot oder Bitte) → *Would you like some coffee?*

• Zur Unterstützung wird *lif* S. 112 herangezogen.   *TB, S. 112*

• Schriftliches Vervollständigen des Dialogs in Einzelarbeit.

• Lesen des Dialogs mit verteilten Rollen als Ergebniskontrolle.

Lösungen: *some, any, much, some, some, many, many, some, any, anything, some, someone, anyone, any, something, any, something*

> **Erweiterung:**
> *Copymaster 5* bietet eine Tandemübung. L kopiert die Vorlage so oft, dass für jedes Paar eine Kopie vorliegt, zerschneidet die Kopien und gibt S1 die obere und S2 die untere Hälfte. Somit verfügt S1 über die Informationen, die S2 fehlen, und umgekehrt. Durch gegenseitiges Fragen finden S heraus, wo sich die Gegenstände/Nahrungsmittel befinden, die am unteren Rand ihres Bildes abgebildet sind. Redemittel: *Where is/are the ...? – The ... is/are on/in/behind/in front of/next to ...* Aufgrund der erhaltenen Informationen zeichnen oder kleben S die Gegenstände/Nahrungsmittel in ihre Zeichnung ein. Ergänzender Wortschatz: *teapot, pot/saucepan, frying pan,* ggf. *mugs* (anstatt *cups*).

TB PP India   **Lesen**   *TB, S. 21*

In **Bayswater 1** und **2** waren die Texte zu Land und Leute jeweils auf Deutsch, nun ab Band 3 sind die Texte auf Englisch, die Rubrik heißt entsprechend *People and places.*

• Im Text sind zwar viele neue Vokabeln enthalten, jedoch sind die meisten aus dem Kontext sowie aufgrund der Sprachverwandtschaft zum Deutschen zu erschließen, zudem gehören sie nicht zum produktiv zu beherrschenden Wortschatz.

• Klassengespräch (ggf. auf Deutsch): Weshalb taucht im Englischlehrbuch ein Text über Indien auf, welche Zusammenhänge gibt es zwischen den beiden Ländern?

- S lesen den Text still, versuchen ihn ohne Wörterbuch zu verstehen.
- Eine kurze deutsche und anschließend englische Zusammenfassung des Textes hilft, sich einige der genannten Fakten einzuprägen, die anschließend für PB B3 benötigt werden.

> **Zusatzinformationen:** *India*
> Geschichtliche Fakten: Zunächst zum mongolischen Reich gehörend, wurde Indien nach der Entdeckung des Seeweges durch Vasco da Gama 1497 unter portugiesische Herrschaft gestellt, im 17. Jahrhundert wurde es niederländisch und britisch. Durch die *East Indian Company* wurde die Herrschaft Großbritanniens ständig ausgebaut, 1876 wurde *Queen Victoria* Kaiserin von Indien. Nach vielen vergeblichen Versuchen, die Unabhängigkeit zu erlangen, konnte diese 1949 proklamiert werden. Pandit Nehru wurde 1950 erster Ministerpräsident der Republik Indien.
> Aktuelle Daten: Die indische Gemeinde in London ist mit über 400 000 Menschen die größte ihrer Art in Europa. Es gibt überall indische Restaurants, die indische Kultur ist ein wesentlicher Bestandteil des britischen Lebens.

PB B3   Britain and India   **Lesen/Schreiben**   *PB, S. 16*

a) S korrigieren die falschen Sätze mithilfe des Textes *India*, TB S. 21.
Lösungen:
1. English is still one of the official languages and is spoken by many people.
2. Cricket and hockey are two of the most popular sports in India.
5. There are many shops and supermarkets in Britain where you can buy Indian spices.
6. A vindaloo is the hottest curry.

b) Auch für diese Teilaufgabe nehmen S den Text im TB zur Hilfe.
Mögliche Lösungen: *India became independent in 1949. Many people from India came to work in Britain in the 1950s and 1960s because Britain needed more workers in factories, hotels and hospitals. A sari is a sort of Indian dress. Today people of Indian origin play a big part in British life.*

> Erweiterung:
> Da die Beziehungen zwischen Indien und Großbritannien auch heute noch sehr eng sind, lohnt sich eine intensive Beschäftigung mit Geschichte und Gegenwart dieses Landes. S begeben sich auf die Suche nach weiteren Informationen, z. B. in Reisebüros, Lexika, Internet, und gestalten ein Poster mit Landkarte, wichtigen Städten und kleinen Texten zur Geschichte und aktuellen Situation wie auch zu den Beziehungen zwischen Indien und Großbritannien. Authentisches Material hilft, fremdsprachige Atmosphäre zu verbreiten, und stellt außerdem eine gute Vorbereitung auf *Theme 8B (English as a world language)* dar. Das Material kann auch für ein Quiz genutzt werden.

TB B3   What dishes can you make?   **Sprechen/Schreiben**   *TB, S. 21*

a) • L lässt zunächst aufzählen, was an Nahrungsmitteln zur Verfügung steht, dann werden im Unterrichtsgespräch mithilfe der vorgegebenen Redemittel Ideen gesammelt.
  • Alternative: Nach dem Vorbild der Fernsehsendung „Kochduell" arbeiten S in Gruppen zusammen. Die Gruppe, die nach einer bestimmten Zeit (fünf bis acht Minuten) die besten und realistischsten Vorschläge unterbreitet, ist Sieger des *cooking contest*.

b) Diese Zusatzaufgabe kann in die schriftliche Hausaufgabe verlegt werden. S lassen ihrer Fantasie freien Lauf, einige der „Kreationen" werden dem Rest der Lerngruppe in der Folgestunde vorgestellt.

TB B4   Sweet carrot halva   **Lesen/Erproben**   *TB, S. 21*

Idealerweise wird das Rezept gemeinsam in der Schulküche ausprobiert. In der vorhergehenden Stunde bespricht L mit S, wer welche Zutaten mitbringt. Wenn die räumlichen Bedingungen in der Schule das gemeinsame Kochen nicht zulassen, finden sich sicherlich einige S bereit, das Karottenhalva zu Hause zuzubereiten und in die Schule mitzubringen.

PB B4   Gujarati carrot salad   Lesen/Schreiben   *PB, S. 17*

- S bearbeiten die Aufgabe in Einzelarbeit. Auch hier lohnt sich die Umsetzung des Rezepts.
- Aussprache: Gujarati [ˌguːdʒəˈrɑtɪ]

Lösungen: *Mix the grated carrots with the salt in a bowl. Heat the oil in a small pan. When the oil is very hot, put in the mustard seeds. After ten seconds pour the oil and the mustard seeds over the carrots. Add the lemon juice and mix it with a fork. Serve warm or cold.*

TB B5   Eating habits around the world   Lesen/Sprechen   *TB, S. 22*

- S lesen die beiden kleinen Texte, zunächst jede/r still für sich, dann laut. Anschließend werden die angeschlossenen Fragen im Unterrichtsgespräch beantwortet.

TB B6   YOUR favourite party meal   Schreiben   *TB, S. 23*

Wie das Symbol in der Randspalte des TB zeigt, ist der zu erarbeitende Text für das Portfolio gedacht.

- Vorbereitend sammeln S in einem kurzen Unterrichtsgespräch mögliche Antworten und notieren Stichpunkte für ihren zu erstellenden Text.
- Die schriftliche Beantwortung der Fragen eignet sich für die Hausaufgabe.
- Wenn S es wünschen, können sie ihre Texte in der Folgstunde mit L oder anderen S besprechen. Dieses Editieren von Texten vor ihrer Fertigstellung ist ein wichtiger Schritt, um beim Schreiben unterschiedlichste Aspekte der Textgestaltung zu beachten, und bringt S nützliche Hinweise in Bezug auf Satzanfänge, Verknüpfung von Wörtern, Wortwahl und Satzstrukturen. Die endgültige Fassung wird in Ruhe zu Hause geschrieben, mit Zeichnungen oder Fotos versehen und ins Portfolio eingeheftet (vgl. TM S. 7f.).

PB B5   Party food   Lesen/Schreiben   *PB, S. 18*

Übung zur Festigung der Satzstellung

- S bearbeiten die Aufgabe in Einzel- oder Partnerarbeit, mündliche Kontrolle.

Lösungen: *My favourite party food is called Biryani. You need rice, lamb, onions, yoghurt, garlic and Indian spices. This dish is very popular in India and Pakistan. It takes three or four hours to prepare a good Biryani. Biryani is quite difficult to make.*

TB B7   YOUR cookbook   Projekt   *TB, S. 23*

Bei diesem ersten Projekt im Schuljahr ist es ratsam, von dem *tip* in der Randspalte des TB ausgehend mit S auf Deutsch Hinweise und Regeln für die Projektarbeit zu besprechen. Die erarbeiteten Punkte werden (möglichst auf Englisch!) auf einem Poster festgehalten, das während der gesamten Dauer des Projekts als Orientierung im Klassenraum hängt.

Mögliche Erweiterung des *tip* im TB:

1. Plan it.
- *Talk about and plan the project (use a mind map).*
- *Plan the work! Have ideas! Be creative!*
- *Who must do what?*

2. Do it.
- *Talk to people.*
- *Visit places and people.*
- *Look for material (library, Internet, …).*

3. Check it.
- *Discuss the results with your group.*
- *Make sure you haven't forgotten anything.*
- *Start to work on the presentation.*
- *Find the best and most interesting way to present it (use photos or music).*

4. Present it.
- *Organize a good time and/or place for your presentation.*
- *Work as a group.*
- *Do your best.*

Neben dem Aneignen von Fähigkeiten in der Planung, Organisation und Durchführung selbstbestimmten Arbeitens ist der soziale Aspekt ein entscheidender Faktor bei der Projektarbeit. S werden in diesen Phasen des Unterrichts zu Teamfähigkeit, Eigen- und Mitverantwortung, Disziplin und Kritikfähigkeit erzogen. Darüber hinaus ist es erfreulich zu sehen, wie begeistert sich S bei ausreichendem Freiraum für eine Idee einsetzen können, ohne sich von Hindernissen fachlicher Art aufhalten zu lassen.

Nach Abschluss der Arbeit müssen die Bemühungen der S gebührend gewürdigt werden. Da S oft sehr kritisch mit den eigenen Produkten, aber auch mit denen anderer S umgehen, muss L für eine ausgewogene Einschätzung sorgen. Sicherlich wird es in Inhalt und Ausführung Unterschiede geben, und es ist gut, wenn alle S diese Unterschiede wahrnehmen und diese Unterschiede auch benannt werden, doch meist gibt es in jedem Beitrag auch Positives zu entdecken. Gerade am Anfang des Schuljahres ist den S Mut für weitere Aufgaben dieser Art zu machen.

Besonders schöne Arbeitsergebnisse können an entsprechender Stelle in der Schule ausgestellt werden.

TB Optional   Fish and chips   **Lesen**   *TB, S. 24*

Der Text wird von S selbstständig gelesen und bearbeitet, L bietet zwei Niveaus der Textauswertung auf Karteikarten an. Beispiele:

↓:*Read the text and try to understand most of the information. There are not many new words, and it's not necessary to understand every word, but you can use the word list on page 143 of your textbook if you like.*

When you have read the text, write a few sentences about it. (You can do that in German.)

Or, if you don't want to do that, draw a picture of a fish and chips shop or of people eating fish and chips.

↑:*Read the text and try to understand most of the information. Don't use a dictionary. It's not necessary to understand each word in the text. Here is some help:*

'chippy' is another name for a fish and chips shop.

'haddock', 'cod' and 'plaice' are kinds of fish.

When you have read the text, write a few sentences about it in English but use your own words, please.

Medium	Nummer	Seite	Titel	Fertigkeit	Zusatzinfo
copy 6			How fit are you?	Schreiben/Sprechen	Fitnesstest
Folie 3			Fit for fun	Sprechen	Wortschatz: *sports*
TB	A1	26	Sports freak or couch potato?	Schreiben/Sprechen	*mind map*
PB	A1	19	Favourites	Schreiben/Sprechen	
copy 7			What a day!	Sprechen	Brettspiel
TB	A2	26	Who does what?	Sprechen	*adverbs of frequency* (R) und *adverbs of manner*
TB	lif 3	114	Adverbien der Art und Weise		
PB	A2	19	How do they do it?	Schreiben/Sprechen	*adverbs of frequency* (R) und *adverbs of manner*
TB	A3	27	Healthy, lazy, slow …	Sprechen/Schreiben	Adjektiv–Adverb
PB	A3	20	Nice and easy – easily and nicely	Schreiben	Adjektiv–Adverb (kontrastiv)
TB	A4	27	A day in the life …	Schreiben/Sprechen	Textproduktion
PB	A4	20	Where does it go?	Sprechen/Schreiben	*adverbs of frequency* (R)
copy 8			How …? How often …?	Sprechen	*adverbs of frequency* (R) und *adverbs of manner*
TB	A5	28	Sports hero of the week – Anfernee Hardaway	Sprechen/Lesen/Schreiben	Leseverstehen; Textverständnis; Basketball
PB	A5	21	Ask Anfernee	Sprechen/Schreiben	Interview/Fragestellung
Folie 4			Who is it? – An interview	Sprechen	Interview/Fragestellung
TB	A6	28	The most interesting team sport is …	Sprechen	Steigerung von Adjektiven (R)
PB	A6	21f.	Nicer or more dangerous?	Schreiben	Steigerung von Adjektiven (R)
TB/CD	A7	29	The Junior Knights Club	Hören	Eishockey
PB	A7	22f.	What did Scott say?	Schreiben/Lesen	Textverständnis
TB	A8	29	You must be fast to play ice-hockey	Lesen/Sprechen/Schreiben	*must, don't have to* (R) Portfolio
PB	A8	23	Must you …? No, you don't have to …	Sprechen/Schreiben	*must, don't have to* (R)

Die grau unterlegten Felder stellen das Pflichtpensum dar, die weißen die Kür.

Theme 2: How fit are you?

Teil A: • **Lebensgewohnheiten beschreiben**
Über Sportarten reden
Über Idole sprechen

Als Einstieg fordert L die S zu einigen kurzen gymnastischen Übungen auf, um (wieder) munter zu werden, die Anspannung der vorangegangenen Stunden abzuschütteln und sich vom Stillsitzen zu erholen. Da L die Übungen demonstriert, stellt unbekanntes Vokabular keine Hürde für S dar, gleichzeitig wird der Wortschatz *parts of the body* immanent wiederholt. Falls S die Übungen bereits kennen, übernimmt ein/e S die Rolle des „Vorturners".
Beispiele:
Swing your right/left arm/leg.
Shake your arms/hands/legs.
Jump up and down.
Stamp your feet.
Stretch your arms.
Sit down./Stand up again.
Snap your fingers.
Clap your hands.
Bend your knees.
Touch your ears/toes/right elbow/left knee/...

Auch das Bewegungs- und Konzentrationsspiel *Simon says* eignet sich gut als Einstieg in das *Theme*. S dürfen die Bewegungen nur dann ausführen, wenn die Aufforderung mit *Simon says* eingeleitet wird. Beispiel:
Simon says touch your right ear. → S berühren ihr rechtes Ohr.
Simon says touch your left toes. → S berühren ihre linken Zehen.
Touch your right elbow. → S dürfen keine Bewegung ausführen. Wer es dennoch tut, scheidet aus oder erteilt nun die Aufforderungen.

Copymaster 6 testet die sportliche Leistungsfähigkeit der S. Zunächst schätzen S sich selbst ein, danach wird der Test paar- oder gruppenweise durchgeführt (auch L macht mit!). Selbsteinschätzung und Realität werden anschließend verglichen, im Unterricht erfolgt ein kurzes auswertendes Klassengespräch: *How fit are you really? Was it easy/difficult/hard/no problem to jump up and down for 30 seconds/to step on and off a chair 10 times/...? Were you out of breath after exercise 3?* Auch bietet sich eine immanente Wiederholung der Steigerung von Adjektiven an, ohnehin eines der Wiederholpensen in *Theme 2: Which exercise was easiest/most difficult? Was lifting up your chair easier or more difficult than touching your left foot with your right hand? ...*
Abschließend werden die Gesamtergebnisse der Klasse an der Tafel zusammengefasst *Tafel* (*Is class ... fit?*) und versprachlicht: *15 pupils were out of breath after exercise 1./Everybody thought exercise 2 was the most difficult exercise./...*

Zur Vorbereitung auf TB A1 und zur Reaktivierung bekannten Wortschatzes zum Wortfeld *sports* wird Folie 4 eingesetzt, die mit bildlichen Impulsen die englischsprachigen Bezeichnungen von Sportarten ins Gedächtnis ruft und S zu Aussagen über bevorzugte Sportarten anregt.

TB A1   Sports freak or couch potato?   **Schreiben/Sprechen**   *TB, S. 26*
• *sports freak* erschließt sich von selbst, L führt *couch potato* ein, lässt S jedoch zunächst Vermutungen zur Bedeutung anstellen.
• S erstellen in Einzel- oder Partnerarbeit je eine *mind map* zu *sports freak* und *couch potato*. Alternativ erstellen sie nur eine *mind map* – welche, bleibt ihnen überlassen.
• Nach dieser Phase der Still-/Partnerarbeit werden die Ergebnisse an der Tafel zusammen- *Tafel* getragen, S ergänzen ihre *mind maps*.

- Klassengespräch: *What are sports freaks/couch potatoes interested in? What do they like eating? Where do they spend a lot of their time?* Da es in fast jeder Klasse übergewichtige S gibt, sollte mit der notwendigen Sensibilität vorgegangen werden, L achtet darauf, dass keine abwertenden/hänselnden Bemerkungen fallen.

PB A1   Favourites   **Schreiben/Sprechen**   *PB, S. 19*

a) S ordnen die vorgegebenen Wörter und Wendungen in Einzelarbeit, die Ergebnisse werden im Plenum abgerufen. Zur Versprachlichung der Ergebnisse verwenden S folgende Redemittel:
Couch potatoes/Sports freaks like eating …/They don't like eating …
Couch potatoes like sitting …/Sports freaks like going to …
… like/don't like …
Lösungen:
couch potato: favourite food: chocolate, chips and cream; favourite places: on the sofa, in front of the fridge/television; favourite words: relax, don't worry, take it easy; favourite activities: eating, sleeping and watching TV
sports freak: favourite food: salad, muesli and melon; favourite places: in the gym, at the sports centre/football stadium; favourite words: winner, first, champion; favourite activities: running, training, winning

b) Im Anschluss an das S-S-Gespräch stellen S die Vorlieben des Partners/der Partnerin dem Plenum vor: *(Patrick) likes/doesn't like …*

Copymaster 7 besteht aus zwei Seiten – dem Spielfeld *(Copymaster 7.1)* und den Anweisungen *(Copymaster 7.2)*. Das Spiel ist für zwei bis vier Spieler gedacht, festigt Wortschatz und Wendungen und kann für Phasen der Freiarbeit genutzt werden. Damit das Spielfeld haltbarer wird, kann es auf Pappe geklebt und laminiert werden. Zusätzlich werden Spielfiguren und ein Würfel benötigt.   *Spielfiguren, Würfel*

TB A2   Who does what?   **Sprechen**   *TB, S. 26*

- S ordnen die Sätze mündlich im Unterrichtsgespräch.
- Erst in einer zweiten Phase wird die Aufmerksamkeit der S auf die in jedem Satz verwendeten Adverbien *(adverbs of manner/adverbs of frequency)* gelenkt: L bereitet die Sätze auf Folienstreifen vor, mit Lücken zum Einsetzen der Adverbien. S lesen die Sätze ohne Adverbien laut, erkennen, dass die Sätze auch ohne Adverb grammatisch vollständig sind. L legt die fehlenden Adverbien auf *(quickly, regularly, well, rarely* (2x), *very fast, happily, very slowly, lazily, healthily, permanently, usually)*, S setzen ein.   *Folienstreifen*
- L unterscheidet an der Tafel zwischen Adverbien der Häufigkeit *(regularly, rarely, permanently, usually)*, Adverbien der Art und Weise *(quickly, happily, slowly, lazily, healthily)* und unregelmäßigen Adverbien *(well, fast)*.   *Tafel*
- Übergang zu *lif 3,* TB S. 114.   *TB, S. 114*
Lösungen:
A sports freak walks up and down stairs quickly without getting out of breath/goes swimming regularly/plays tennis and swims well/rarely eats crisps and burgers/can run very fast/happily eats salads and fresh fruit.
A couch potato gets out of bed very slowly/sits lazily in front of the television/doesn't eat healthily/permanently plays computer games/rarely moves from his/her chair/usually goes everywhere by car.

lif 3   Adverbien der Art und Weise   **Lesen**   *TB, S. 114*
Leistungsstarke Lerngruppen arbeiten die Regeln zu Bildung und Gebrauch der Adverbien selbstständig durch, in anderen Lerngruppen werden sie im Plenum gelesen und besprochen. Eine Festigung der erworbenen Kenntnisse findet in den anschließenden Übungen in TB und PB statt.

PB A2 How do they do it? Schreiben/Sprechen *PB, S. 19*
- L erläutert an der Tafel die unterschiedliche Stellung von Adverbien der Häufigkeit (zwischen Subjekt und Verb) und Adverbien der Art und Weise (üblicherweise am Satzende). *Tafel*
- S bereiten die Übung mündlich vor, L weist darauf hin, dass jedes Adverb mindestens einmal verwendet werden soll.
- Die Ergebnisse werden im Unterrichtsgespräch abgerufen, schriftliche Sicherung in der Hausaufgabe.

Mögliche Lösung:
A sports freak rarely plays computer games.
A couch potato rarely eats fresh vegetables.
A sports freak does everything quickly.
A couch potato sits in front of the television lazily.
A sports freak lives and eats healthily.
A couch potato walks everywhere slowly.
A sports freak regularly trains at a fitness studio.
A couch potato goes to school lazily.
A sports freak can run fast.
A couch potato is permanently half asleep.
A sports freak usually likes to walk.
A couch potato can't play any sport well.

TB A3 Healthy, lazy, slow ... Sprechen/Schreiben *TB, S. 27*
Übung zur Bildung von Adverbien
- Eine Kontrastierung Adjektiv–Adverb erfolgt hier noch nicht, der erste Satz erfordert jeweils das Adjektiv, der zweite das Adverb.
- Sätze 2 und 3 werden mündlich im Plenum erarbeitet, der Rest schriftlich in Einzelarbeit.
- Die Ergebnisse werden zunächst in Partnerarbeit verglichen und ggf. korrigiert, anschließend gemeinsam im Plenum.

Lösungen: *2. lazy, lazily 3. slow, slowly 4. quick, quickly 5. regular, regularly 6. good, well 7. fast, fast 8. happy, happily*

PB A3 Nice and easy – easily and nicely Schreiben *PB, S. 20*
Erste kontrastierende Übung zur Verwendung von Adjektiv und Adverb
- Falls die Übung in die häusliche Arbeit verlegt wird, bereitet L für die Folgestunde eine Folie mit den Sätzen und Folienstreifen mit den Adjektiven und Adverbien vor, so dass eine gemeinsame Überprüfung und eventuelle Korrekturen möglich sind. *Folie, Folienstreifen*
- S begründen jeweils den Einsatz von Adjektiv oder Adverb.

Lösung: *regularly, healthy, slowly, healthily, well, slow, quickly, happily, lazily, good, lazy, regular, quick*

TB A4 A day in the life ... Schreiben/Sprechen *TB, S. 27*
a) • S erarbeiten in Gruppen einen Text über *couch potatoes*. Alternativ wird es S freigestellt, ob sie über *couch potatoes* oder über *sports freaks* schreiben möchten.
  • Idealerweise verwenden S in ihren Texten viele Adverbien, allerdings soll diese Vorgabe S nicht in ihrem Schreibfluss stören, die Textproduktion steht im Vordergrund.

b) Die Texte eignen sich – abgesehen vom Vortrag in der Klasse – auch für das Portfolio. Für diesen Zweck können S sie durch Zeichnungen oder Fotos ergänzen. *Portfolio*

 c) Zusatzaufgabe: S diskutieren in Gruppen bzw. in der Klasse die positiven und negativen Seiten eines Lebens als *couch potato*. S bereiten ihre Argumente stichwortartig vor, dies ermöglicht auch langsameren S die Teilnahme an der Diskussion.

Erweiterung:
Wenn die Thematik allgemein interessiert, erstellen S mit Texten und Zeichnungen/Fotos in Gruppenarbeit Poster, auf denen das Leben von *couch potatoes* und *sports freaks* anschaulich und lustig gegenübergestellt wird. Die Ergebnisse werden im Klassenzimmer ausgehängt.

PB A4   Where does it go?   Sprechen/Schreiben   *PB, S. 20*

Festigung der Stellung der Adverbien der Häufigkeit

Ein/e S wiederholt die Stellung der Adverbien der Häufigkeit (zwischen Subjekt und Verb), zwei Beispiele werden gemeinsam besprochen, die weiteren Sätze in der schriftlichen Hausaufgabe erarbeitet.

Lösungen:

Miss Lazybones never gets up before eleven o'clock. She regularly watches television all day. She never has to run to school. She always goes to school by bus. She is always in bed when I telephone her. She often misses lessons at school. She regularly sits on the sofa all day.

Miss Fitness is always awake early. She regularly goes to bed before ten o'clock. She never sits in front of the television all day. She regularly goes to the gym. She always runs or cycles to school. She has always enjoyed sport. She often plays tennis in the summer.

Copymaster 8 bietet 28 Tätigkeiten und 2 x 18 Adverbien und festigt Gebrauch und Stellung der Adverbien. Das Behalten wird durch das Anfassen und „Be-greifen" der Karten unterstützt.

Partnerspiel: Jedes Paar bekommt eine Kopie des Blattes und schneidet zunächst die Kärtchen aus: Beide S bekommen einen Satz der Adverbien, die Tätigkeitskärtchen werden verdeckt auf den Tisch gelegt. S1 zieht eine Tätigkeit und stellt S2 eine Frage, die entweder nach der Art und Weise oder nach der Häufigkeit fragt, z. B.: *How do you do gym exercises?/How often do you sit in front of the television?* S2 antwortet mit einem vollständigen Satz mit Adverb und legt dann die Adverbkarte und die Tätigkeitskarte beiseite. Nun zieht S2 eine Tätigkeit und fragt S1. Usw.

Das Spiel kann auch zu dritt oder viert gespielt werden. Ebenso können S die Tätigkeitskärtchen um eigene ergänzen.

TB A5   Sports hero of the week – …   Sprechen/Lesen   *TB, S. 28*
Tafel
• L beginnt einen Basketballkorb an die Tafel zu zeichnen, S erraten, was gezeichnet wird (*Guess what I'm drawing.*). Anschließend fragt L die S nach ihrem Vorwissen: *Do you like basketball? What do know about basketball? Do you know any players, teams, …?* Auch ein mitgebrachter Basketball oder Fotos von Spielern können das Gespräch anregen.

• S lesen den Text still.

• L verweist auf den *tip* in der Randspalte, S und L rechnen ihre Körpergröße in *foot* und *inch* um.

• Der Text weist noch weitere Zahlen auf, so bietet er Anlass für eine Wiederholung der Datumsangabe und der Jahreszahlen.

a) S lesen den Text nochmals jede/r für sich, die falschen Sätze werden im Unterrichtsgespräch verbessert.
   Lösungen: *1. Anfernee was born in Memphis, Tennessee. 3. His father showed him how to play basketball. 4. Penny became top scorer at his high school in Memphis. 5. Penny's career almost ended when he was shot by robbers. 7. Penny became Player of the Year in college. 8. Penny is still young and one of the most famous basketball players in the United States.*

b) • In leistungsstarken Lerngruppen wird die Aufgabe in die Hausaufgabe gegeben, in leistungsschwachen Gruppen wird sie im Unterricht in Partnerarbeit erarbeitet. Die Ergebnisse werden anschließend in der Klasse vorgelesen. Bei Interesse der S können die Texte schön gestaltet und im Klassenzimmer ausgehängt/ausgelegt werden.

   • Alternativ halten S ihren Lebenslauf als berühmte Sportler lediglich stichwortartig fest und interviewen sich anschließend gegenseitig zu ihren „berühmten Sportlerkarrieren".

Erweiterung:
Vielleicht gibt es in der Klasse ein/e S, der/die Basketball spielt und/oder besonders von dieser Sportart begeistert ist. Dann bittet L diese/n S, in einer der nächsten Stunden ein Mini-Referat (ca. drei Minuten) über den Sport zu halten (Anzahl der Spieler pro Mannschaft, einfachste Regeln, bekannte Sportler, Mannschaften, Besonderheiten, …).

Zusatzinformationen: *Basketball*
Basketball is one of the most exciting indoor sports. With a basket on a wall and a large ball it is easy to play. The basic rules are: no running with the ball except when dribbling, you may use your hands only for passing the ball and throwing it towards the basket.
There are five players in each team. The players try to throw the ball through the basket, an open net fixed to a metal ring high up off the ground.
In 1891 the YMCA training instructor Dr James Naismith in Springfield/Massachusetts hung peach baskets from the balcony at opposite ends of the gym when it was not possible to play sports outside in the freezing New England winter. The game became popular in North America and then internationally. 21 nations sent their teams to the 1936 Olympic Games. The 1972 USA – USSR final has gone down in history as one of the most sensational matches of all time. Since 1976 basketball has been an Olympic Games sport for women, too.
Today, 193 countries belong to the FIBA, the world's main basketball association.

PB A5   Ask Anfernee   Sprechen/Schreiben   *PB, S. 21*
a) Erarbeitung in schriftlicher Einzelarbeit.
  Lösungen: *I'm (abhängig vom aktuellen Jahr)./I'm from Memphis, Tennessee./I lived in Memphis, and I grew up with my grandmother./When I became Player of the Year in college, I scored 729 points in one season./I'm 6'7''./It's my dream to get to the NBA Hall of Fame.*

b) In leistungsschwachen Lerngruppen können die Fragen und Antworten in Partnerarbeit erarbeitet werden.
  Mögliche Lösungen:
  Who showed you how to play basketball? – One day my father came to visit me in Memphis and he showed me.
  Have you got a golden rule? – Yes, I always stayed away from the drugs and violence on the streets of Memphis.
  Why do people call you Penny? – When I was a little boy, I was smaller than the other boys.

Erweiterung:
Folie 5 bietet ausreichend Gesprächsanlässe für Interview und Fragestellung. S haben die Möglichkeit, eine reale, bekannte oder fiktive Person zu interviewen. Ebenso kann das Interview als Rätsel gestaltet werden, die Fragesteller müssen die wahre Identität der befragten Person in Erfahrung bringen.

TB A6   The most interesting team sport is …   Sprechen   *TB, S. 28*
Übung zur Wiederholung der Steigerung von Adjektiven
• Einleitendes Klassengespräch: *What sport do you like? Is it dangerous/difficult/…?*
• S vergleichen im Unterrichtsgespräch die verschiedenen Sportarten, sowohl die Adjektive als auch die Sportarten können beliebig erweitert werden. Schriftliche Sicherung von mindestens fünf Sätzen in der Hausaufgabe.
• Ein/e oder zwei leistungsstarke S wiederholen die Regeln zur Steigerung von Adjektiven. Zur Unterstützung kann *lif* herangezogen werden.   *TB, S. 116*

PB A6   Nicer or more dangerous?   **Schreiben**   *PB, S. 21f.*
a) S ergänzen die fehlenden Formen in Einzelarbeit, begründen ihre Ergebnisse anschließend im Unterrichtsgespräch, das von einer kleinen, leistungsstarken Gruppe geleitet werden kann, und bieten L so einen guten Einblick in ihre Kenntnisse.
  Lösungen: *beautiful–more beautiful–most beautiful, busy–busier–busiest, bad–worse–worst, brilliant–more brilliant–most brilliant, cheap–cheaper–cheapest, difficult–more difficult–most difficult, clever–cleverer–cleverest, violent–more violent–most violent, good–better–best, early–earlier–earliest*

b) Beantwortung in Einzelarbeit. Ein Abrufen der Ergebnisse ist nicht notwendig, da die Ergebnisse in Teilaufgabe c) gesichert werden.

c) Um die Teilaufgabe vorzuentlasten, können die zehn Adjektive zunächst im Plenum gesteigert werden, anschließend Erarbeitung der Vergleiche in Einzelarbeit.

TB A7   The Junior Knights Club   Hören   *TB, S. 29*
S hören den Text bei geschlossenem TB von der CD mit folgender Aufgabe: Was erfahrt ihr über Eishockey? Was ist neu für euch? Was wusstet ihr schon? S beantworten die Fragen auf Deutsch.

PB A7   What did Scott say?   Schreiben/Lesen   *PB, S. 22f.*
a) S entwirren zunächst gemeinsam die *scrambled words (helmet, foul, ice-skates, stick, puck, rink, padded clothing)*, erst dann vervollständigen sie die Sätze und lesen sie anschließend laut vor.
Lösungen: *ice-skates, puck, helmet, rink, stick, foul, padded clothing*

b) S lesen das Interview im TB und verbessern dann die falschen Aussagen.
Lösungen: *2. Professional ice-hockey players sometimes have three or four games a week – that's a lot more than professional footballers. 3. It's a hard game, but you don't have to be violent. 5. The padded clothing and the helmet weigh about seven kilos.*

TB A8   You must be fast to play ice-hockey   Lesen/Sprechen/Schreiben   *TB, S. 29*
a) S lesen das Interview mit Scott ein weiteres Mal jede/r für sich (auf lautes Lesen sollte aufgrund der hohen Anzahl neuer Wörter verzichtet werden) und beantworten die Frage unter Verwendung der Strukturen *you must* und *you don't have to*. Sollte dies Schwierigkeiten bereiten, wird *lif* zur Unterstützung herangezogen.   *TB, S. 116*
Lösungen:
You must be very fast/very fit/very good on ice-skates/flexible/strong enough to wear all the padded clothing and helmet/quite hard.
You don't have to be tall/violent.

b) S übertragen die Ergebnisse aus Teilaufgabe a) im Gespräch mit einem Partner/einer Partnerin auf andere Sportarten.

c) Mithilfe einer Sportzeitschrift oder des Internets finden S so viel wie möglich über ihre/n Lieblingssportler/in heraus, Musterinformationen bieten TB A5 und PB A5. Der Text (einschließlich Begründung, weshalb man diese/n Sportler/in gewählt hat!), geht mit Zeichnungen und/oder Fotos gestaltet in das Portfolio ein.

PB A8   Must you ...? No, you don't have to ...   Sprechen/Schreiben   *PB, S. 23*
Übung zur Wiederholung von *must* und *don't have to*
a) S formulieren mindestens sieben Fragen, die Vorgaben können beliebig ergänzt werden.
Mögliche Lösungen:
Do you have to study hard to go to university?
Do you have to be rich to be happy?
Do you have to eat healthy food to look good?
Do you have to be clever to make a lot of money?
Do you have to be fit to become a good footballer?
Do you have to eat a lot to be a strong athlete?
Do you have to be clever to play computer games?

b) L achtet darauf, dass S die Fragen in Langsätzen *(No, you don't have to be rich to be happy.)*, nicht in Kurzantworten *(No, you don't.)* beantworten.

Medium	Nummer	Seite	Titel	Fertigkeit	Zusatzinfo
TB/CD	B1	30	The story of Christy Brown	Hören/Lesen	Lebensgeschichte eines behinderten Autors
copy 9			The story of Christy Brown	Lesen	Textverständnis
TB	B2	31	Christy's life	Schreiben	*summary*
PB	B1	24	The story of Helen Keller	Schreiben	
TB	B3	31	My Left Foot	Lesen	Film über Christy Brown
TB	B4	32	What could he do?	Lesen/Sprechen	*to be able to, can/can't, could/couldn't*
TB	lif 4	115	to be able to		
PB	B2	24f.	When were you able to …?	Sprechen/Schreiben	*to be able to*
TB	PP	32	The Paralympics	Lesen	Geschichte der Paralympics
PB	B3	25	Olympics and Paralympics	Schreiben	Wortfamilie *able*
TB	B5	33	Disabled people in the community	Lesen/Sprechen/ Schreiben	Projekt: Broschüre über Behinderte in unserer Gesellschaft
TB/CD	Optional	34	Kieran	Hören/Lesen	Gedicht über einen Rollstuhlfahrer

Die grau unterlegten Felder stellen das Pflichtpensum dar, die weißen die Kür.

Teil B: • Über Behinderungen und Behindertensport sprechen

TB B1   The story of Christy Brown   Hören/Lesen   *TB, S. 30*

S entscheiden selbst über ihr Vorgehen bei der Texterschließung. L entwickelt mit S Fragen an der Tafel, S übernehmen sie in ihre Hefte (Rubrik: Lernstrategien/Arbeitstechniken).   *Tafel*
Mögliche Fragen:
- Leseziele: Willst du den Text vollständig, mit einigen Details oder nur grob verstehen?
- Vorgehensweise: Willst du den Text zunächst einmal hören – bei geschlossenem oder geöffnetem TB? Oder möchtest du ihn lieber nur lesen?
- Umgang mit unbekanntem Vokabular: Welche Techniken zum Verstehen unbekannter Wörter kennst du?
  - Die Verwandtschaft zum Deutschen: *feed*–füttern, hier: ernähren; *bricklayer*–ein Mensch, der Ziegelsteine „legt", ein Maurer.
  - International verwendete Wörter: *control, modern*.
  - Aus dem Zusammenhang erschließen: *His mother always found time – and patience – to help Christy …:* die Mutter hatte immer Zeit, ihrem Sohn zu helfen; was gehört noch dazu außer Zeit? Geduld.
  - Das *Vocabulary* (S. 145f.) oder das *Dictionary* (ab S. 168) im TB.
  - Ein ‚normales' Wörterbuch E-D.
- Selbstkontrolle: Wie überprüfe ich, ob ich den Text verstanden habe?
  - Mithilfe eines vorbereiteten Arbeitsblatts (*Copymaster 9*).
  - Durch ein Gespräch mit einem Partner/einer Partnerin.
  - Durch ein Gespräch mit L/Klassengespräch.

Nach dieser vorbereitenden Phase entscheiden sich S für ihr Verfahren und finden sich ggf. mit anderen zusammen, die dasselbe Verfahren gewählt haben. (L stellt CD zur Verfügung.)

Die Textauswertung erfolgt gemeinsam und konzentriert sich auf folgende Fragen: *What could Christy Brown do? What couldn't he do? How did his family help him?*

TB B2   Christy's life   Lesen/Schreiben   *TB, S. 31*
- Nochmaliges Lesen des Textes.
- Vervollständigen der Sätze mithilfe des Textes und unter Verwendung eigener Formulie-rungen.
- Nach dem Vergleich der Ergebnisse im Plenum lesen S die 15 Sätze einmal zusammen-hängend, um ein Gespür für Struktur und Länge eines *summary* zu bekommen.

Mögliche Lösung: *1. Christy Brown was born in Dublin in 1932. 2. He had many brothers and sisters. 3. The family was poor. 4. It became clear that Christy was handicapped when he was a few months old. 5. He could not move properly. 6. His mother decided to help him. 7. She helped him to learn the alphabet and to write with his left foot. 8. He could draw pictures. 9. People bought his pictures. 10. An American doctor, who worked in a clinic for children and young people like Christy, visited him one day. 11. Christy went to the clinic. 12. He learned how to control his body a little. 13. He wrote a book about his family, "My Left Foot". 14. It was a bestseller. 15. He won many prizes as a writer.*

PB B1   The story of Helen Keller   Schreiben   *PB, S. 24*
- Nach dem Vorbild des Textes über Christy Brown ergänzen S die fehlenden Elemente. Eine Kontrolle erfolgt über OHP oder durch Vorlesen des vervollständigten Textes.   *Folie*
- Nach dem Lesen schließen S für einige Minuten die Augen und stellen sich vor, sie wären blind: Welche Probleme ergeben sich daraus? Welche Sinne werden geschärft, wenn man nicht sehen kann?

Lösung: *Helen Keller was born in Tuscumbia, Alabama in the U.S.A. in 1880. When she was nineteen months old, she became ill. After that she was not able to hear and she couldn't see; she was completely deaf and blind. When she was seven years old, her family found a teacher called Anne Mansfield Sullivan. She was able to teach Helen to read and write using a special machine. Helen was also able to "listen" to people talking by putting her hands on their faces. First she learned to read and write, and then she started to learn how to speak. After one month she was able to speak very well. She went to high school and became a writer. In her books she describes her disabilities and how she learned to read, write and speak. One of her most famous books is called "Out of the Dark". She died in 1968.*

Erweiterung:
Um die Erfahrung des „Blindseins" zu konkretisieren, gehen S paarweise zusammen, S1 verbindet sich die Augen und bewegt sich „blind" im Raum oder auf dem Schulgelände, begleitet von S2, der/die aufpasst, dass nichts passiert. S2 ermöglicht S1 besondere Tast- und Geruchserlebnisse (Gras, Erde, Plastik, Radiergummi, …). Anschließend wird getauscht.
Aus der kurzen Selbsterfahrung heraus, sich nur auf das Ohr, auf Tast- und Geruchssinn zu verlassen, können bei S interessante kleine Gedichte entstehen. Das Schreiben beginnt mit der Sammlung von Wörtern und Wendungen, z. B.: *black around me, dark/darkness, sun–trees–flowers–what colours are they?, I can see with my ears, What is blue/red …?* Die Ergebnisse, die sich keineswegs reimen müssen, finden mit weiteren Gedichten, die im Laufe des 7. Schuljahres entstehen, Eingang in ein *book of poems*.

TB B3   My Left Foot   Lesen   *TB, S. 31*

a) S entscheiden sich wie in TB B1 selbstständig für ihr Vorgehen bei der Texterschließung. Die knappe Kontrolle des Verstehens erfolgt im Klassengespräch oder in Partnerarbeit.

b) Diese anspruchsvolle Aufgabe kann in Partnerarbeit erledigt werden. Kinoprogramme oder Jugendzeitschriften sind hierfür hilfreich. Besonders gut gelungene Darstellungen – evtl. mit Fotos aus Filmen – werden im Klassenraum, in der *English Corner*, veröffentlicht oder auf großen Poster allen zugänglich gemacht. Weniger leistungsstarke S beschränken sich u. U. auf das Leben ihres Lieblingsschauspielers/ihrer Lieblingsschauspielerin.

TB B4   What could he do?   Lesen/Sprechen   *TB, S. 32*

Bewusstmachung *to be able to*

a) S lesen die Sätze, übersetzen sie und verallgemeinern, was ausgedrückt wird: die Fähigkeit, etwas zu tun (Eintrag ins Heft unter dieser Redeabsicht!). Die Umformulierung der Sätze erfolgt im Unterrichtsgespräch.
Lösungen: *Christy couldn't go to school. Christy's brothers made him a box so that he could play with them. When he was older, Christy could draw and write with his left foot. Christy could sell the pictures he drew. If you break your leg, you can't play football. She can write with her left hand and her right hand. Can you swim?*

b) • S formulieren Sätze mit *When I was five …* Stützender Tafelanschrieb:
   When I was five,
   I could …, but I couldn't …
   I was able to …, but I wasn't able to …
 • In leistungsschwachen Lerngruppen werden bejahte Aussage und Verneinung zunächst getrennt, erst in einem zweiten Schritt erfolgt die Kontrastierung.
 • Hausaufgabe: Jede/r S schreibt fünf Sätze, die über die Vorgaben im TB hinausgehen.

lif 4   to be able to   Lesen   *TB, S. 115*

 • Stilles Lesen der Angaben bis zur Überschrift *simple past*.
 • Wiedergabe des Erfassten mit eigenen Worten.
 • Alternativ erarbeitet eine kleine Gruppe von S die Strukturen gemeinsam mit der Klasse .

PB B2   When were you able to …?   Sprechen/Schreiben   *PB, S. 24*

 • L achtet darauf, dass S nicht ihre eigenen, sondern die Antworten des Partners/der Partnerin eintragen.
 • Gemeinsames Gespräch in der Klasse für Vergleich und evtl. Korrekturen.
 • Interessierte S gestalten für ihr Portfolio einen Text mit Fotos: *When I was one (year old), I was/wasn't able to … When I was three (years old), I was/wasn't able to …*   *Portfolio*

TB PP   The Paralympics   Lesen/Sprechen   *TB, S. 32*

 • S lesen den Text in Stillarbeit und beantworten anschließend folgende Fragen:
   What are the Paralympics? In what kinds of sports do the athletes compete? When did the Paralympics begin? What do athletes show the world? What are their dreams?
 • Aktualisierung: An den *Paralympics* 2000 in Sydney nahmen 4000 Aktive teil.

> **Erweiterung:**
> S sammeln Informationen über die letzten oder kommenden *Paralympics* (Winterspiele: Nagano/Japan 1998 und Salt Lake City/USA 2002, Sommerspiele: Sydney/Australien 2000 und Athen 2004).
> Nützliche Internetadressen: www.paralympic.org, www.saltlake2002.com, www.rollstuhlsport.de, www.behindertensport.de

PB B3   Olympics and Paralympics   Schreiben   *PB, S. 25*

Übung zu den Wortbildungsmöglichkeiten mit dem Wortstamm *able*.
- L klärt zunächst die Bedeutung der einzusetzenden Wörter, danach Vervollständigen der Sätze in Einzelarbeit.
- Vergleich mit dem Partner/der Partnerin; bei Schwierigkeiten erfolgt die Klärung im Klassengespräch oder im individuellen Gespräch mit L.

Lösungen: *disabled, disabilities, able, unable, able, able-bodied, able, ability, disabled, unable, able-bodied, ability*

TB B5   Disabled people in the community   Projekt   *TB, S. 33*

Dieses Projekt ermöglicht die Öffnung des Englischunterrichts in mehrfacher Hinsicht:
- Zusammenarbeit mit anderen Fächern (Deutsch, Religion, Ethik)
- Bewusstes Wahrnehmen der Lebensbedingungen für Behinderte in der eigenen Umgebbung, der Stadt, dem Dorf, dem Stadtteil
- Sensibilisierung für die Bedürfnisse und Erfahrungen Behinderter und ihrer Familien
- Schulung von Schlüsselkompetenzen wie Eigenverantwortlichkeit und Teamfähigkeit (Arbeits- und Zeiteinteilung, Sammeln und Auswerten authentischer Materialien aus unterschiedlichen Medien).

S legen eigenständig Themen und Schwerpunkte für die Projektarbeit fest und teilen sich in Gruppen auf, L übernimmt lediglich beobachtende und beratende Funktion.

Die angegebenen Schritte im TB eröffnen S die Möglichkeit, all ihre Talente und Fähigkeiten einzubringen. Für die Ausformulierung und Gestaltung der Texte ist eine Arbeitsphase in der Klasse einzuplanen, in der S Probleme thematisieren können und von L Hilfe und Hinweise erhalten.

Punkt 6 der Liste im SB kann um eine Präsentation der gefundenen Materialien erweitert werden, um S auch in dieser Fähigkeit zu schulen. Die Gruppen berichten jeweils über ihre Vorgehensweise und möglichen Probleme bei der Beschaffung der Materialien.

Überlegungen sind schließlich auch zur gegenseitigen Bewertung der Ergebnisse erforderlich: zum Anteil der einzelnen Gruppenmitglieder, zu den Ergebnissen im Vergleich zu anderen Gruppen, zur Wirksamkeit auf den Betrachter/Leser der Broschüre. Diese Überlegungen stellt L gemeinsam mit S an.

TB Optional   Kieran   Hören/Lesen   *TB, S. 34*

S stimmen ab, ob sie das Gedicht lieber hören, bei geschlossenem oder geöffnetem TB, oder lesen möchten. Da es bei diesem Text in erster Linie um die emotionale Wirkung geht, sollte auf auswertende Aufgaben verzichtet werden, bei Verständnisschwierigkeiten fasst ein/e leistungsstarke/r S oder L den Inhalt auf Englisch (oder Deutsch) zusammen.

Medium	Nummer	Seite	Titel	Fertigkeit	Zusatzinfo
Folie 5			Carnival here and there	Sprechen	Wortschatzwiederholung und -erweiterung
TB	A1	36	Here comes Carnival	Lesen/Sprechen	*Notting Hill Carnival*
TB	A2	37	Notting Hill Carnival	Lesen/Sprechen	
PB	A1	26	Carnival sights and sounds	Schreiben	Wortschatzfestigung
PB	A2	26	Are you sure?	Lesen/Schreiben	Textverständnis
TB	lif 5	118	Relativsätze		
PB	A3	27	What can you remember?	Schreiben	Relativsätze
copy 10			Who or which?	Lesen	Relativpronomen
TB	A3	38	Who's who and what's what?	Sprechen	Textverständnis; Relativsätze
TB	A4	38	Carnival and the people of Notting Hill	Hören/Sprechen/ Schreiben	
PB	A4	28	Do you know who ...?	Schreiben	Allgemeinbildung
PB	A5	29	Carnival love	Lesen	Gedächtnistraining
TB/CD	A5	39	Steelband jump up	Hören	
TB	A6	40	The dark side of Carnival	Lesen	
TB	PP	40	The Metropolitan Police	Lesen	Landeskunde
PB	A6	29	Missing letters	Lesen/Schreiben	Wortschatzfestigung
TB/CD	A7	41	At Notting Hill police station	Hören/Schreiben	Hörverstehen; *past progressive*
TB	lif 6	119	Past progressive		
PB	A7	30f.	The wrong words	Hören/Schreiben/Lesen	Hörverstehen; *past progressive*
Folie 6			What happened while ...?	Sprechen	*past progressive*
PB	A8	31	Pairs	Sprechen/Schreiben	*past progressive*
copy 11			While I was sleeping ...	Sprechen	Spiel
TB	A8	41	YOUR street festival	Lesen/Schreiben	Portfolio
PB/CD	A9	32	The village festival	Hören	Hörverstehen

Die grau unterlegten Felder stellen das Pflichtpensum dar, die weißen die Kür.

Theme 3: Going public

Teil A: • Veranstaltungen kommentieren
           • Über Vor- und Nachteile von Großveranstaltungen sprechen

Obgleich die Begeisterung für Karneval oder Fasching in Deutschland regional sehr unterschiedlich ist, wird der Bericht über *Notting Hill Carnival*, Europas größtes Straßenfest mit jährlich über zwei Millionen Besuchern, die S sicherlich interessieren. Sie lernen London von seiner sehr farbenfrohen Seite kennen: ein weiteres Beispiel für London als multikulturelle Gemeinschaft.

Notting Hill Carnival geht auf die Initiative der afro-karibischen Gemeinde zurück, alle Einwohner des Stadtteils *Notting Hill*, unabhängig von ihrer Herkunft und ihrem Kulturkreis, zu einem gemeinsamen Fest zusammenzubringen und die alltäglichen Probleme, den Rassismus, den Mangel an Arbeitsmöglichkeiten und die schlechten Wohnbedingungen für einen Tag zu vergessen. Sich tanzend, musizierend und singend auf der Straße zu treffen und gemeinsam zu feiern, war Ausdruck ihrer kulturellen Identität und half, soziale Spannungen zwischen ethnischen Gruppierungen abzubauen.

Wie erhofft, war schon das erste Fest 1964 ein großer Erfolg. Mittlerweile ist daraus ein multikulturelles Großereignis geworden: ein farbenfroher Umzug mit fantasievollen Wagen zieht fünf Kilometer durch die Straßen von *Notting Hill*. Hunderte von Ständen bieten neben Kunst und handwerklichen Produkten exotische Köstlichkeiten an. Als Besonderheit treten auf drei großen Bühnen internationale Stars auf.

Das fröhliche Fest am letzten August-Wochenende schließt den darauf folgenden Montag, den sog. *August Bank Holiday*, ein. *Bank Holidays* sind öffentliche Feiertage, an denen Banken, Postämter, Betriebe, Geschäfte etc. geschlossen bleiben. Es gibt folgende *Bank Holidays* in England und Wales: *New Year's Day* (1. Januar, bzw. der erste darauf folgende Werktag, falls der 1. Januar auf einen Samstag oder Sonntag fällt), *Good Friday, Easter Monday, May Day Holiday* (der erste Montag im Mai), *Spring Holiday* (der letzte Montag im Mai), *August Bank Holiday* (der letzte Montag im August), *Christmas Day, Boxing Day* (bzw. jeweils der erste darauf folgende Werktag). In Schottland und Nordirland gelten z. T. andere Feiertage.

Der Einstieg in das *Theme* erfolgt über Folie 5. Anhand der beiden Fotos vom Karneval in Deutschland und in London sprechen sie über eigene Erfahrungen mit dem Karneval/ Fasching und gewinnen einen ersten Eindruck vom *Notting Hill Carnival*. Die Folie reaktiviert nicht nur bekannten Wortschatz, sondern kann zudem genutzt werden, um neues Vokabular einzuführen und somit TB A1 vorzuentlasten.

TB A1   Here comes Carnival   **Lesen/Sprechen**   *TB, S. 36*
Drei Gruppen von S lesen jeweils einen Abschnitt des Textes. Eine vierte Gruppe sammelt Informationen aus dem Stadtplan (Route der Umzüge, gesperrte Straßen, Zentrum der Polizei, Toiletten, Kinderfundstätte, …). Anschließend informieren sich die vier Gruppen gegenseitig im Plenum über ihre gewonnenen Kenntnisse, z. B.: *I've read that Notting Hill Carnival is always in August, it's the biggest street festival in Europe. …*

TB A2   Notting Hill Carnival   **Lesen/Sprechen**   *TB, S. 37*
• Die drei Fragen beziehen sich auf jeweils einen der drei Abschnitte. Entsprechend sind die drei Gruppen (siehe oben) die Experten für die Beantwortung der jeweiligen Frage.
• Alternativ überfliegen alle S den gesamten Text und beantworten die Fragen.

PB A1   Carnival sights and sounds   **Schreiben**   *PB, S. 26*
Die Entschlüsselung der *scrambled words* wird im Plenum gesichert *(crowds, costumes, singer, musician, recorded music, disk jockey, float, calypso, steel band, dancer)*, erst dann tragen S die Wörter in die Tabelle ein und ergänzen weitere.
Lösungen:
people who take part in the carnival: singer, musician, disk jockey, dancer; tourists, bands
music you can hear: recorded music, calypso, steel band; live music
things you can see: crowds, costumes, float; steelpans, steel drums

Erweiterung:
Nachdem der Wortschatz zum Wortfeld *carnival* erweitert und gefestigt wurde, sollte auch an eine Lernerfolgskontrolle gedacht werden. Möglich ist es, einen Kurztest zur Vokabelsicherung von einer Schülergruppe bzw. einer/m S vorbereiten, durchführen und kontrollieren zu lassen. Soll dies regelmäßig geschehen, wird der Wortschatz eingegrenzt (Wortfeld, ein Abschnitt im *Vocabulary* oder *Dictionary* im TB, regelmäßige/unregelmäßige Verben etc.). Eine bestimmte Anzahl Vokabeln wird festgesetzt, auch das Bewertungsschema wird gemeinsam beschlossen: Wie wird mit Rechtschreibfehlern umgegangen? Gibt es Zusatzpunkte? Wie viele Punkte sind für eine 1, 2, 3 etc. erforderlich?
Auch auf diese Weise übernehmen S Verantwortung für ihr Lernen und gewinnen dabei einen Einblick in die Schwierigkeiten beim Korrigieren und Bewerten ihrer Leistungen. U. U. geben sie sich dann mehr Mühe, leserlich zu schreiben und sich an die vorgegebene Form zu halten.

PB A2 Are you sure? Lesen/Schreiben *PB, S. 26*
Nach der vorangegangenen intensiven Beschäftigung mit dem Text im TB stellt diese Übung keine Schwierigkeit dar. S schreiben die korrigierten Sätze in ihr Heft.
Lösungen: *1. The floats are beautifully decorated lorries. 3. Over 50,000 people take part in Carnival. 4. Some of the music is live, and some of the music is recorded music which popular DJs play in the streets. 5. Carnival first started in Trinidad. 6. Black slaves had a carnival when they became free in 1833. 8. Just a few people took part in the first London carnival. 9. Young men found empty oil drums on the beaches of the Caribbean. American sailors had left them there. The young men made steelpans from the empty oil drums. 11. Steel bands have musicians of all ages. 12. There are usually between 40 and 50 musicians in a steel band.*

lif 5 Relativsätze Sprechen *TB, S. 118*
Bewusstmachung der Relativsätze
- Zunächst Erarbeitung der Struktur im Klassengespräch, Tafelanschrieb durch L: *There's* *Tafel* *somebody in your class who has got a cat/dog/new mountain bike/...* L: *Who is the boy/the girl who has got a ...?* S: ... L: *Yes, that's right. ... is the boy/girl who has got a ...* Nach einigen Sätzen antworten S in ganzen (Relativ-)Sätzen.
- Verallgemeinerung: L: Was geschieht in diesen (Neben-)Sätzen? S: Über eine Person wird eine nähere Aussage gemacht. L: Das Gleiche ist auch für Sachen möglich. Tafelan- *Tafel* schrieb: *There's something in our town that's very interesting for tourists.* L: *What is it that's very interesting for tourists?* S: *It's the castle/museum/tower/... that's interesting for tourists.*
- In *lif 5* werden weitere Beispiele gelesen. S fassen die Regel kurz: *who* steht für Personen, *which* für Sachen, *that* für Sachen und Personen.
- Es folgt der Eintrag ins Heft unter der Redeabsicht: ‚Nähere Aussagen/Angaben über eine Person oder eine Sache machen'.

PB A3 What can you remember? Schreiben *PB, S. 27*
Anwenden der Relativsätze
- S betrachten die Zeichnung zwei Minuten lang, schließen dann das PB und sammeln im Unterrichtsgespräch, woran sie sich erinnern, zunächst ohne Berücksichtigung des grammatischen Pensums.
- Anschließend gilt es, die Personen und Gegenstände näher zu beschreiben. S lesen die Beispiele im PB, sammeln gemeinsam zwei weitere Beispiele, die zur Stütze an der Tafel *Tafel* festgehalten werden, und formulieren schriftlich weitere Äußerungen in Einzelarbeit.
Mögliche Lösungen: *There are many tourists who are watching the carnival. There are many people who are dancing. There is a girl that is crying. There is a child that is talking to a policeman. There is a boy who is eating an ice-cream. There is a man who is running away with a woman's handbag. There are three people who are standing at the window. There is a steel band that is playing on steel drums. There is a man who is filming a woman with a fish on her head. There are many people who are laughing.*

copy
10

Copymaster 10 bietet eine Einsetzübung zur Einschleifung der Relativpronomen. S tragen die Relativpronomen ein oder schneiden sie aus und kleben sie ein.

TB A3   Who's who and what's what?   **Sprechen**   *TB, S. 38*
Festigung der Relativsätze
Die Übung bietet eine weitere Auswertung des Textes TB A1 unter Verwendung von Relativ-
pronomen. Die Ergebnisse werden nach der mündlichen Erarbeitung schriftlich gesichert.
Lösungen: *There are many people who are having fun. There are many tourists who take
photos. There are many steel bands that play steel band music. There are floats which are large,
decorated lorries. There is an official carnival map that shows you where things are happening.
There is recorded music which DJs play. There were costumes that looked like the slave masters.
There are band costumes that fit the bands' themes. There are musicians of all ages who stand
behind their instruments on floats.*

TB A4   Carnival and the people of ...   **Hören/Sprechen/Schreiben**   *TB, S. 38*
a) S hören jeweils einen Sprecher/eine Sprecherin, geben wieder, was sie über die Personen
    gehört haben und verwenden dabei Relativsätze analog zum vorgegebenen Muster.
    Mögliche Lösungen: *Gilbert is the boy who says Carnival is his favourite time of year. Peter
    is the boy who likes dancing in the streets. Samuel is the boy who says you can forget your
    problems and have a great time at Carnival. Tina is the girl who loves Carnival because she
    gets to wear a costume and take part with her band.*

b) Erarbeitung in schriftlicher Einzelarbeit, in leistungsschwachen Gruppen in Partnerarbeit.

c) Mit dieser Aufgabe schließt sich der Kreis zum Einstieg in das *Theme* (vgl. TM S. 42), nur
    steht S nun ein größerer Wortschatz zur Verfügung. Falls S ihre Antworten schriftlich dar-
    legen, wäre dies ein Text für das Portfolio: *Carnival and me.*   *Portfolio*

PB A4   Do you know who ...?   **Schreiben/Sprechen**   *PB, S. 28*
a) S werden die Aufgabe ohne Nachschlagen vermutlich nicht lösen können, daher eignet
    sie sich gut für die Erarbeitung als Hausaufgabe.
    Lösung: *Armstrong, The Titanic, Beethoven, elephant, Saint Helena, van Gogh, Norway,
    Juliet, Greenland, red, white, blue*

b) Schriftliches Beantworten der Fragen in Einzelarbeit, Abrufen der Ergebnisse im Plenum.

PB A5   Carnival love   **Lesen/Sprechen**   *PB, S. 29*
Diese Aufgabe trainiert das Gedächtnis. S lernen zunächst in Partnerarbeit auswendig,
anschließend versuchen sich einzelne Paare daran, die ganze Geschichte vor der Klasse auswendig aufzusagen.

TB A5   Steelband jump up   **Hören**   *TB, S. 39*
Die Aufnahme vermittelt einen guten Eindruck von der Atmosphäre des *Notting Hill
Carnival.* Eine Auswertung sollte nicht stattfinden.

TB A6   The dark side of Carnival   **Lesen**   *TB, S. 40*
• Lesen des Textes jede/r für sich, Wiedergabe des Inhalts: Worum geht es?
• Der Stadtplan von TB S. 36 wird herangezogen, um die Standorte der Polizei, die Toiletten und die beiden „Fundstätten" für verloren gegangene Kinder ausfindig zu machen
   und sich im Beschreiben von Wegen zu üben: *Tell a young mother in Portobello Road who
   has lost her little boy where the nearest lost and found children centre is./Tell some people in
   Harrow Road who are looking for toilets where the nearest toilets are./...*

> Erweiterung:
> S erstellen ähnliche Regeln für Besucher von größeren Festen und Umzügen in der Hei-
> matregion. Dabei ist auf die Verstärkung einer Forderung/eines Ratschlags durch *Do* hin-
> zuweisen: *Do take care .../Do check ...*
> Allgemeiner gehaltene Ratschläge, die auf die Gefahren bei größeren Menschenansamm-
> lungen aufmerksam machen (und die auch für das Verhalten unter S gelten!) können als
> Poster für das Schulhaus oder als Handzettel mit Zeichnungen gestaltet werden.

TB PP   The Metropolitan Police   Lesen   *TB, S. 40*
                                                                                Tafel

- Tafelanschrieb: S C O T L A N D   Y A R D
  L: *Which words come to your mind when you see or hear these words?* Gemeinsame Wort-schatzsammlung an der Tafel.

- Lesen des Textes mit folgender Aufgabenstellung: *What are the tasks of the men and women of the Metropolitan Police? (They are there to control crowds and traffic and keep big events safe.) Who works at New Scotland Yard? (Detectives who solve murders, search for criminals and find stolen jewels or paintings.) How many people work at New Scotland Yard? (about 2,000) Where does the name Bobby for a British policeman come from? (Short form of Robert, after Sir Robert Peel, who founded the Metropolitan Police Force in 1828.)*

> **Zusatzinformationen:** *New Scotland Yard*
> *New Scotland Yard is the main office of the division of the London police dealing with serious crime. It is also the name of the headquarters of the Metropolitan Police in London.*

PB A6   Missing letters   Lesen/Schreiben   *PB, S. 29*

Festigung von neuem Wortschatz
Lösung:
detective: A police officer who solves murders.
New Scotland Yard: The headquarters of the Metropolitan Police.
guns: Police officers do not carry them.
truncheon: A stick which police officers carry.
bobby: A name which people call a policeman.
criminal: A person who commits a crime.

TB A7   At Notting Hill police station   Hören/Schreiben   *TB, S. 41*

Bewusstmachung des *past progressive*
Der Hörtext lautet:

Policewoman:	*Hello, Notting Hill police station – how can I help you?*
Emily Stevens:	*Hello, this is Emily Stevens. I'm at the Carnival and I'd like to report a stolen bag.*
Policewoman:	*Can you tell me what happened?*
Emily Stevens:	*Well, while I was buying a drink, a man snatched my handbag.*
Policewoman:	*And can you tell me where and when …*

Policewoman:	*Hello, Notting Hill police station – how can I help you?*
Andrew Brookes:	*Hello, this is Andrew Brookes. I hope you can help me. I'm in Notting Hill with my family and we've lost our youngest son, Samuel. He's only eight and we're very worried.*
Policewoman:	*When did you notice he was gone?*
Andrew Brookes:	*About half an hour ago. While we were talking to friends, he went to buy a snack.*
Policewoman:	*Can you describe him to me and tell me …?*

Policeman:	*Hello, Notting Hill police station – how can I help you?*
Amy Eastwick:	*Oh, hello, this is Amy Eastwick. I'd like to report a theft. While I was listening to a steel band, a man stole a camera from my pocket. He was about …*

Policeman:	*Hello, Notting Hill police station – how can I help you?*
Jay Greenhill:	*Hello, this is Jay Greenhill. When I was walking down Oxford Gardens, I found an expensive camera. Someone must have lost it and …*

a)
- S hören die vier Telefonate mit kurzen Pausen zum Notieren der Ereignisse. L ruft die Ergebnisse ab und schreibt die vier Lösungssätze untereinander an die Tafel.   *Tafel*
- Bewusstmachung der grammatischen Struktur: L fordert S auf, die Struktur der vier Lösungssätze zu analysieren. S erkennen im Hauptsatz *simple past* und im Nebensatz eine ihnen bislang unbekannte Zeitform. L nennt den Namen, lernstarke S leiten die Regeln zur Bildung des *past progressive* ab, stellen Vermutungen über den Gebrauch an und überprüfen die Vermutungen mithilfe von *lif 6.*   *TB, S. 119*
- Eintrag im Heft unter „Über den Ablauf vergangener Ereignisse berichten".

Lösungen: *While we were talking to friends, he went to buy a snack./While I was listening to a steel band, a man stole a camera from my pocket./When I was walking down Oxford Gardens, I found an expensive camera.*

b) • S schreiben unter Verwendung des *past progressive* kurze Texte über eines der Bilder und lesen sie vor.
   • S formulieren eigene Erlebnisse, z. B.: *While I was waiting for the bus last week, it began to rain/a car stopped in front of me. While I was listening to music on my walkman, … While my friend and I were playing football, …*
   Mögliche Lösung: *While Karim was taking a photo, his keys fell out of his pocket. A man picked them up and gave them back to Karim./While Sharon and Josephine were taking part in the Carnival, a little girl started to cry. They took her to one of the lost and found children centres./When Gillian and Vera were waiting at the bus stop, a man stole a handbag from a woman. Gillian ran after him but the man was too fast for her. Then they went to one of the crime reporting centres with the woman.*

PB A7   The wrong words   **Hören/Schreiben/Sprechen**   *PB, S. 30f.*
Weitere Auswertung des Hörtextes aus TB A7
a) • Nochmaliges Anhören der ersten beiden Telefonate, S machen Notizen.
   Lösungen:
   1. what do you want → how can I help you?; here is → this is, in a phonebox → at the Carnival, some stolen money → a stolen bag; why it happened → what happened; ticket → drink, woman → man, purse → handbag.
   2. I know → I hope, with my friends → with my family, our eldest son → our youngest son, six → eight, angry → worried; Who noticed → When did you notice; an hour ago → half an hour ago, walking with our friends → talking to friends, an ice-cream → a snack

b) Festigung des *past progressive*
   • S sortieren den Dialog in Einzelarbeit.
   • Nachstellen der Szene mit Variieren der Vorfälle, Namen etc.
   Lösung: *Notting Hill police station. How can I help you? – Hello, this is Lesley Rowing. I'd like to report a lost gold watch. – Can you tell me what happened? – When I was watching the dancers, I noticed it was gone. – When did you last see it ? – About two hours ago. – I'm sorry, but we haven't got it here.*

Folie 6 bietet eine weitere Möglichkeit der Festigung des *past progressive*. S beschreiben die dargestellte andauernde Handlung im *past progressive (While the boy was sleeping, …)*, die hinzukommenden Handlungen im *simple past*. S ergänzen die Situation um weitere hinzukommende Handlungen.

PB A8   Pairs   **Sprechen/Schreiben**   *PB, S. 31*
Mündliches Kombinieren der Sätze, anschließend schriftliche Sicherung.
Lösung: *We were sunbathing in the garden when it began to rain. The tourist was taking a photo of the parrot when it flew away. While we were looking at the river, a monster swam towards us. The cat was watching the hole when a mouse came out. While we were laughing and shouting, the teacher came in. I wasn't expecting anything nice to happen when I met you, so it was great! The thief was running away with the money when he fell over and broke his leg.*

Copymaster 11 bietet eine weitere Möglichkeit zur Festigung der grammatischen Struktur. Die Kärtchen werden ausgeschnitten und nach *simple past* und *past progressive* geordnet verdeckt auf zwei Stapel gelegt. Die zwei bis vier Spieler ziehen nacheinander je eine Karte von beiden Stößen und fügen die beiden Sätze mit *when* oder *while* zusammen. Dabei achten sie auf evtl. erforderliche Änderungen der Personal- und Possessivpronomen sowie manchmal notwendige Ergänzungen.
Bei diesen Verbindungen entstehen z. T. recht lustige Kombinationen. Es wird eine Dauer von fünf Minuten festgesetzt, das Paar/die Gruppe, die zuerst alle Karten aufgearbeitet hat, hat gewonnen. Das Spiel kann um weitere Kärtchen, ggf. auch Blankokärtchen, erweitert werden.

Erweiterung:
Es wird in zwei bis vier Gruppen gespielt, die gegeneinander antreten. L oder eine weitere kleine Gruppe von S geben einen Satzanfang im *past progressive* vor, z. B.: *While I was lying in the sun near the swimming pool, ...* Die Gruppen versuchen nun schnellstens eine Ergänzung im *simple past* zu finden, z. B.: *..., a child started to cry./somebody called my name./...* Die Gruppe, die zuerst eine korrekte Ergänzung gegeben hat, bekommt einen Punkt. Ziel des Spiels ist das lockere und spontane Sprechen, bei dem die Inhalte im Vordergrund stehen und nicht mehr das grammatische Pensum.

TB A8   YOUR street festival   **Lesen/Schreiben**   *TB, S. 41*

• Lesen des Textes.
• Schreiben eines analogen Textes über ein Fest in der Region nach vorgegebenem Muster. Folgende Fragen sind als Stütze denkbar:
  – *What kind of carnival/festival/street party have you been to?*
  – *When/Where was it?*
  – *Who was there with you?*
  – *What did you do there? Did anything special happen?*
  – *What was the weather like?*
  – *What were people able to see/hear/buy/do there?*
  – *How many people were there?*
• Um den geschriebenen Text mit möglichst wenig Fehlern für das Portfolio aufzubereiten, wird er mit einem Partner/einer Partnerin besprochen. In Zweifelsfällen hilft L. Häufige Fehler werden mit der gesamten Lerngruppe besprochen. Das gemeinsame Redigieren eines Textes (von Freiwilligen!) über OHP ist ebenfalls möglich.   *Folie*
• S ergänzen ihren Text durch Zeichnungen, Fotos, Zeitungsausschnitte etc.

PB A9   The village festival   **Hören**   *PB, S. 32*
Der Hörtext lautet:
In our village we have a festival called a fête once every two years. It's in August, so the weather is usually good. In the morning everyone helps to put up the stalls and it begins at 2.30 when crowds of people arrive.
A band plays old music and there are all kinds of races and competitions. One of the strangest is called "Throwing the boot". The winner is the person who can throw the boot the furthest.
Last year there were pony rides, but a small pony ran away with one of the children. Local painters show their pictures in one tent and in another everyone drinks tea, coffee or juice and eats cakes and biscuits.
There are things to buy from the stalls like jars of sweets and plants and funny hats. At one stall a woman uses face-paints to make your face look like a lion, a dog or a cat but I decided not to visit her!

• Anhören des Textes von der CD, parallel Kennzeichnen der richtigen Antworten.
• Nur bei großen Schwierigkeiten sollten S den Text ein zweites Mal hören. Der einmalige Hörvorgang entspricht der natürlichen Kommunikation, so dass sich S auch daran gewöhnen müssen, zumal wenn es sich wie hier um einen relativ einfachen Text handelt.
Lösungen: *1. every two years 2. fine 3. after lunch 4. old music 5. throwing the boot 6. ran away with one of the children 7. tea, coffee 8. paint your face*

Medium	Nummer	Seite	Titel	Fertigkeit	Zusatzinfo
TB	B1	44f.	London for teenagers	Sprechen/Lesen	Landeskunde
PB	B1	32f.	London puzzle	Lesen/Schreiben	Wortschatzfestigung
PB	B2	33	How well do you know London?	Lesen	Landeskunde
Folie 7			Taller, larger, more famous	Sprechen	Landeskunde
TB	B2	46	Where to go in London	Sprechen	
TB/CD	B3	46	A tour through London	Sprechen/Schreiben/ Hören	Hörverstehen
TB	PP	46	The Tower of London	Lesen	Landeskunde
PB	B3	34	The Tower of London	Lesen/Schreiben	Textverständnis; Fragestellung
PB	B4	34f.	Finding out about London	Lesen	Textpassagen ordnen
TB	B4	47	Find out more about London	Lesen/Schreiben/ Sprechen	Projekt
TB	B5	47	Sightseeing in YOUR area	Schreiben	Textproduktion
PB	B5	35	A postcard	Schreiben	
TB	Optional	48	The skating ramp	Lesen/Sprechen	lautes Lesen

Die grau unterlegten Felder stellen das Pflichtpensum dar, die weißen die Kür.

Teil B: • **Sightseeing in London planen**
Meinungen äußern und begründen
Heimatort beschreiben

TB B1   London for teenagers   Sprechen/Lesen   *TB, S. 44f.*
- S betrachten die Fotodoppelseite TB S. 42/43 und geben ihre Eindrücke wieder, sagen, was sie bereits von London kennen bzw. über London gehört und gelesen haben. In einer *mind map* um das Wort *London* können diese Nennungen an der Tafel oder auf Poster *Tafel* festgehalten und später kontinuierlich erweitert werden.
- Klassengespräch: *What would you like to see in London? What would you like to know more about?*
- S lesen die Informationen der Doppelseite TB S. 44/45 und ordnen die Texte den nummerierten Zeichnungen zu.
- Anschließend versuchen S, die Gebäude auf TB S. 42/43 zu benennen *(London Dungeon, Natural History Museum, Royal Albert Hall, The Beatles/Madame Tussaud's, Tower Bridge, Buckingham Palace, the Tower).*
Lösung: *1–London Zoo, 2–Madame Tussaud's, 3–Hyde Park, 4–Segaworld, 5–Buckingham Palace, 6–London Transport Museum, 7–Covent Garden, 8–Trafalgar Square, 9–Tower Bridge, 10–The Tower of London, 11–London Dungeon*

PB B1   London puzzle   Lesen/Schreiben   *PB, S. 32f.*
- S lösen die Aufgabe in Einzelarbeit.
- Anschließend geben sie kurze Auskünfte zu den Sehenswürdigkeiten, z. B.: *London Dungeon is near London Bridge and London Bridge Station. It's a museum of horror … The Royal National Theatre is near Waterloo Bridge. …* L fragt nach: *Who of you has heard of Shakespeare?/Do you know the names of the people in Queen Elizabeth's family?*
Lösungen: *Thames, Tower Bridge, Notting Hill, Segaworld, Royal National Theatre, Madame Tussaud's, Paddington, Charing Cross, St. Paul's Cathedral, Zoo, Trafalgar Square, Buckingham Palace, Hyde Park*

Zusatzinformationen: *Trafalgar Square*
Der berühmte Londoner Platz soll bald ohne Tauben zu bestaunen sein – der letzte Taubenfutterverkäufer auf dem *Trafalgar Square* musste seinen Stand Anfang 2001 schließen. Auf Betreiben des Bürgermeisters Livingstone, der die Tauben als „fliegende Ratten" bezeichnet, soll der Platz taubenfrei werden, doch diese Bemühungen stoßen bei Tierfreunden und Gästen der Stadt auf wenig Gegenliebe. Für den Bürgermeister sind die Tauben eine „die Gesundheit bedrohende Last", und es kostet die Stadt jedes Jahr mehr als 300 000 DM, die etwa eine Tonne Taubendreck von bis zu 40 000 Tauben entfernen zu lassen. Die Zukunft wird zeigen, ob es gelingt, die Tauben zu vertreiben.

PB B2   How well do you know London?   Lesen   *PB, S. 32*
S lösen die Aufgabe in Partnerarbeit. S1 liest jeweils beide Sätze vor, S2 gibt an, welcher den Tatsachen entspricht. Nach der Hälfte werden die Rollen getauscht.
Lösungen:
When the Queen is at the Palace you can see a flag flying.
Covent Garden used to be famous as a fruit and vegetable market.
There are over 10,000 animals at the zoo.
At one museum you can be a film star or read the news.
People stand up and talk at Speakers' Corner.
At the London Transport Museum you can travel on a tall bus with two floors.
Tower Bridge does not open every day now.
The Norwegians give a Christmas present to the people of London every year.

Folie 7   Taller, larger, more famous   Sprechen
Die Folie erweitert das Allgemeinwissen der S und festigt immanent die Steigerung der Adjektive.

TB B2   Where to go in London   Sprechen   *TB, S. 46*
- Stellen und Beantworten der Fragen in Partner- oder Gruppenarbeit mithilfe von TB A1 und PB B1 und B2.

TB B3   A tour through London   Sprechen/Schreiben/Hören   *TB, S. 46*
a) • S übernehmen die Tabelle in ihr Heft, füllen sie aus und bereiten sich damit auf die mündliche Darstellung und Begründung ihrer Favoriten vor. Letzteres erfolgt in Partner- oder Gruppenarbeit.
- Mithilfe einer Strichliste an der Tafel werden die drei beliebtesten Besuchermagnete bestimmt: *The top three London sights in our class are …*   *Tafel*

b) Zusatzaufgabe: S gestalten einen Text über einen Tag in London. Der Text kann, durch Zeichnungen/Fotos von Sehenswürdigkeiten bereichert, in das Portfolio aufgenommen werden.   *Portfolio*

c) Der Hörtext lautet:
Guide: Good afternoon, ladies and gentlemen. Can you all hear me? Yes.
We are now driving down Knightsbridge. On the left, down Brompton Road, is Harrods, and to the right you can see Hyde Park.
Now we are on Kensington Road and if you look to your left you can see the Royal Albert Hall, which is famous for music and sports events. Behind the Royal Albert Hall, there is the Natural History Museum. On the right is Kensington Gardens, with the Albert Memorial. There's a statue of Prince Albert, Queen Victoria's German husband – can you see him? In the park, behind the memorial is the statue of Peter Pan, but unfortunately you can't see that from the bus.
And now we're coming to Kensington Palace, with its beautiful gardens …

- Anhören der Stadtführerin und Verfolgen der Route auf dem Stadtplan, TB S. 44/45.
- Zweites Anhören mit Pausen und Notieren der genannten Sehenswürdigkeiten.

> **Zusatzinformationen:** *Albert Memorial*
> *The Albert Memorial is a large monument in Kensington Gardens opposite Royal Albert Hall, erected in commemoration of Prince Albert, Queen Victoria's German husband, who died in 1861. Prince Albert married Queen Victoria (1837–1901) in 1840. He introduced the tradition of the Christmas tree to Britain. Prince Albert and the Queen had their first Christmas tree at Windsor Castle in 1841. A few years later nearly every home in Britain had one.*

TB PP   The Tower of London   Lesen   *TB, S. 46*
Lesen des Textes mit anschließender kurzer Wiedergabe der Fakten bei geschlossenem TB.

PB B3   The Tower of London   Lesen/Schreiben   *PB, S. 34*
- Nochmaliges Lesen des Textes TB S. 46.
- Formulieren der Fragen mündlich, anschließend schriftliche Sicherung.
- Abschließendes Lesen der Fragen und Antworten in Partnerarbeit.
Lösungen:
How many towers are there?
When did William the Conqueror start to build the Tower?
What has the Tower been used for since the 16th century?
What's the name of the famous Indian diamond in Queen Elizabeth the Queen Mother's crown?
How much does the St Edward's crown weigh?
What's the name of the famous guards in the Tower?

> **Erweiterung: Assoziationsspiel**
> Spiel in Vierergruppen: Zunächst schreibt jede/r S für sich Sehenswürdigkeiten und/oder bekannte Details einzeln auf kleine Karten. Die Karten der vier S werden gemischt und verdeckt auf den Tisch gelegt. S1 zieht ein Kärtchen (z. B. *raven*) und nennt seine/ihre Assoziation dazu (z. B. *Tower of London*), ggf. mit Begründung. Wenn ihm/ihr nichts einfällt, geht das Kärtchen an S2 weiter. Das Spiel ist beendet, wenn alle Karten gezogen sind. Sieger ist, wer die meisten Karten hat.

PB B4   Finding out about London   Lesen   *PB, S. 34f.*
- Ordnen der beiden Briefe in Einzelarbeit.
- Zusammenhängendes lautes Lesen beider Briefe.
Lösungen: *Letter asking for information: 7–2–5–9, Answering letter: 4–6–1–8–3*

TB B4   Find out more about London   Projekt   *TB, S. 47*
- Als Vorbereitung empfiehlt es sich, das Verfassen höflicher Briefe mit der Bitte um Informationen im Plenum zu besprechen und zu üben. Muster bieten das TB und PB B4.
- Wichtig ist die Abstimmung darüber, welche Sehenswürdigkeiten von den einzelnen Gruppen bearbeitet werden, um Dopplungen zu vermeiden.
- Auch Bekannte und Verwandte, die bereits in London waren, sind gute Informationsquellen, die es zu erschließen gilt.
- Adressen, bei denen Informationsmaterial erbeten werden kann:
  Britische Zentrale für Fremdenverkehr (BTA), Taunusstr. 52–60, 60239 Frankfurt/Main
  British Tourist Authority, Thames Tower, Black's Road, London W6 9EL, England
  London Tourist Board and Convention Bureau, Glen House, Stag Place, Victoria SW1E 5LT, London, England.

> Erweiterung:
> Für S der 5. und 6. Klasse kann ein Brettspiel über London entwickelt werden, das mit Ereigniskarten und ersten Infos Neugier und Interesse weckt.

TB B5   Sightseeing in YOUR area   Schreiben   *TB, S. 47*
- Für das Portfolio wird ein Transfer des Gelernten auf die eigene Lebenswelt geleistet: eine englischsprachige Führung durch die Stadt/Region mit kleinen Texten, die durch Zeichnungen, Ansichtskarten oder eigene Fotos ergänzt werden können.
- Als Vorbereitung empfiehlt sich die gemeinsame Beantwortung folgender Fragen, die an der Tafel festgehalten werden, um während der Bearbeitung als Stütze zu dienen: *What is interesting for visitors in your town/village/area? What do you know about these sights and places? Where can you get information about …? Who/What can be helpful? (parents, friends, tourist information centre, books, …)*   *Tafel*
- Die besten Arbeiten werden ausgestellt.

PB B5   A postcard   Schreiben   *PB, S. 35*
Nachdem in TB B5 eine *guided tour* für die Heimatregion erarbeitet wurde, ist die Aufgabe nicht schwer zu lösen. S tauschen ihre Ergebnisse untereinander aus.

> Erweiterung: *London Quiz*
> Zum Abschluss der Arbeit über London ist eine Rätselphase angezeigt: S beschreiben Sehenswürdigkeiten Londons, ohne ihren Namen zu nennen, die anderen S erraten, welche Attraktion gemeint ist. Damit die Sprechzeit für alle S erhöht wird, wird das Spiel in Gruppen durchgeführt.

TB Optional   The skating ramp   Lesen/Sprechen   *TB, S. 48*
- Stilles Lesen des Textes.
- Klassengespräch: *Have you got similar problems in your area? Where do YOU go to meet friends/enjoy the day?*
- Falls S ähnliche Probleme haben, verfassen sie in Partnerarbeit Briefe an die Lokalzeitung.

> Erweiterung:
> Wenn S gerne laut lesen, kann der Brief für das spielerische *stop reading* genutzt werden. Die Klasse wird in zwei Gruppen geteilt, S1 der ersten Gruppe beginnt zu lesen, bei einem Aussprache- oder Lesefehler unterbricht die andere Gruppe durch kurzes Klopfen. S2 der ersten Gruppe liest weiter, angefangen am Anfang des letzten Satzes von S1. Die Gruppe, die mit weniger S durch den Text kommt, hat gewonnen.

Medium	Nummer	Seite	Titel	Fertigkeit	Zusatzinfo
Folie 8			Alone on a high mountain	Sprechen	*Difficult situations*
TB	A1	50	A problem shared	Lesen	Probleme junger Leute
PB/CD	A1	36	Jason and his dad	Hören/Schreiben	Hörverstehen
TB	A2	50f.	Three people – three problems	Lesen/Sprechen	Textverständnis; Gefühle ausdrücken
copy 12			When do YOU feel like this?	Sprechen	Wortfeld *adjectives of feeling*
TB	A3	51	I've got a problem	Lesen/Schreiben	Textproduktion
TB	A4	51	YOUR advice	Lesen/Sprechen/ Schreiben	Ratschläge erteilen
PB	A2	37	No means no	Lesen/Sprechen	Persönliche Stellung-nahme; Ratschläge erteilen
TB	A5	52	How to handle bullies	Lesen/Sprechen	Leseverstehen
TB	A6	52	Charlotte's story	Lesen/Schreiben/ Sprechen	Textverständnis
PB	A3	38	Wordsquare	Lesen/Schreiben	Wortschatzfestigung
TB/CD	A7	53	The class trip thief	Hören/Schreiben/ Sprechen	Hörverstehen; Text-produktion; persönliche Stellungnahme
PB	A4	38	Sorry, could you say that again?	Hören/Schreiben	Hörverstehen
PB	A5	39	Difficult decisions	Sprechen/Schreiben	Verhalten in schwierigen Situationen
TB/CD	A8	53	Being lonely	Hören/Sprechen	Gedicht
PB	A6	39	A mobile phone	Sprechen	Auswendiglernen
TB	A9	53	It's good to have friends	Sprechen	Textproduktion
TB	lif 7	121	each other		

Die grau unterlegten Felder stellen das Pflichtpensum dar, die weißen die Kür.

Theme 4: No man is an island

Teil A: • **Persönliche Probleme beschreiben**
Verständnis äußern
Ratschläge geben
Sorgen/Befürchtungen äußern
Antworten bewerten

Die Probleme Jugendlicher sind Gegenstand vieler Jugendzeitschriften, und die Kummerkastenseite gehört zu den am intensivsten gelesenen Seiten. Sie zeigt, dass Heranwachsende ähnliche Schwierigkeiten haben – Probleme in der Schule, zu Hause, mit der Figur, mit Freundschaften – und dieser Tatbestand verbindet. Anlässe, sich dazu in der Fremdsprache zu äußern, gibt es nur selten. Jedoch werden sich S nur dann zu ihren Sorgen und Nöten äußern, wenn ein gutes vertrauensvolles Verhältnis zur Lehrkraft besteht.

Folie 8   Alone on a high mountain   Sprechen
Die Folie regt S an, sich in eine Situation zu versetzen, in der sie auf sich allein gestellt sind.

TB A1   A problem shared   Lesen/Sprechen   *TB, S. 50*
• Lesen der drei kurzen Briefe, die Jugendliche an die Zeitschrift geschrieben haben (Fettdruck), anschließend kurze Zusammenfassung.
• Wenn Gesprächsbereitschaft vonseiten S besteht, äußern sie sich zu Fragen wie: *What do you do when you have problems? Who do you talk to? Have you ever written to a magazine? Have you ever called a helpline phone number?*
• S sammeln gemeinsam Ratschläge für die drei Jugendlichen im TB.
• Lesen der Antwortschreiben von Jane.

> Erweiterung:
> Die drei Briefe und Antworten bieten eine gute Gelegenheit zur Entwicklung des extensiven zügigen Leseverstehens. L gibt jeweils ein Zeitlimit vor und erklärt S, dass es nicht darum geht, jedes Wort der Texte zu verstehen, sondern ein Grobverständnis zu erlangen.

PB A1   Jason and his dad   Hören/Sprechen   *PB, S. 36*
Der Hörtext lautet:
Jason: I have always wanted a dog but you won't let me have one.
Dad: You know our flat is too small.
Jason: But Dad, I will feed it and take it for long walks.
Dad: You can't leave a dog at home all day.
Jason: Oh please, Dad! I'm sure I can find someone who will look after it while we're away.
Dad: Jason, I said no.
Jason: Maybe I could take it to school with me?
Dad: Your teachers wouldn't let you take a dog to school.

• S hören den Text von der CD, in einem kurzen Unterrichtsgespräch wird das Verständnis geklärt.
• S hören den Text erneut und schreiben das Gespräch mithilfe der Stichwörter auf. Alternativ bietet TB A1 Hilfe.
• Das Gespräch wird vor der Klasse nachgestellt, wobei auch die emotionale Seite zu beachten ist.

TB A2   Three people – three problems   Lesen/Sprechen   *TB, S. 50f.*
a) S geben die in TB A1 geschilderten Probleme mündlich wieder.
Mögliche Lösungen:
Jason in the first letter has problems with his dad. He'd love to buy a dog. He wants to take the dog to school. He wants to feed the dog and take it for long walks.

Kan in the second letter has problems with her parents. She wants to run away because she loves her boyfriend. She is scared to tell her parents about her boyfriend.
Sarah in the third letter has problems with her nose. She wants to get the magnetic bit of the earring out her nose. She'd hate to talk to her doctor about it. She doesn't want to have her nose pierced.

b) • Bevor sich S äußern, wird mithilfe von *Copymaster 12* entsprechendes Sprachmaterial in Erinnerung gerufen und erweitert.
  – S ordnen die Adjektive den Gesichtern zu: *The person/face in number … is/feels … frustrated* und *horrified* sind unbekannt, können aber erschlossen werden.
  – S überlegen, wann sie sich wie fühlen: *I'm …/I feel … when …*
  – S gestalten ihren Gesichtsausdruck sowie Gestik und Körpersprache einem Adjektiv entsprechend, die anderen S erraten das Adjektiv. Dieses Spiel kann um *positive adjectives of feeling* ergänzt werden.

• S geben Auskunft über die Gefühle der Personen, die die Briefe geschrieben haben und nutzen die vorgegebenen Satzanfänge.

c) S äußern sich zu den Antwortbriefen und begründen ihre Meinung.

TB A3 I've got a problem Lesen/Schreiben *TB, S. 51*
a) S wählen ein Problem aus, das sie selbst betrifft oder für das sie Verständnis haben, und fertigen knappe Notizen dazu an, wie am Beispiel im TB gezeigt.

b) Das Schreiben der Briefe wird in die Hausaufgabe gelegt.

TB A4 YOUR advice Lesen/Sprechen *TB, S. 51*
a) • S tauschen die Briefe, die sie in TB A3 geschrieben haben, untereinander aus.
  • L spielt mit S an einem der sechs Probleme aus TB A3 die vorgegebenen Redemittel durch: *Why don't you look for a job after school?/Have you ever thought of talking to your parents about it?/I'd suggest you talk to your parents again./Why don't you try to understand your parents a bit?*
  • S erteilen sich in Partnerarbeit mündliche Ratschläge zu ihren Briefen.
  • S präsentieren die Probleme des Partners/der Partnerin und ihre Ratschläge der Klasse: *Fabian's problem is that … I'd suggest she …/I think she should …/My advice is …*

b) Zusatzaufgabe: Leistungsstarke oder besonders interessierte S verschriftlichen ihren Ratschlag in Form eines Antwortbriefes einer Jugendzeitschrift.

PB A2 No means no Lesen/Sprechen *PB, S. 37*
a) S lesen die Texte und nehmen anschließend unter Verwendung der vorgegebenen Redemittel im Unterrichtsgespräch Stellung zu den Positionen der Eltern.

b) S sammeln im Unterrichtsgespräch Lösungsvorschläge.

> Erweiterung: *A problem shared*
> *Try to find classmates who have the same problem(s) as you. Sit down and discuss how to solve your problem(s). Report the results of your talk to your class.*

TB A5 How to handle bullies Lesen/Sprechen *TB, S. 52*
• Die Überschrift des Textes, *Charlotte, 11, says she is a prisoner in her home because of bullies,* eignet sich gut, um S Vermutungen über den Text anstellen zu lassen und Erwartungshaltungen bei S auszubilden. Damit S nicht schon in den Text schauen, sondern sich auf die Überschrift konzentrieren, schreibt L diese an die Tafel und führt ein kurzes *Tafel* Klassengespräch, z. B.: *What could the text be about?/Why do you think Charlotte is a prisoner in her home?/What could 'bullies' be?*
• S lesen den gesamten Text still. Danach fragt L sie nach ihren Eindrücken: *What do you think about the situation?/Are there bullies at our school, too?* Da es sich hier um ein sensibles Thema handelt, sollte L auch deutsche Meinungsäußerungen zulassen.

TB A6   Charlotte's story   Lesen/Schreiben/Sprechen   *TB, S. 52*

a) S lesen den Text nochmals und erarbeiten die Antworten in Partnerarbeit.
Lösungen: *They waited after school because they knew Charlotte had no one to walk home with. They walked behind her and talked about her all the time. They called her at home and put the phone down when she answered. They rang the doorbell and ran away. They stood outside the house and shouted. They wrote words on the back of Charlotte's parents' car with their fingers.*

b) S sammeln die Gefühlswörter in Stillarbeit aus dem Text, das anschließende Gespräch erfolgt im Plenum.
Mögliche Lösung: *frightened, to panic, to cry, scared, confidence*

c) Gegenstand des Gesprächs sind Fragen wie: Sollte in der Schule nicht mit allen Beteiligten gesprochen werden? Welche Gründe gibt es für *bullying*? Was kann man als Betroffene/r selbst dagegen tun? Wie kann ein vernünftiges Verhältnis zwischen S entwickelt werden? (Hierüber ist durchaus ein Gespräch auf Deutsch akzeptabel, damit es nicht oberflächlich bleibt und betroffenen S wirklich helfen kann.)

PB A3   Wordsquare   Lesen/Schreiben   *PB, S. 38*

Wortschatzfestigung: Wortfeld *adjectives of feeling*
Lösungen:
→ : *happy, sad, unhappy, angry, bad, frightened, silly, afraid, better, lonely, excited, blue*

> Erweiterung:
> An dieser Stelle empfiehlt sich wieder ein von S erarbeiteter und womöglich zumindest vor-korrigierter Vokabelkurztest (z. B. in Gestalt eines Lückentextes o. Ä.), um die neue Lexik fest einzuprägen.

TB A7   The class trip thief   Hören/Sprechen/Schreiben   *TB, S. 53*

Der Hörtext lautet:

Hazel:	*Look at the swimming pool, Sally. Doesn't it look great? And there's no one in it. Is the water warm?*
Sally:	*Yes, it is. Shall we go for a swim?*
Steve:	*Yes, let's. There are the changing rooms over there. See you in a minute, girls.*
Sally:	*I'm really looking forward to a swim after our long walk.*
Hazel:	*Me too.*
Sally:	*Are you ready to go?*
Hazel:	*Almost. Do you think it's OK to leave my discman here?*
Sally:	*Well, the door doesn't lock, … but I'm sure no one would take it. There are only people from our class around.*
Hazel:	*OK, let's go. Steve and Martin are in the pool already.*
…	
Martin:	*Sally, do you have your ball with you? Maybe we could play a game.*
Sally:	*Yes, it's in the changing rooms. I'll just go and get it.*
…	
Sally:	*Janet, what are you doing? That's Hazel's discman!*
Janet:	*I was – er, just – er, …*

a) • Einführendes Klassengespräch: *Have you ever gone on a class trip? When was it? Where did you go? How long did you stay there? And what did you do there? Did anything special happen? Did you like the trip to …? Why/Why not?*
   • S hören den Text von der CD und fassen das Gehörte kurz zusammen.

b) Leistungsstarke Lerngruppen sammeln in Einzelarbeit mögliche Reaktionen von Sally, notieren Stichpunkte und formulieren anschließend aus. In leistungsschwächeren Gruppen arbeiten S paarweise zusammen.

c) S lesen verschiedene Varianten vor und begründen jeweils, warum sie sich für diese Form der Fortsetzung der Geschichte entschieden haben. Die Lerngruppe nimmt jeweils Stellung, begründet und ergänzt.

PB A4   Sorry, could you say that again?   **Hören/Schreiben**   *PB, S. 38*
- Zweites Anhören des Textes von der CD bei geöffnetem PB. Leistungsstarke Gruppen markieren und ersetzen parallel die falschen Wörter, in leistungsschwächeren Gruppen stoppt L die CD jeweils an den entsprechenden Stellen.
- Vorlesen des korrigierten Gesprächs mit verteilten Rollen.

Lösungen: *hot → warm; down there → over there; quite → really, Nearly → Almost; will → would; school → class; water → pool; have a game → play a game; Martin's → Hazel's*

PB A5   Difficult decisions   **Sprechen/Schreiben**   *PB, S. 39*
- Zu den ersten beiden Beispielen diskutieren S im Plenum mögliche Verhaltensweisen.
- Über die Sätze 3 bis 7 unterhalten S sich in Partnerarbeit und schreiben die von ihnen bevorzugte Variante auf.
- In einem weiteren Klassengespräch werden die Ergebnisse verglichen und besprochen.

TB A8   Being lonely   **Hören/Sprechen**   *TB, S. 53*
- Anhören des Gedichts von der CD bei geschlossenem TB, S äußern ihre Eindrücke.
- Klassengespräch: *How do you feel when you are lonely? Is 'lonely' the same as 'alone' for you? What must you do to have/to make friends?*

PB A6   A mobile phone   **Sprechen**   *PB, S. 39*
Um ihr Gedächtnis zu trainieren, sollten S gelegentlich auswendig lernen. Beim Abrufen des Gelernten kann Chor- oder Gruppensprechen eingesetzt bzw. der Text in Sprechketten zerlegt werden. Dabei müssen S gut auf den Text des Vordermannes achten und ihren Teil der Verszeile unmittelbar anschließen, so dass nicht zu hören ist, dass es sich um unterschiedliche Sprecher handelt. Bei der Aufnahme auf Kassette ist am besten zu hören und zu überprüfen, ob es unnötige Pausen gab oder nicht.

TB A9   It's good to have friends   **Sprechen/Schreiben/Lesen**   *TB, S. 53*
Bewusstmachung *each other*
a) • Kurzes Klassengespräch bei geschlossenem TB, in dem L gut miteinander befreundete S befragt: *(Katharina) and (Maike), I know you are good friends. Do you help each other with your homework?/Do you give advice to each other?/Do you talk about your problems to each other?/Do you lend money, videos or CDs to each other?/...* S antworten mit Kurzantworten *(Yes, we do./No, we don't.)* oder wiederholen die von L vorgegebenen Sachverhalte: *We help each other./We lend money/videos/CDs to each other./We give advice to each other if there is a problem./We go swimming/for long walks with each other./...*
- L übernimmt zwei, drei ausführliche Antworten an die Tafel, S übersetzen die Sätze.   *Tafel*
- S lesen *lif 7*, TB S. 121.   *TB, S. 121*
- S nennen weitere Aspekte einer guten Freundschaft – gemeinsame Unternehmungen, Umgangsweise etc. – und äußern ihre Vorstellungen möglichst unter Verwendung von *each other.*

b) Für das Portfolio verfassen S einen Text über sich und ihren besten Freund/ihre beste Freundin. Um S Unterstützung zu geben, die sich mit freier Textproduktion schwer tun, können folgende Impulse hilfreich sein: *Who (is your best friend)? Since when (has he/she been your best friend)? Why (is he/she your best friend)? What (do you do together/for each other)?*

Medium	Nummer	Seite	Titel	Fertigkeit	Zusatzinfo
TB	B1	54f.	Robinson Crusoe	Sprechen, Lesen	Comic
PB	B1	40	Robinson Crusoe	Schreiben	*simple past* **(R)**
TB	B2	56	Interviewing Robinson Crusoe	Sprechen	Fragen stellen; Textproduktion
Folie 9			Creative use of things	Sprechen	bekannte Gegenstände ungewöhnlich nutzen
PB	B2	40	Simple past	Schreiben/Sprechen	*irregular verbs*
copy 13			Irregular verbs	Sprechen	Spiel
TB	B3	57	What happened before?	Sprechen/Schreiben	Bewusstmachung *past perfect*
TB	lif 8	122	Past perfect		
PB	B3	41	What did you do after you had done that?	Sprechen	*past perfect*
TB	B4	57	Robinson's adventure in the paper	Schreiben	Textproduktion
PB	B4	42	The last class trip	Schreiben	Textproduktion
TB	B5	57	Lonely and homesick	Sprechen	
PB	B5	42	Lucky seven	Schreiben/Sprechen	Textproduktion
TB/CD	B6	58	Home on the range	Sprechen/Lesen/Singen	Lied
PB	B6	42	Home	Sprechen	
TB	B7	59	What is home? Where is home?	Lesen/Sprechen/ Schreiben	Portfolio
copy 14			Poems, poems, poems	Schreiben	Textproduktion
PB	B7	43	My home is your home	Schreiben	Wortschatzfestigung
PB	B8	43	Ladybird, ladybird	Lesen	Reim
TB	Optional	60	Split between two houses	Lesen	Leseverstehen; Textproduktion
PB	Portfolio	44f.		Hören/Sprechen/Lesen/ Schreiben	Selbsteinschätzung

Die grau unterlegten Felder stellen das Pflichtpensum dar, die weißen die Kür.

Teil B: • **Ein Interview führen**
Einen Zeitungsbericht schreiben
Über Einsamkeit reden
Familie und Zuhause beschreiben

TB B1   Robinson Crusoe   **Sprechen/Lesen**   *TB, S. 54f.*
• Um Spannung zu erzeugen, erfolgt an der Tafel die Einstimmung mit einem *acrostic*.   *Tafel*
  Find the English expressions for these German words:

Beziehung	R	*elationship*
Meinung	O	*pinion*
Eine/r, die/der Schwächere schikaniert	B	*ully*
Insel	I	*sland*
Zeitung	N	*ewspaper*
Naturwissenschaft	S	*cience*
Reihenfolge	O	*rder*
Notizbuch, Heft	N	*otebook*

• Klassengespräch: *Have you ever heard of Robinson?/Who is Robinson?/Have you heard of the book* Robinson Crusoe*?/Have you read the book?/What is it about?/Who wrote it?/When did Daniel Defoe write the book? (In 1719.)*
• Bei geöffnetem TB werden die Jahreszahlen im Englischen geübt. S lesen den *tip* in der Randspalte, L gibt weitere Jahreszahlen an der Tafel vor.   *Tafel*
• S lesen den Comic in Stillarbeit.

PB B1   Robinson Crusoe   **Schreiben**   *PB, S. 40*
a) • S überfliegen den Comic im TB nochmals und bestimmen die Zeitform, in der er geschrieben ist *(simple past)*.
  • S ergänzen die Formen des *simple past* in Einzelarbeit.
  Lösungen: *1. had, rescued 2. came 3. arrived 4. called, taught 5. lived 6. left, travelled 7. sank 8. swam, survived 9. left 10. showed, taught*

b) S ordnen die zehn Sätze in Einzelarbeit, das Ergänzen der Gefühle bleibt ggf. leistungsstärkeren S vorbehalten.
  Lösung: *6–9–7–8–5–2–1–4–10–3*

TB B2   Interviewing Robinson Crusoe   **Sprechen**   *TB, S. 56*
a) • Einleitung durch L: *Robinson Crusoe arrived back in York in 1687. How many years had he been away? (36 years) Look at the comic on page 54 if you don't remember when he left.*
  • S lesen zunächst nur die Fragen laut, L achtet auf korrekte Intonation (Entscheidungsfrage (= ohne Fragewort): Stimme heben; Ergänzungsfrage (= mit Fragewort): Stimme senken).
  • S lesen mit verteilten Rollen jeweils eine Frage und Antwort vor (eine Antwort ist in der Zeichnung enthalten). Da es nicht zu allen Fragen eine Antwort gibt , müssen S eigene Antworten ergänzen.
  Mögliche Lösungen:
  What did you eat? – Bananas, potatoes, plants, coconuts.
  Would you go there again? – Just for a holiday.
  What did you miss most? – I missed my home and my family most of all.
  How did you kill animals for food? – With a gun.
  What did you hate most about the island? – I didn't hate anything. But I was lonely at first.
  What did you like about the island? – I learned how to use plants as medicine.
  What has changed here while you were away? – A lot of things – the houses, the people ...
  Did you brush your teeth? – Of course, with a small stick.
  Where did you sleep? – I slept outside. Sometimes I slept on the beach.
  How did you teach Man Friday to speak English? – Well, I pointed to things and he learned the words.

b) • S überlegen sich weitere Fragen, zu denen die anderen S u. a. mithilfe des Comics Antworten finden.

• Ein Interview auf Kassette aufzuzeichnen, ist für S interessant, da sie sich sprechen hören und einschätzen können, wie englisch es klingt. Das gemeinsame Anhören und kritische Betrachten der Aufnahmen ist für die Ausspracheschulung ein ausgezeichnetes Mittel. Jede/r S sollte wenigstens einmal im Jahr eine solche Chance bekommen. Mögliche Lösungen: *What did you learn on the island? Why did you bring Man Friday with you? How did you feel when the English ship arrived? Were you often afraid? Did you have any accidents on your island?*

Erweiterung:

Als Robinson mit Freitag die Insel verlassen und nach England zurückkehren konnte, stellten die Menschen natürlich nicht nur ihm, sondern auch Freitag viele Fragen. Welche könnten das gewesen sein?

S sammeln in Partnerarbeit Fragen zu Herkunft, Familie, Alter, Muttersprache, wie er auf die Insel kam, wie er Englisch lernte etc. Anschließend erhalten S von L folgenden Text, der einige Antworten liefert.

When I walked through the forest one day, some cannibals from another island caught me. They brought me to a strange island. There was a white man with a gun. The cannibals ran away. The white man rescued me and called me Man Friday. His name was Robinson Crusoe. He taught me English and I learned to read and write. One day a ship arrived. Robinson was very happy because the white men rescued us from the island. In 1687 Robinson and I arrived in England.

Folie 9   Creative use of things   Sprechen

Folie 9 zeigt verschiedene Gegenstände des Alltags. S überlegen, wie man sie zu anderen, ungewohnten Zwecken einsetzen kann, wenn es ums Überleben geht.

PB B2   Simple past   Schreiben/Sprechen   *PB, S. 40*

Festigung der drei Stammformen unregelmäßiger Verben

Bei Schwierigkeiten greifen S auf die Liste der unregelmäßigen Verben, TB S. 209, zurück.

Erweiterung: Weitere Möglichkeiten zur Festigung der unregelmäßigen Verben
• S ordnen die Verben nach Gruppen:
  – „Hühnerverben": *put–put–put; hit, cost, cut, fit, let, set, shut, hurt*
  – *sing–sang–sung; begin–began–begun; ring, drink, sing, sink, swim*
  – 1. und 3. Form sind gleich: *become–became–become; come, run*
  – 2. und 3. Form sind gleich: *bring–brought–brought; buy, catch, fight, teach, think*
  – drei unterschiedliche Formen: *blow–blew–blown; draw, grow, know, throw; bite–bit–bitten; hide, ride, eat, forget, give*

• *Copymaster 13* festigt Infinitiv und *simple past.* S schneiden die Dreiecke aus und legen sie wieder so zusammen, dass Infinitiv und *simple past* aneinander stoßen. In Partnerarbeit können S weitere Dreiecke erarbeiten und mit anderen Paaren austauschen.
• Memory: vgl. TM S. 23.
• Die Klasse wird in drei Gruppen geteilt. Die erste Gruppe nennt einen Infinitiv, die zweite das *simple past*, die dritte Gruppe das *past participle*. Pro Gruppe notiert ein/e S die erzielten Punkte, für jede korrekt genannte Verbform einen Punkt. Im zweiten Durchgang beginnt die zweite Gruppe, danach die dritte mit einem Infinitiv usw.
  Variante: L nennt ein Verb auf Deutsch, die erste Gruppe nennt den englischen Infinitiv usw.
• Die Klasse wird in zwei Gruppen geteilt. Ein/e S der ersten Gruppe beginnt mit einem Verb und seinen Stammformen, z. B. *teach–taught–taught*, ein/e S der zweiten Gruppe nennt ein Verb, das sich darauf reimt, z. B. *catch–caught–caught*. Dann beginnt die zweite Gruppe usw.
• S erarbeiten ein Domino mit Verbformen. Beispiel:

TB B3   What happened before?   Sprechen/Schreiben   *TB, S. 57*

Bewusstmachung *past perfect*

- S ordnen die Satzhälften im Unterrichtsgespräch einander zu.
- L lässt S die ersten beiden Sätze übersetzen und die Zeitform bestimmen, dabei fällt S auf, dass sie dies bei der Zeitform *had* + 3. Verbform nicht können. Sie sollten jedoch in der Lage sein, sie im Deutschen zu benennen (Vorvergangenheit, Plusquamperfekt).
- S lesen die Beispielsätze in *lif* 8 und geben die Regeln zu Bildung und Verwendung des   *TB, S. 122* *past perfect* mit eigenen Worten wieder.
- Schriftliche Sicherung der Übung in der Hausaufgabe.

Lösungen:

After Robinson Crusoe had lived in London for some years, he left on a ship for the Caribbean.
After Robinson Crusoe's ship had sunk, he swam to an island.
After Robinson Crusoe had lived alone for many years, some cannibals came to the island with a prisoner.
After Robinson Crusoe had rescued the prisoner, he named him Man Friday and taught him to speak English.
After Robinson Crusoe had taught him to speak English, Man Friday taught Robinson Crusoe how to use plants as medicine.
After Robinson Crusoe and Man Friday had lived on the island for more than 20 years, an English ship rescued them and they returned to England in 1687.

PB B3   What did you do after ...?   Sprechen   *PB, S. 41*

Festigung *past perfect*

S erarbeiten die Fragen und Antworten in Partnerarbeit, einige Paare präsentieren ihre Ergebnisse anschließend im Plenum.

Lösungen:

Day 1: After he had lain in the sun for a few hours, he found some wood./After he had found some wood, he made a kind of boat./After he had made a kind of boat, he went back to the ship on boat./After he had gone back to the ship on boat, he found some food and a big box./After he had found some food and a big box, he brought the food and the box back to the island./After he had brought the food and the box back to the island, he had a meal./After he had had a meal, he collected grass, leaves and sticks./After he had collected grass, leaves and sticks, he made a house./After he had made a house, he went to sleep.

Day 2: First he got up./After he had got up, he washed in the sea./After he had washed in the sea, he ate some fruit./After he had eaten some fruit, he opened the box from the ship./After he had opened the box from the ship, he found a gun in the box./After he had found a gun in the box, he saw some wild goats./After he had seen some wild goats, he decided to try and shoot one./After he had decided to try and shoot a wild goat, he found some pens and paper in the box./After he had found some pens and paper in the box, he decided to write something every day./After he had decided to write something every day, he wrote about the first two days on the island./After he had written about the first two days on the island, he went to sleep.

> Erweiterung: *A long, long story*
> L beginnt folgende Geschichte, die von S unter Verwendung von *past perfect* und *simple past* weitergesponnen wird : *Yesterday morning I got up at six. After I had got up, I went to the bathroom. – After I had gone to the bathroom, I cleaned my teeth. – After I had cleaned my teeth, I had a shower. – ...*

TB B4   Robinson's adventure in the paper   Schreiben   *TB, S. 57*

- Anfertigen von Notizen in zeitlich korrekter Abfolge der Ereignisse. Wenn S über zusätzliche Informationen über Robinson Crusoe verfügen, können sie diese hier einfließen lassen (vgl. auch den Film *Cast Away*).
- Vor dem Schreiben des Artikels erarbeitet L gemeinsam mit S Unterschiede zwischen einem mündlichen Bericht und einem Zeitungsartikel: Der Zeitungsartikel ist ausführlicher und versucht, Spannung zu wecken und aufrechtzuerhalten.

PB B4   The last class trip   Sprechen/Schreiben   *PB, S. 42*
- Klassengespräch, um die Ereignisse der letzten Klassenfahrt wieder lebendig werden zu lassen, z. B.: *When/Where did you go? What did you do there? What was the most exciting thing? What was the weather like?*
- In Einzel- oder Partnerarbeit entsteht ein schriftlicher Bericht, der das Portfolio bereichern kann.   *Portfolio*

TB B5   Lonely and homesick   Sprechen   *TB, S. 57*
Die beiden Teilaufgaben werden im Klassen- oder Partnergespräch bearbeitet. Die Auswahl der mitzunehmenden Gegenstände wird je nach Zielort sehr unterschiedlich ausfallen. Deshalb finden sich nach der ersten Auswahl S zusammen, die das gleiche Ziel gewählt haben, und begründen ihre Wahl bzw. tauschen sich mit den anderen darüber aus.

PB B5   Lucky seven   Sprechen/Schreiben   *PB, S. 42*
- S wählen sieben Gegenstände aus und begründen schriftlich, warum sie gerade diese mitnehmen würden.
- S vergleichen und diskutieren ihre Auswahl in Gruppen.

> Erweiterung: *Kim's game*
> S schreiben die in der Aufgabe genannten Gegenstände auf Karten, die auch noch von weitem lesbar sind, und heften sie an die Tafel. S schließen für einen Moment die Augen, L nimmt eine Karte von der Tafel. S öffnen die Augen, L fragt: *What's missing?* Wer als erstes die fehlende Karte nennt, darf an die Tafel und das Spiel fortführen.
> Das Spiel ist auch mit Folienstreifen auf dem OHP möglich.   *Tafel*

TB B6   Home on the range   Sprechen/Lesen/Singen   *TB, S. 58*
- Anhören des Liedes von der CD bei geschlossenem TB.
- Stilles Lesen des Textes.
- Klassengespräch: Worauf bezieht sich der Wunsch *O give me a home, where the buffaloes roam, ...?* Der Sänger wünscht sich ein Heim in der weiten Prärie, wo Büffel, Antilopen und andere Wildtiere leben, wo der Himmel selten bedeckt ist, die Sterne nachts am Himmel zu sehen sind, die Luft sauber ist und das Atmen leicht fällt. Er würde sein Heim niemals mit einem in der Stadt tauschen.
- Lautes Lesen des Textes – einzeln und im Chor. Letzteres sollte bereits den Rhythmus des Liedes einbeziehen.
- Abspielen der CD, S summen und singen dann bald mit. Falls L oder ein/e S Gitarre spielen können, wäre eine Begleitung natürlich reizvoll.

PB B6   Home   Sprechen   *PB, S. 42*
- Überleitung vom Lied durch L: *Where do YOU want to live? What do you like better – the city or the village or would you like to live on a lonely ranch? Do you love YOUR home here in ...?*
- S formulieren im Plenum zu jeder der vorgegebenen Fragen ein Beispiel, dann arbeiten sie paarweise zusammen, einige Paare präsentieren ihre Mini-Dialoge anschließend im Plenum.

TB B7   What is home? Where is home?   Lesen/Schreiben/Sprechen   *TB, S. 59*
a) S erlesen sich die Sprichwörter zum Thema *home*, klären den Sinn im Klassengespräch, falls erforderlich, und notieren, was das Wort *home* für sie bedeutet. Danach erstellen sie eine *mind map* zu *home*, die anschließend an der Tafel noch einmal entsteht und in die S ihre Ideen eintragen. Die eigene *mind map* wird dabei ergänzt und erweitert.   *Tafel*

b) S nutzen die *mind map*, um Aussagen über eines oder zwei der Sprichwörter zu machen. Mit dem Partner/der Partnerin diskutieren sie, was sie von der einen oder anderen Aussage halten. Schriftliche oder zeichnerische Ergebnisse werden im Portfolio abgeheftet.

c) Zusatzaufgabe: Leistungsstarke oder besonders interessierte oder kreative S fügen ihre in Teilaufgabe a) entstandenen Äußerungen zu einem Gedicht zusammen, das sie ebenfalls in ihr Portfolio aufnehmen können.

Portfolio

Um S von der Vorstellung zu befreien, dass sich bei einem Gedicht die Zeilen reimen müssen, setzt L *Copymaster 14* ein.

> Erweiterung:
> Falls S für das Schreiben eines Gedichts nicht zu gewinnen sind, erstellen sie eine Collage mit Fotos/Zeichnungen unterschiedlichster Orte, die für Menschen das Zuhause sind: Wohnwagen, Hausboot, Iglu, Hütte, Beduinenzelt, Häuserblock, Villa, Reihenhaus, Höhle, zerstörte Häuser (Erdbeben, Kriege), … Damit kann die besondere Bedeutung und intensive Beziehung der Menschen zu ihrem Zuhause herausgestrichen werden. Auch die Wunschvorstellungen vom eigenen Zuhause können dargestellt werden.

PB B7   My home is your home   **Schreiben**   *PB, S. 43*

Zuordnen der Tiere in Einzelarbeit, Vergleich der Ergebnisse in Partnerarbeit.
Mögliche Lösung:
in a tree: fly, bird, rabbit, mouse
in the air: fly, bird
in the water: fish, crocodile, duck
on the ground: spider, horse, pony, fly, bird, rabbit, crocodile, duck, pig, lamb, mouse, tiger, elephant

PB B8   Ladybird, ladybird   **Lesen**   *PB, S. 43*

Die deutsche Entsprechung ist: Maikäfer flieg, dein Vater ist im Krieg, dein(e) Mutter ist in Pommerland, Pommerland ist abgebrannt, Maikäfer flieg!

TB Optional   Split between two houses   **Lesen**   *TB, S. 60*

- Dieses heikle Thema, das Leben von Kindern, deren Eltern geschieden sind, erfordert viel Einfühlungsvermögen und sollte nicht Thema eines Klassengesprächs sein.
- S entscheiden individuell, ob sie sich mit dem Text beschäftigen wollen oder nicht. Wenn ja, können sie ihre eigenen Empfindungen und Erfahrungen aufschreiben, Parallelen zum gelesenen Text aufzeigen oder gänzlich andere Verhältnisse schildern. L erklärt sich bereit, die Texte durchzusehen und mit den Verfassern individuell zu besprechen.

PB Portfolio   Selbsteinschätzung nach der Hälfte des Schuljahres/nach *Theme 4*   *PB, S. 44f.*

Die vier Einschätzungsbogen dienen der Selbsteinschätzung der S, den Stand ihrer Kenntnisse und Fertigkeiten im Gebrauch der englischen Sprache bzw. ihren Lernfortschritt im Vergleich zum Ausgangsniveau zu Beginn des Schuljahres festzustellen (vgl. PB S. 4f.). L nimmt keinen Einblick in die Einschätzung, dies ist eine Angelegenheit, die S allein zu verantworten haben.

- S lesen die Angaben zu den vier Fertigkeiten und schätzen ihre Fähigkeiten ein. Dies kann mit größerer Ruhe zu Hause erledigt werden.

Im Anschluss sollte S Gelegenheit gegeben werden, ihre Einschätzung mithilfe einiger kurzer Aufgaben noch einmal zu überprüfen und ggf. zu revidieren.

- **Hören**
  - L fordert einzelne S auf, bestimmte nicht sprachliche Tätigkeiten auszuführen, wie z. B. gymnastische Übungen, einen Gegenstand im Zimmer verstecken, einen Gegenstand an die Tafel zeichnen und die Klasse erraten lassen, ein Bilddiktat ausführen.
  - Kurze Ausschnitte aus Hörtexten späterer *Themes* oder anderer (älterer) Lehrwerke werden angespielt, S versuchen, so viel wie möglich zu verstehen, auch wenn sie nicht mit dem Kontext des Textes vertraut sind.
  - Auch kurze Mitschnitte von Radiosendungen sind geeignet, wobei S nur herausfinden sollen, welche Orte, Ereignisse, Jahreszahlen etc. Gegenstand der Sendung/Nachrichten sind *(listening for gist)*.

- **Sprechen**
  - Ein Interview mit einem Sportler, einem Behinderten, einem Star aus dem Showgeschäft führen.
  - Ein Gespräch mit verschiedenen Partnern über das Wetter, den zuletzt gesehenen Film, das vergangene Wochenende etc. führen.
  - Kurze Texte aus dem TB oder aber Originalbriefe von Briefpartnern aus Großbritannien/den USA laut vorlesen.
  - Ein Gedicht der Klasse vortragen.
  - Etwas über sich sagen: Alter, Wohnort, Familie, Hobbys, Schule, Freunde, Urlaubspläne etc.
  - Wendungen des *classroom discourse* einsetzen, z. B. um sich für vergessene Dinge zu entschuldigen, Nichtverstehen zu signalisieren, die Bedeutung eines unbekannten Wortes zu erfragen, um etwas zu bitten, etwas vorzuschlagen.

- **Schreiben**
  - Kurze Texte, die S nicht kennen, z. B. aus älteren Lehrwerken, abschreiben.
  - Eine (Post-)Karte schreiben (je nach Nähe zu einem Feiertag, Geburtstag von Klassenkameraden etc. z. B. eine *Valentine's card, Get well soon card, Easter card, birthday card*).
  - Notizen zu einem bereits behandelten Thema anfertigen – mit oder ohne Hilfe von Nachschlagewerken.
  - Ein lustiges, trauriges oder aufregendes Ereignis schildern.
  - Ein Gedicht verfassen.

Die Selbsteinschätzung zum **Lesen** kann mit Texten des TB oder kleinen Lektüren überprüft werden, es eignen sich aber auch hier Texte aus älteren Lehrwerken zu den bereits behandelten Themen.

Medium	Nummer	Seite	Titel	Fertigkeit	Zusatzinfo
Folie 10			The past in our daily life	Sprechen	
TB	A1	62	Something for a rainy day	Lesen/Sprechen	Informationen über britische Museen
TB	A2	63	Where to start	Sprechen	Wünsche begründen
PB	A1	46	Small city – a lot of museums	Schreiben	
PB/CD	A2	46f.	A tourist guide	Hören/Schreiben	Hörverstehen
PB	A3	47	Compare the museums	Schreiben	Textproduktion; Festigung des Komparativs
TB	A3	63	A great day out	Lesen/Sprechen	Leseverstehen
PB	A4	47	A great day out	Lesen/Schreiben	Leseverstehen
TB	A4	64	Inventions	Sprechen/Schreiben	Nützlichkeit von Erfindungen
PB	A5	48	Who invented …?	Schreiben/Sprechen	Daten von Erfindungen
PB	A6	48	Useful inventions	Sprechen	persönliche Stellungnahme
TB	PP	65	Museums can be fun	Lesen	Landeskunde
PB	A7	49	What can you do?	Schreiben	
TB	A5	65	Are YOU a successful inventor?	Schreiben/Sprechen	Wie kreativ sind S? – Evtl. Portfolio

Die grau unterlegten Felder stellen das Pflichtpensum dar, die weißen die Kür.

Theme 5: Learning from the past

Teil A: • Ein Museum beschreiben
  Über Erfindungen sprechen
  Funktionen erklären

Wenn S das Wort Museum hören, zeigen sie in der Regel spontane Abneigung. Dies ist bedingt durch wenig reizvolle Erfahrungen, die S bei Museumsbesuchen mit langweiligen oder zu langen Texten und wenig interessanten Ausstellungsstücken gemacht haben. Deutsche Museen bieten nur selten die Möglichkeit, aktiv zu werden. Eine interessante Einführung in das Thema ist daher äußerst wichtig, um S trotz ihrer Abneigung für das Thema zu gewinnen. Hierfür sind Originalmaterialien aus britischen (und deutschen) Museen geeignet, die Interesse wecken können, oder einzelne Gegenstände aus längst vergangenen Tagen, die S Rätsel aufgeben.

Der Einstieg in das *Theme* erfolgt über ein Klassengespräch bei geöffnetem TB S. 61. L: *Theme 5 is called* Learning from the past. *What does it mean, learning from the past? What can you see in the picture? What do these things have to do with the past? What do you think of the past? What do you know about the history of the telephone/TV/...? Do you think it is a good idea to look back to the past? Or should we only look to the present and future?*

> Erweiterung:
> Anhand von Folie 10 sprechen S über die Schätze und Rohstoffe der Natur und darüber, wie wichtig es ist, sorgsam mit ihnen umzugehen, über die lange Geschichte unserer hoch technisierten Welt und über den Erfindungsreichtum und die Ideen unzähliger Forscher, Entdecker und Erfinder, die Geräte entwickelten, die wir heute tagtäglich benutzen.

TB A1 Something for a rainy day   Lesen/Sprechen   *TB, S. 62*
• Ein/e lesestarke/r S liest den einleitenden Text vor, die Museumsbroschüre studieren S jede/r für sich. Die auswertenden Fragen werden im Klassengespräch beantwortet.

TB A2 Where to start   Sprechen   *TB, S. 63*
a) Beantworten der Fragen im Klassengespräch.
  Lösungen: *1. 5 2. Yes, you can. 3. In the Museum Café on the ground floor. 4. Yes, they can. They can use the lift, and there are toilets for the disabled. 5. No, you can't. You have to go to the third floor for that. 6. ships: 2nd floor (navigation), space: ground floor (the exploration of space), 3rd floor (flight/flight lab), sport: ground floor (science of sport), medicine: 4th floor (glimpses of medical history), 3rd floor (health matters)*

b) Erarbeitung in Partnerarbeit.

> Erweiterungen:
> • S erarbeiten Gespräche am *information desk* des Museums. In Gruppenarbeit bereiten sich 12 S auf ihre Arbeit an der Information vor, prägen sich den Plan des Museums ein und machen sich Notizen, wo sich was befindet, um schneller Auskunft geben zu können. Die anderen S bereiten ihre Fragen vor, bemühen sich dabei um einen höflichen Gesprächseinstieg *(Excuse me, please.)*. Anschließend führen S ihre Gespräche. Beispiel:
> *Visitor 1: Excuse me, please. I need the cash machine first. Where is it?/Where can I find it?*
> *Clerk: It's behind the shops and the post office over there. It's easy to find.*
> *Visitor 2: Good morning.*
> *Clerk: Good morning, Sir/Madam. Can I help you?*
> *Visitor: I'm interested in papermaking/the picture gallery/... Can you tell me where it is?*
>
> • Wenn L Originalmaterialien von britischen Museen hat, überlässt er/sie sie S für kurze Zeit zur Einsicht. Sie vermitteln einen Eindruck von den äußerst lebendig gestalteten britischen Museen, in denen man auf vielfältige Art und Weise als aktiv Beteiligte/r einbezogen wird – sei es durch Geräusche, Gerüche, Rauch, oder z. B. durch die Übernahme der Rolle eines Filmstars im *Museum of the Moving Image (MOMI)* in London.

Zusatzinformationen: Britische Museen
Andere interessante Beispiele sind: *The Whispering Gallery* in *St. Paul's Cathedral*, die audio-visuelle Darstellung des *Great Fire of London* im Jahre 1666, das vier Fünftel der *City* zerstörte, sowie die goldglänzende Kutsche des *Lord Mayor*, die alljährlich beim Umzug des Bürgermeisters zum Einsatz kommt und viele andere Attraktionen, die man im *Museum of London* bestaunen kann. Mit dem Zeitwagen des *Tower Hill Pageant* kann man 2000 Jahre Londoner Geschichte unterhaltsam und mit allen Sinnen erleben.

Erweiterung: *A questionnaire*
S befragen sich in Vierergruppen zu ihren bisherigen Museumsbesuchen. Die Ergebnisse werden im Plenum präsentiert und diskutiert. Mögliche Fragen:
1. *Have you ever been to a museum?*
2. *What kind of museum was it?*
3. *Who did you go with?*
4. *What did you see there?*
5. *Was the museum interesting/boring/exciting?*
6. *What was most interesting?*
7. *Did you learn any interesting facts about the past?*
8. *Would you like to go there again?*
9. *What should a museum be like?*

PB A1   Small city – a lot of museums   **Schreiben/Sprechen**   *PB, S. 46*
- Auf einer Englandkarte (TB, Innendeckel hinten) finden S die Stadt Bath.
- In Einzelarbeit formulieren S ihre Vermutungen. Dafür sollten Wörterbücher bereitliegen.
- In Partnerarbeit werden die Vermutungen ausgetauscht und evtl. ergänzt.

Zusatzinformationen: *The Roman Baths in Bath*
The Roman Baths are about 2,000 years old. A lot of people from the large Roman Empire came to Bath to recover. They came there because of the warm mineral springs. The main spring was called after Sulis Minerva, the Goddess of trade, but also of war. There are only two real things today that show that Romans were in Britain a long, long time ago: Hadrian's Wall in the North of England and the Roman Baths in the South West. People only found the first parts of this early history of Bath in the 18th and 19th century. Still today many people are cured by the water from the springs.

PB A2   A tourist guide   **Hören/Schreiben**   *PB, S. 46f.*
Der Hörtext lautet:
Good morning Ladies and Gentlemen. Before we start our sightseeing tour, I'd like to tell you a little bit about what you can see in the many museums you can find in Bath. The museum that most people want to visit is, of course, the Roman Baths Museum. There you can see the original hot water baths that the Romans used; you can also see parts of Roman buildings, Roman jewellery, a beautiful mosaic floor and some wonderful Roman glass bottles. The Costume Museum is the place to go if you are interested in clothes. You can see dresses, shoes and hats from hundreds of years ago. Finally, the Museum of the Royal Photographic Society is a fantastic place if you like photography. You can see hundreds of old photographs and old cameras there. Oh, I nearly forgot to mention the smallest museum in Bath – The Bath Postal Museum – they have old stamps and equipment from an old post office and a marvellous collection of model post boxes. Now I think we'll start our tour in the Roman Baths ... if you'd like to come this way ...

- Erstes Anhören des Textes.
- Zweites Anhören und Ergänzen der Informationen.
Mögliche Lösungen:
Roman Baths Museum: the original hot water baths, parts of Roman buildings, Roman jewellery, a mosaic floor, Roman glass bottles
Costume Museum: clothes, dresses, shoes, hats from hundreds of years ago
Museum of the Royal Photographic Society: old photographs, old cameras
Bath Postal Museum: old stamps, equipment from an old post office, collection of model post boxes

PB A3   Compare the museums   Schreiben/Sprechen   *PB, S. 47*
Festigung des Komparativs
- S schreiben jeweils sechs Sätze (denkbar als Hausaufgabe), L ruft die Ergebnisse im Klassengespräch ab: *What's your opinion? What do you think?*

TB A3   A great day out   Lesen/Sprechen   *TB, S. 63*
- Stilles Lesen des Textes.
- Klassengespräch: *What did Susan like best? Did she like the same things you would like?*
Lösung: *The highlight for Susan was sitting in a real aeroplane cockpit.*

PB A4   A great day out   Lesen/Schreiben   *PB, S. 47*
- Nochmaliges Lesen des Textes im TB, Korrektur der Fehler in Einzelarbeit.
- Vorlesen der korrigierten Sätze oder Austausch mit einem Partner/einer Partnerin.
Lösungen: *Chichester → Kensington; boyfriend → cousin; boring → fantastic; inventor → pilot; Austria → Australia; saw → didn't see*

TB A4   Inventions   Sprechen/Schreiben   *TB, S. 64*
a) S schauen sich die Erfindungen an und sagen, was sie für wichtig, gut oder nicht wichtig erachten (neuer Wortschatz: *invention, light bulb, match, ballpoint, penicillin, mobile phone, zip*), anschließend Verschriftlichung der Ergebnisse.

b) L stellt für die Erarbeitung dieser Teilaufgabe Wörterbücher bereit (für weitere Ideen/Erfindungen ggf. Vorgriff auf Folie 11).

c) Der Text sollte Antwort auf folgende Fragen geben: *What does it look like? (colour, size) What is it used for? How does it work? How important is it for you/your family/your class?*

PB A5   Who invented …?   Schreiben/Sprechen   *PB, S. 48*
a) Ohne Recherche ist diese Aufgabe vermutlich nicht zu lösen, sie eignet sich daher gut als Hausaufgabe.

b) S notieren ihre Ergebnisse in vollständigen Sätzen.
Lösungen:
J. Presper Eckert & John W. Mauchly invented the electronic digital computer in 1946 in the USA.
William Webb Ellis invented rugby in 1823 in Great Britain.
Ts'ai Lun invented paper in 105AD in China.
Alexander Graham Bell invented the telephone in 1876 in the USA.
James Naismith invented basketball in 1891 in the USA.
Anton von Schrotter invented safety matches in 1845 in Germany.
Levi Strauss invented the jeans in 1872 in the USA.
Walter Hunt invented the safety pin in 1849 in the USA.
Whitcomb L. Judson invented the zip fastener in 1893 in the USA.
Sir Rowland Hill invented postage stamps in 1837 in Great Britain.
Nicholas Jacques Conté invented the pencil in 1795 in France.
Zacharias Janssen invented the microscope in 1590 in the Netherlands.
Major Walter Clopton Wingfield invented lawn tennis in 1873 in Great Britain.

PB A6   Useful inventions   Sprechen   *PB, S. 48*
Die Sätze werden im Klassengespräch vervollständigt, besonderes Augenmerk wird auf die Begründungen gelegt.

TB PP   Museums can be fun   Lesen/Sprechen   *TB, S. 65*
- S erlesen den Text in Stillarbeit.
- L befragt S nach den für sie interessantesten Informationen und lässt Vergleiche zu deutschen Museen anstellen: *Do you know museums like that in Germany? What can you do in museums here?*

PB A7 What can you do?   **Schreiben**   *PB, S. 49*

S erarbeiten die Sätze in Einzelarbeit schriftlich.
Lösungen:
You can watch the old machines working in a watermill.
You can see old trains in a steam railway museum.
You can wear a helmet with a light on it in a show mine.
You can see very old children's games in a toy museum.
You can learn about wild animals in a wildlife centre.
You can see maps showing the interesting trees in a forest visitor centre.
You can see old boats in a canal museum.

Erweiterung:
Es kann für S eine interessante Aufgabe sein, über ein Museum der Region einen englischsprachigen Führer zu erarbeiten. Folgende Tätigkeiten sind erforderlich:
- Informationen über das Museum sammeln (schriftlich, mündlich)
- Material sichten und auswählen
- sich über Schwerpunkte des Museumsführers einigen
- Texte/Vorschläge für Aktivitäten schreiben/übersetzen
- Fotos machen, Zeichnungen anfertigen
- einzelne Seiten gestalten und heften
- fertige Exponate ausstellen.

Etwas weniger aufwendig ist ein großes Poster für das Schulhaus oder den Fachunterrichtsraum, doch in jedem Fall sollten S die benötigten Infos selbst besorgen.

TB A5 Are YOU a successful inventor?   **Schreiben/Sprechen**   *TB, S. 65*

a) • S erarbeiten die Teilaufgabe als Hausaufgabe. Sie schreiben einen Text für das Portfolio und illustrieren ihn.
    • Zeichnerisch begabte S können ihre Erfindung auf eine Leerfolie bringen und in der Folgestunde über OHP der Klasse vorstellen.   *Folie*

 b) Zusatzaufgabe: Sprechfreudige S diskutieren ihre Ideen im Plenum.

Erweiterung:
Auf einer Ideenbörse in der Schule stellen S ihre Kreationen vor.

Medium	Nummer	Seite	Titel	Fertigkeit	Zusatzinfo
TB/CD	B1	68	Front page	Sprechen/Hören	Gestalten einer Klassenzeitung
PB	B1	49	A quiz	Schreiben/Sprechen	Wortschatzfestigung
PB	B2	50	True or false?	Schreiben	Textverständnis
PB	B3	50	Riddles	Lesen/Sprechen	Sprachspiel
copy 15			Riddles, riddles, riddles	Lesen/Sprechen	Sprachspiel
TB	B2	68	Reporting reporters	Lesen/Schreiben/ Sprechen	Textverständnis
TB	B3	69	Headlines	Lesen/Sprechen/ Schreiben	Textverständnis; Textproduktion
TB	B4	69	Do it yourself	Lesen/Sprechen	Bewusstmachung *reflexive pronouns*
TB	lif 9	125f.	Reflexivpronomen		
PB	B4	50f.	They about themselves	Schreiben/Sprechen	*reflexive pronouns*
TB	B5	69	Motto of the month	Schreiben/Sprechen	Textproduktion
PB	B5	51	Mottos for everybody	Sprechen/Schreiben	Textproduktion
Folie 11			If there is no electricity, …	Sprechen	
TB	B6	70	Life without electricity	Schreiben/Sprechen	Was wäre ein Leben ohne Elektrizität?
PB	B6	51	Water, water everywhere	Schreiben	Was wäre ein Leben ohne Wasser?
TB	B7	70	David in Wales	Lesen/Sprechen/ Schreiben	alternative Energien
TB	B8	71	David's article	Schreiben	Textproduktion
TB	B9	71	YOUR class magazine		Projekt
TB	Optional	72	Levi's invention	Lesen	Geschichte der Jeans

Die grau unterlegten Felder stellen das Pflichtpensum dar, die weißen die Kür.

Teil B: • Ideen sammeln
Über alternative Technologien reden

In britischen Schulen sind Schülerzeitungen weitaus häufiger anzutreffen als in Deutschland. Mehrere Gründe sprechen jedoch für ein solches Unternehmen:

- S gestalten einen Teil ihrer Freizeit sinnvoll.
- Sie üben sich beim Verfassen der Artikel im schriftlichen Ausdruck und schulen bei der Diskussion über Themen und Beiträge ihre mündlichen Fähigkeiten.
- S haben ein Publikationsorgan, dem sie ihre Sorgen und Nöte wie auch Erlebnisse und Meinungen anvertrauen können.
- Neben dem Schreiben unterschiedlicher Textsorten (Bericht, Aufruf, Tauschannonce etc.) sind auch andere Talente gefordert, wie z. B. das Zeichnen, das Einrichten der Seiten, das Gestalten mit dem Computer.
- Die Schülerzeitung stellt ein ausgezeichnetes Mittel dar, um das Verhältnis der S untereinander und zu L zu festigen und entwickelt so auch soziale Kompetenzen.

Vielleicht gibt das Projekt, TB S. 71, den Anstoß, eine eigene Klassenzeitung herauszugeben.

TB B1   Front page   **Sprechen/Hören**   *TB, S. 68*
- Klassengespräch: *Have you ever thought of making a school or class magazine? Do you think it's a good idea or a bad idea? Do you have any ideas what you could write about in a class magazine? …*
- Anhören des Textes von der CD, in leistungsstarken Lerngruppen bei geschlossenem, in leistungsschwachen bei geöffnetem TB. Grobe Wiedergabe des Inhalts.

PB B1   A quiz   **Schreiben/Sprechen**   *PB, S. 49*
- S erarbeiten die Übung in Einzelarbeit, ggf. greifen sie auf TB B1 zurück.
Lösung:
A text in a newspaper: an article
Very clever or very good: brilliant
A religious festival in the spring: Easter
To tell someone your name when you first meet them: to introduce yourself
A ball game which was invented in England: rugby
A type of question you ask people for fun. It has an amusing or clever answer: riddle
The person who reads a text: reader
The answer to a problem or puzzle: solution

PB B2   True or false?   **Schreiben**   *PB, S. 50*
- S schreiben die korrigierten Sätze zum Textverständnis ins Heft.
Lösungen:
1. Vera says she has written a report about the day centre for old people.
2. Susan says she went to the Science Museum last weekend.
3. Susan says she has already written her report.
4. James says his German teacher will forget about the homework he owes her.
5. Roy says they should talk to Georg, the German Assistant teacher from Cologne.
6. Vera says she'd love to interview the new boy from Wales.

PB B3   Riddles   **Lesen/Sprechen**   *PB, S. 50*
Stilles Lösen der Rätsel als kleiner Wettbewerb: *Who can match the riddles and solutions first?*
Lösung:
When can you say, "I is"? – I is the letter after H in the alphabet.
What has a mouth but doesn't say anything? – A river.
What has 6 legs but only walks on 4? – A horse with a rider.
What kind of phone can you find in an orchestra? – A saxophone.
What has four fingers and a thumb but isn't a hand? – A glove.
What kind of tables do people eat? – Vegetables.
What kind of umbrella does the Queen of England carry on a rainy day? – A wet one.

copy
15

Erweiterungen:
Copymaster 15 bietet weitere Rätsel für die S, die Freude daran haben und die Rätsel in PB B3 schnell lösen konnten. L ermuntert S zudem, sich eigene Rätsel zu überlegen.
Lösungen:
What is red, blue and purple all over? – I don't know but it certainly would look funny.
Why did the woman throw the butter out of the window? – She wanted to see a butterfly.
Why did the man with one hand go into town? – To go to the second-hand shop.
Why did the computer get some cheese? – To give it to the mouse.
Find an animal in CONGRATULATE. – Rat.
Change a letter in MOUSE to make a building. – House.
Which word can you put in front of -book, -shop, -man, -day? – Work.
Add a letter to LIGHT to make a trip in a plane. – FLIGHT.
Change a letter in MONEY to make something very sweet. – Honey.
What is in the middle of Italy? – The letter A.
It comes and comes but never will arrive. – Tomorrow.
Which word can you put in front of -dresser, -dryer, -brush and -cut? – Hair.
What time is it when ten men are running after five chicken? – Ten after five.
Why was 6 afraid of 7? – Because 7 8 9.
Add a letter to PLACE to make a building. – Palace.
How would you get your purse back if it fell into a river? – You would get it back wet.
Add a letter to DIVER to make a job. – Driver.
When is a green book not green? – When it is read.
What has a face and hands but can't speak? – A clock.
Which is faster – hot or cold? – Hot – because you can catch a cold.

TB B2 Reporting reporters   **Lesen/Schreiben/Sprechen**   *TB, S. 68*

a) L teilt die Klasse in fünf Gruppen, die die Informationen über die fünf Reporter in arbeitsteiliger Gruppenarbeit zusammentragen.

b) Die Gruppen tauschen ihre Ergebnisse im Plenum oder in neu gebildeten Gruppen aus, in denen sich je ein Mitglied der fünf Gruppen befindet.
Mögliche Lösungen:
Roy would like to talk to Georg, the German Assistant teacher from Cologne, because he's leaving soon. And he is sure it would be interesting if they could get the new science teacher to talk about herself and her Amnesty International activities. He also thinks it's important to have something about school on the front page.
Vera has written a report on the day centre for old people because they plan to close it. She'd love to interview this good-looking new boy in G10.
Susan has written an article about the Science Museum in Kensington because she went there with her cousin Michael last weekend. She thinks they shouldn't give the readers the solution to the riddles this time because it was too easy last time.
Judy wants to decide what's on page one of the school magazine.

TB B3 Headlines   **Lesen/Sprechen/Schreiben**   *TB, S. 69*

a) S ordnen die Überschriften im Unterrichtsgespräch den Themen aus TB B1 zu.
Mögliche Lösung:
'A fun-tastic museum' is for an article about the Science Museum in Kensington.
'New science teacher at Holland Park' is for an article about the new science teacher who worked for Amnesty International.
'Goodbye to Wales' is for an article about the good-looking new boy in G10.
'Day centre closure protest' is for an article about the day centre for old people.
'More fun in German lessons' is for an article about Georg, the German Assistant teacher from Cologne.
'Strain your brain' is for the page with the riddles.
There is no article about 'Do it yourself', 'Teaching the tango' and 'Post from penfriends'.

b) S wählen eine der verbleibenden Überschriften und notieren in Stichpunkten, wovon der Artikel handeln könnte. S mit der gleichen Wahl tauschen ihre Ideen aus.

> Erweiterung:
> Die Ergebnisse aus TB B3 können im Hinblick auf das bevorstehende Projekt (TB B9) genutzt werden: S sammeln zu den gewählten Überschriften Ideen, Infos und Anschauungsmaterial, so dass einige Beiträge für die Klassenzeitung bereits vorbereitet sind, der zeitliche Aufwand für das Projekt somit reduziert ist.

TB B4   Do it yourself   **Lesen/Sprechen**   *TB, S. 69*
Bewusstmachung *reflexive pronouns*

a) • Bis auf Satz 7 sind alle Sätze dem Text TB B1 entnommen, so dass die Aufgabe S keine Schwierigkeiten bereiten wird. Die Ergebnisse werden schriftlich gesichert.
    • Anschließend übersetzen S die sieben Sätze mündlich.
    Lösungen: *1. herself 2. ourselves 3. yourself 4. myself 5. themselves 6. himself 7. yourselves*

b) • Die Personal- und Reflexivpronomen werden an der Tafel einander zugeordnet.   *Tafel*
    • S lesen *lif 9* in Stillarbeit und fassen das Gelesene anschließend zusammen, wahlweise   *TB, S. 125f.*
    auf Deutsch. L ergänzt den Tafelanschrieb um einige Beispielsätze.   *Tafel*
    • S übernehmen den Tafelanschrieb unter der Redeabsicht ,Ausdrücken, was jemand für sich, an sich, mit sich, … tut' ins Heft.
    Lösungen: *I–myself, you–yourself, he–himself, she–herself, it–itself, we–ourselves, you–yourselves, they–themselves*

PB B4   They about themselves   **Schreiben/Sprechen**   *PB, S. 50f.*
Anwenden und Festigung *reflexive pronouns*
• S erarbeiten die Lösungen in Partnerarbeit.
• Es empfiehlt sich eine mündliche Kontrolle, u. U. mit nochmaligem Rückgriff auf *lif 9*.   *TB, S. 125f.*
Lösungen:
They are looking at themselves in the mirror.
Rosemary is enjoying herself at the disco.
The duck can see itself in the water.
You can read about yourselves in the school magazine.
He is writing about himself in the letter to his penfriend.
The children are watching themselves on the video.
I can see you are enjoying yourselves.
Why are you talking to yourself?
I made it myself without any help.
Let's introduce ourselves.

• L führt mit S ein Klassengespräch, was sie und andere in der Familie zu Hause tun: *I make my bed myself./My mum waters her plants herself./…*

TB B5   Motto of the month   **Schreiben/Sprechen**   *TB, S. 69*
• Jede/r S schreibt ein Motto in großen Buchstaben auf ein DIN-A4-Blatt, in weniger kreativen Lerngruppen arbeiten S paarweise zusammen.
• S sammeln die Blätter ein, befestigen jeweils drei oder vier an der Tafel und diskutieren: *Tafel*
I think … is a very good motto for our class because … Die Klasse wählt die fünf besten Mottos, die während der nächsten fünf Wochen reihum im Klassenzimmer ausgehängt werden und helfen können, bestimmte Verhaltensweisen auszuprägen.

PB B5   Mottos for everybody   **Sprechen/Schreiben**   *PB, S. 51*
• Gemeinsam werden die vorgegebenen Mottos gelesen und durch je ein weiteres ergänzt.
• In Stillarbeit schreiben S noch zwei oder drei weitere Mottos für jede Spalte in ihr Heft.

Folie 11   If there is no electricity, …   **Sprechen**
Mit Folie 11 wird TB B6 vorbereitet.

TB B6   Life without electricity   Schreiben/Sprechen   *TB, S. 70*

a) S erstellen die Liste in Einzelarbeit und vergleichen sie anschließend mit einem Partner/einer Partnerin.

b) S bereiten die Teilaufgabe in Einzelarbeit vor, wahlweise mündlich oder schriftlich, die Ergebnisse werden im Plenum zusammengetragen und besprochen.

c) In Gruppen diskutieren S, wo Energie herkommt und fertigen eine *mind map* an. Da nicht alle Energieformen S auf Englisch bekannt sind, sollten Wörterbücher bereitliegen *(solar energy, wind power, geothermal energy, energy from the tides, …)*.
Ein möglicher Punkt der Diskussion: *Which of these kinds of energy is best for nature/the cheapest/the cleanest/the most dangerous/…?*

Erweiterung: *Story-telling*
In der Diskussion ergibt sich u. U. folgende Frage: *Would you like to try living without electricity for a weekend? What wouldn't be possible? What would you have to do?*
Daran kann sich folgende Aufgabe anschließen: *Let's try to tell a story of some friends or a family who spent a weekend without electricity.*

- S erarbeiten mündlich eine Geschichte: L oder ein/e S beginnen, der/die Nächste mit einer Idee fährt fort. Dabei ist aufmerksames Zuhören wichtig, um an geeigneter Stelle etwas zum Verlauf der Geschichte beisteuern zu können.   *Tafel*
- Wenn die Geschichte schriftlich festgehalten werden soll, ist es ratsam, sie ein zweites Mal zu erzählen. Dabei hält L Stichpunkte an der Tafel oder auf Folie fest.
- Diese Stichpunkte werden von S zu der vollständigen Geschichte ausgeschrieben, die (evtl. mit einer Zeichnung) in das Portfolio aufgenommen werden kann.   *Portfolio*

PB B6   Water, water everywhere   Schreiben   *PB, S. 51*

a) S arbeiten die sechs Sätze in Einzelarbeit aus.
Mögliche Lösungen:
We couldn't live without water.
We wouldn't be able to wash our face/body without water.
You couldn't make/drink tea without water.
You need water to do the washing-up.
We couldn't swim without water./You swim in water.
Fish couldn't live without water./Fish live in the water.

b) Erarbeitung in Einzelarbeit, Abrufen der Ergebnisse im Plenum.

Erweiterungen:
- Klassengespräch: *What can we do to save water in and around our school/our flat or house?*
- S erarbeiten eine Folie oder ein Arbeitsblatt zum Thema *Life without water*. Ein Anlass ist z. B. der „Tag des Wassers" jedes Jahr am 22. März. Zur Illustration eignen sich Fotos/Bilder aus Dürregebieten in Afrika, Asien etc., die S zum sparsamen Umgang mit Wasser anhalten.

TB B7   David in Wales   Lesen/Sprechen/Schreiben   *TB, S. 70*

a) • S lesen den einführenden Text.
- S schlagen im *Vocabulary*, TB S. 157, nach, wie die neuen Wörter ausgesprochen werden. L überprüft die Aussprache und bekommt so einen Überblick, inwieweit S zum Lesen der Lautschrift in der Lage sind.
- S geben Auskunft darüber, wo sich die einzelnen Anlagen befinden und verwenden dabei Präpositionen wie *next to, on the left/right, at the top/bottom, in the middle of …*

b) Zusatzaufgabe: S informieren sich über ähnliche Anlagen in der eigenen Umgebung.

c) Zusatzaufgabe: S arbeiten paarweise zusammen.

Erweiterung:
Da dieses Thema durchaus für die Klassenzeitung in TB B9 interessant sein kann bzw. sich für ein großes Poster eignet, holen S Informationen über Anlagen in ihrer Umgebung ein, vergleichen diese mit der von *David in Wales* besuchten und berichten über Kostenaufwand, Nutzen, Größe etc. Diese Vorleistung kann auch für TB B8 genutzt werden.

TB B8   David's article   Schreiben   TB, S. 71
Diese Zusatzaufgabe kann von nur einem Teil der Klasse übernommen werden, während schreibschwächere S über Anlagen in der Heimatregion berichten (siehe Erweiterung oben).

TB B9   YOUR class magazine   Sprechen/Schreiben   TB, S. 71
In beiden Teilen von *Theme 5* finden sich Anregungen für eine Schul- bzw. Klassenzeitung. Darüber hinaus gibt es stets Interessenten für Rezepte, Fitnessratschläge, Sportereignisse, wichtige Themen der Stadt/Gemeinde, Feste und Feiertage (hier und anderswo), Probleme junger Leute, Gedichte, Rätsel, die neuesten Hits etc., die Gegenstand einer solchen Zeitung sein können, so dass jede/r S einen Beitrag in Gestalt eines Textes, eines Bildes oder einer Zeichnung leisten kann.
Hilfe durch L ist u. U. erforderlich bei der technischen Herstellung, aber auch hier ist zu prüfen, ob S nicht selbst bestimmte Teile drucken (eine Druckerei in der Nähe kann um Unterstützung gebeten werden) oder die Herstellung vollständig über den Computer bewerkstelligen können (mit Scanner für Fotos, Farbdrucker etc.).
Während des Schreibens der Beiträge sollte L Korrekturphasen ansetzen, denn eine Korrektur der Beiträge erst nach ihrer Fertigstellung ist für S nicht motivierend. Falls die Klasse mehrere leistungsstarke S in ihren Reihen hat, können auch sie in Gruppen für notwendige sprachliche Unterstützung sorgen.

TB Optional   Levi's invention   Lesen   TB, S. 72
Da jede/r S eine Beziehung zu Jeans hat, ist dieser Text neben dem extensiven Lesen gut zum Anfertigen von Notizen geeignet (Lern- und Arbeitstechnik).
- S lesen den Text, ohne im Wörterbuch oder Wörterverzeichnis nachzuschlagen. L erinnert an verschiedene Techniken zur Bedeutungserschließung unbekannter Lexik (vgl. TM S. 38).
- Für L ist es interessant zu erfahren: *What was new in the text for you? What did you already know?*
- S fertigen Notizen in Stichpunkten an und ergänzen dabei nicht explizite Fakten, z. B.:
  Levi Strauss – born in Bavaria in 1830
  first job – sell kitchen things and cloth
  in 1849 Californian Gold Rush
  route of the ship: east coast of South America, round Cape Horn, north to San Francisco
  sold a lot of things on the ship, made money on his journey
  bought land in California
  rolls of strong canvas cloth
  people didn't need tents, but trousers
  first trousers in 1853
  people liked 'Levi's pants'
  small factory
  cloth from Nîmes (serge de Nîmes) – called denims
  later cloth from Genoa – jeans
  Levi Strauss & Company – one of the largest clothing companies in the world

Medium	Nummer	Seite	Titel	Fertigkeit	Zusatzinfo
copy 16			Money	Sprechen/Schreiben	Wortschatzsicherung
TB	A1	74	Money problems	Sprechen	Vorschläge machen und reagieren
TB/CD	A2	74f.	Karim's trip	Hören/Lesen/Sprechen	Hör-/Leseverstehen
TB	A3	75	Working for money	Lesen/Sprechen	Textverständnis
PB	A1	52	Positive and negative	Sprechen/Schreiben	Vorschläge unterbreiten
PB/CD	A2	52	Jobs	Hören/Schreiben	Hörverstehen
TB	A4	75	Some extra money	Sprechen	Bewusstmachung *if*-Satz Typ 1
TB	lif 10	128f.	*if*-Satz Typ 1		
Folie 12			What happens if …?	Sprechen	*if*-Satz Typ 1
PB	A3	53	How much will I get?	Schreiben	*if*-Satz Typ 1
PB	A4	54	French francs in Brittany	Schreiben/Sprechen	*if*-Satz Typ 1
TB/CD	A5	76	A car-boot sale	Sprechen/Hören	Hörverstehen
Folie 13			What should I sell? What could I buy?	Sprechen	
TB	A6	77	After the sale	Schreiben	Textverständnis; Textproduktion
PB	A5	54	What can I use it for?	Schreiben	Textverständnis; Wortschatzfestigung
PB	A6	55	A vase of flowers	Schreiben/Sprechen	
TB	A7	77	What are they like?	Sprechen	Wortschatzfestigung
TB	A8	77	The best ideas for making money	Sprechen/Schreiben	*if*-Satz Typ 1; Portfolio
TB	A9	78	Why do people sell things?	Sprechen	
TB	A10	78	Buying and selling	Schreiben/Sprechen	Verkaufsgespräch
PB	A7	55	How much is the blue vase in the window?	Schreiben/Sprechen	Verkaufsgespräch
TB/CD	A11	79	Money	Hören	Lied; Hörverstehen

Die grau unterlegten Felder stellen das Pflichtpensum dar, die weißen die Kür.

Theme 6: Cash in hand

Teil A: • Vorschläge machen
          Über Taschengeld sprechen
          Über Möglichkeiten des Geldverdienens reden
          Kaufen und Verkaufen

Das Thema „Geld" beschäftigt Eltern wie Kinder intensiv, denn die Konsumgesellschaft mit ihren Werbestrategien versteht es geschickt, ständig neue Wünsche zu wecken. Kinder erfahren in diesem Bereich schnell die Grenzen des Machbaren, die jedoch zumindest teilweise überwunden werden können, wenn S sich Gedanken machen, wie sie ihr Taschengeld durch eigene Aktivitäten aufstocken und den einen oder anderen Wunsch durch gemeinsame Anstrengung vielleicht doch erfüllen können.

Der Einstieg in das *Theme* erfolgt über *Copymaster 16*. S aktivieren und erweitern ihren Wortschatz zum Wortfeld *money* mit dem Grundgerüst einer *mind map*, die eine lexikalische Grundlage für die weitere Arbeit am *Theme* liefert.

TB A1 Money problems   Sprechen   *TB, S. 74*

• Zur Einstimmung äußern S, wohin sie gerne auf Klassenfahrt fahren würden. L lenkt das Gespräch auf die Kosten und leitet zur Aufgabenstellung über.
• S diskutieren Möglichkeiten des Geldverdienens, verwenden dabei die Formulierungshilfen im TB. Ggf. greifen S auf das Feld *How I could earn money* auf *Copymaster 16* zurück und/oder ergänzen ihre Ergebnisse von dort.

> Erweiterung:
> S erarbeiten einen Fragebogen, welche Jobs von S in der Klasse und darüber hinaus (Parallelklasse, Schule) zum Aufbessern des Taschengeldes ausgeübt werden. In dem Bogen werden die verschiedenen Tätigkeiten in ihrer Häufigkeit (*every day/every week/ every month/...*) eingetragen.
> Bei der Erarbeitung und Auswertung der Fragen werden die unterschiedlichen Tätigkeiten geschrieben und mehrfach gesprochen, so dass eine gute Festigung erzielt wird.

TB A2 Karim's trip   Hören/Lesen/Sprechen   *TB, S. 74f.*

• Anhören des Textes bei geschlossenem TB.
• Knappe Wiedergabe des Inhalts – möglichst auf Englisch – anhand folgender Fragen: *What's Karim's problem? Can Roy help him?*
• Übergang zur Auswertungsaufgabe TB A3.

TB A3 Working for money   Lesen/Sprechen   *TB, S. 75*

• Nochmaliges Anhören des Textes und/oder Lesen des Dialogs mit verteilten Rollen.
• Roys Vorschläge werden in Stichpunkten an der Tafel festgehalten, die beiden anderen   *Tafel* Fragen werden im Plenum beantwortet.
• Anschließend Klassengespräch: *Have you ever worked in a shop/in a supermarket/as a shoeshine boy/...? Have you ever done a paper round/washed your neighbours' car/...? What would YOU do to earn some extra money?*

Mögliche Lösungen:
Roy's ideas: save pocket money, do a paper round, work in a factory, help old ladies with the shopping, sell some old things from the garage, gardening, work as a shoeshine boy
Karim's decision: shoeshine boy
Personal opinion: No, I don't think it's the best decision. Karim will have to buy a few things for cleaning shoes first, and that will cost money.
Yes, I think it's a good idea. There are not many shoeshine boys so I think he will be successful.

PB A1   Positive and negative Sprechen/Schreiben PB, S. 52

a) Partnerarbeit: S1 liest einen Vorschlag, S2 findet die passende Reaktion darauf. Abschließend werden alle Paare nochmals laut vorgelesen.
Lösungen:
Why don't we have a car-boot sale? – Where can we have it? They won't let us use …
What about making cakes …? – I don't think so. We need eggs and milk …
Let's put on a class concert. – I don't think so. Nobody else in our class can play …
Why not put on a play? – I'm not sure. Have we got enough time to learn the words?
What about helping people in their gardens …? – I don't know. Most of the people …
We could wash cars … – I'm not sure. I don't think people will pay so much.

b) • S werden sich der Redeabsicht bewusst, die mit Karims Äußerungen ausgedrückt wird – ‚Vorschläge unterbreiten' –, und tragen mögliche Anfänge unter dieser Überschrift in ihr Heft ein: *Why don't we …?/What about …?/Let's …/Why not …?/We could …*
   • S ergänzen mögliche Anfänge negativer *(I don't know./I don't think so./I'm not sure./But (we could) …* und positiver Reaktionen *(That's a good idea./That's the idea./OK./Super./Great./… I like (gardening/washing cars …)/In my opinion that's the best idea.*
   • S reagieren mit positiven Aussagen auf Karims Vorschläge, z. B.: *Why don't we have a car-boot sale? – Great. We can have it in our garden and in the garage. What about making cakes and selling them? – That's a good idea. I'm sure my mother will help us.*

PB A2   Jobs Hören/Schreiben PB, S. 52

Der Hörtext lautet:

Zoe Peters: … the subject of our phone-in today is jobs – evening jobs, Saturday jobs, part-time jobs, weekend jobs, holiday jobs, Sunday jobs. If you want to tell us about your job, you will find the number in the Radio Times magazine and if you haven't got the Radio Times, I'll give you the number now. Have you got something to write with? Are you ready? Here we go … it's 0800 323232. OK. Here's your first caller. It's Mary from London. Tell us about your job, Mary.

Mary: Well, I work as a shop assistant in a shop that sells newspapers and sweets. I really enjoy my job because I meet a lot of different people. I work every Saturday morning from nine o'clock to one o'clock. The money's very good, too. I get £12.00 for four hours' work.

Zoe Peters: Thanks, Mary. Your job sounds great. Our next caller is Tim from Oxford. Do you enjoy your job, Tim?

Tim: No, Zoe. It's the worst job in the world so I finished last week. I worked in a supermarket every Friday evening. I had to fill up the empty shelves with packets, bottles, cans and jars. It was so boring. I only got £2.00 an hour and I worked for four hours every week. Anyway, I start a new job this Saturday … in a fish and chip shop.

Zoe Peters: Well, good luck with your new job. Bye. And now Peter from Brixham.

Peter: Hi Zoe. I work on my father's boat on Saturday mornings. He takes parties of tourists fishing in his boat. I have to collect the money and help the people with the fishing equipment. We usually go out for about three hours and my dad gives me £7.50. I love my job … it's fantastic. I think I would do it for nothing.

Zoe Peters: Great. What a fantastic job. Now here's our last caller … Muna from Cardiff. What's your job, Muna?

Muna: Hallo Zoe. I've got a Sunday morning paper round. I have to take the Sunday newspapers to thirty houses in three different streets. The Sunday papers are always very heavy because they have two or three extra parts. My round usually takes me about two hours and I get £6.00 every week. It's not a very interesting job but it's OK.

Zoe Peters: Thanks for phoning, Muna. That's all we've got time for this week. Join me next week, same time, same place for Zoe's Phone-in …

• Erstes Anhören des Textes von der CD und Mitlesen.
• Zweites Anhören mit Pausen zum Eintragen der fehlenden Informationen.
• Vergleich mit dem Nachbarn/der Nachbarin, ggf. nochmaliges Hören des Textes.
Lösungen:
Mary from London: Saturday morning 9–1/enjoys her job, money very good
Tim from Oxford: four hours/Friday evening/£2.00/worst job in the world, finished last week
Peter from Brixham: three hours/Saturday mornings/£2.50/fantastic, would do it for nothing
Muna from Cardiff: paper round/two hours/£3

TB A4   Some extra money   Sprechen   *TB, S. 75*
Bewusstmachung *if*-Satz Typ 1
- S erarbeiten die Übung im Klassengespräch.
- Bewusstmachung: L schreibt einen der Sätze an die Tafel, S analysieren (Was wird ausge-   *Tafel*
  drückt? – Unter welchen Bedingungen etwas geschieht. *if*-Satz: *simple present*; Haupt-
  satz: *will-future* und *can, must*).
- S lesen die Beispiele in *lif* 10.   *TB, S. 128f.*
- Schriftliche Sicherung der Übung als Hausaufgabe.

Mögliche Lösungen:
If Karim saves his pocket money, he can't pay for his guitar strings and music.
If Karim does a paper round, he can use his bike.
If Karim works in a factory, he will work hard.
If Karim cleans the neighbours' cars, he can earn some money.
If Karim helps old ladies, he can't do his homework.
If Karim sell the things from the garage, he won't earn a lot of money.
If Karim works as a shoeshine boy, he can invite a beautiful French girl.
If Karim cleans shoes, he can become a millionaire in the end.

Folie 12   What happens if ...?   Sprechen
Folie 12 schleift *if*-Satz Typ 1 im Kontext des *Theme*, Möglichkeiten des Geldverdienens, ein.

PB A3   How much will I get?   Schreiben/Sprechen   *PB, S. 53*
a) Stilles Lesen der Anzeigen, schriftliches Beantworten der Fragen in Einzelarbeit.
   Lösungen:
   If you have a paper round for eight weeks, you can earn £72.
   If you work as a cleaner for two hours every week for eight weeks, you will get £40.
   If you work in a café for two hours for the next eight Saturdays, you can earn £48.
   If you help in the garden for ten hours, you will get £35.

b) Erarbeitung in Einzelarbeit.
   Mögliche Lösungen:
   If you work as a cleaner for two hours every week for eight weeks, you will earn £40.
   If you work in a café for two hours for the next six Saturdays, you will earn £36.
   If you help in the garden for two hours every Saturday for the next five weeks, you will earn £35.
   If you do a paper round for four weeks, you can earn £36.

> Erweiterung:
> S äußern sich mithilfe des *if*-Satzes Typ 1 zu eigenen Möglichkeiten des Geldverdienens:
> *I want to earn about 30 DM a month. If I look after our neighbours' two children, I can earn 8 DM per hour. And if I ..., I can earn ...*

PB A4   French francs in Brittany   Schreiben/Sprechen   *PB, S. 54*
- L und S bringen – soweit von Ferienreisen vor Einführung des Euro noch vorhanden –
  Reste ausländischer Währungen mit.
- Als Vorentlastung ordnen S die Städte den Ländern zu: *Lisbon–Portugal/Brussels–
  Belgium/Copenhagen–Denmark/Ibiza–Spain, island in the Mediterranean* [ˌmedɪtə'reɪnjən]/
  Athens–Greece/Antalya–Turkey/London–Great Britain/Amsterdam–Netherlands.
- S schlagen im Wörterbuch die Aussprache der Städte- und Ländernamen und ihrer Adjek-
  tive nach. Diese werden im Chor, in Gruppen und einzeln gesprochen, um Aussagen über
  die Länder und ihre Währungen machen zu können. Zu beachten sind: *Brussels* ['brʌslz],
  Athens ['æθɪnz], *Copenhagen* [ˌkəupn'heɪgən].
- S vervollständigen die Sätze zunächst mündlich, danach schriftlich.

Lösungen: *1. escudos 2. Belgian francs 3. Danish krone 4. pesetas 5. drachma 6. Turkish lira
7. pounds sterling 8. guilders* (Stand: Juli 2001; ab Januar 2002 gilt für *1., 2., 4., 5.* und *8.* die
Antwort *euros*.)

Erweiterung:
Zur Festigung der Ländernamen leistet das folgende Spiel gute Dienste.
L beginnt mit folgender Äußerung: *I come from Austria, I'm an author and I like apples for breakfast.* S setzen die Äußerungen mit den nachfolgenden Buchstaben des Alphabets fort. S1: *I come from Belgium, I'm a bricklayer and I like a burger/broccoli/baked beans for breakfast.* S2: *I come from China, I'm a champion/cook/climber and I like coconuts/a cocktail/cream/a cup of coffee for breakfast.* S3: …

TB A5   A car-boot sale   **Sprechen/Hören**   *TB, S. 76*
- L erläutert *car-boot sale*: *It's like a flea market. People sell things they don't need anymore from the open boot of a car (that's the back part of a car) or from tables or stalls.*
- Diskussion mit S, ob ein *car-boot sale* auch eine Finanzierungsmöglichkeit für eine Klassenfahrt wäre. (Allerdings ist zu bedenken, dass hierzulande der Kauf aus zweiter Hand nicht so großen Anklang findet wie in Großbritannien.) *Where could you have the car-boot sale? What would you like to sell? Go around your room/flat/house, but ask your parents before you sell anything. Who else could give you things for the sale? What about the prices? How old are your things? Look at the prices for new things.*

- Folie 13 gibt zahlreiche Anregungen, wie das Kinderzimmer entrümpelt werden kann. Allerdings werden sich nicht alle S von ihren Spielen o. Ä. trennen wollen.
- S lesen das Werbeplakat, TB S. 76. Frage: *What will the children do with the money?*
- S hören den Text von der CD bei geschlossenem TB. Höraufgabe (Tafelanschrieb): *What*   *Tafel* *does Rosemary buy? How much does she pay for the things? Who does she buy the things for?*
- S geben den Inhalt kurz wieder und beantworten die drei Fragen *(a vase, a picture and a glass pig./£9 altogether, vase £5, picture £2, pig £2/Aunt Elsie, who has a little antique shop).*

TB A6   After the sale   **Schreiben**   *TB, S. 77*
a) • Lesen oder nochmaliges Hören des Textes.
   • S machen in Einzelarbeit Notizen zu den fünf Fragen.
   Mögliche Lösung: *Karim, Vera, Rosemary/in Karim's garage/organized a car-boot sale/ selling old things/half to a children's charity, half for trip to France*

b) • L weist S darauf hin, dass es hier darum geht, in wenigen Sätzen den Kern des Textes zusammenzufassen *(summary)*. Leistungsstarke Lerngruppen arbeiten selbstständig in Einzelarbeit, in leistungsschwächeren Lerngruppen gibt L die unterstützenden Fragen *Who? What? When? Where? Why? Other important information?* an der Tafel vor.   *Tafel*
   • Zunächst werden die Texte in Partnerarbeit gegenseitig vorgelesen und korrigiert, anschließend im Plenum.
   Mögliche Lösung: *The story* A car-boot sale *is about Karim's and Vera's car-boot sale in Karim's garage. They are selling old things. They want to give half the money to a children's charity and keep the rest for their trip to France.*

PB A5   What can I use it for?   **Schreiben**   *PB, S. 54*
a) Mithilfe von TB S. 76 schreiben S auf, was Karim und Vera verkaufen.
   Mögliche Lösung: a *picture, a vase, a glass pig, books, a CD player, a lamp, plates, picture frames*

b) Lösungen: *1. vase 2. book 3. plate 4. lamp 5. painting/picture 6. CD player*

PB A6   A vase of flowers   **Schreiben**   *PB, S. 55*
- Es bedarf umfangreicher Übung, bevor S sich die Verwendung von Gefäßen und Verpackungen für bestimmte Dinge im Englischen einprägen. L fordert sie auf, die Verpackungen/Gefäße zu malen und die passenden Gegenstände „hineinzuschreiben".
- L weist S darauf hin, dass manche der Gegenstände in mehrere der Gefäße passen.
Mögliche Lösungen:
bag: potatoes; packet: crisps/biscuits; jar: sweets; pot: tea; bottle: wine/milk; cup: tea/milk/ coffee; bowl: soup/ice-cream/milk; box: matches/pencils/chocolates

TB A7 What are they like?   **Sprechen**   *TB, S. 77*

• S suchen in Partnerarbeit Gegenstände und Beschreibungen aus dem Text TB A5 heraus und tragen sie in eine Tabelle ein, wie im TB vorgegeben.

• Zur Wortschatzaktivierung und -festigung werden die Adjektive an der Tafel gesammelt und ggf. gruppiert *(positive/negative).*

Mögliche Lösung: *books: old, new, valuable, interesting, boring, funny; CD player: old, new, broken; picture/painting: valuable, awful*

TB A8 The best ideas for making money   **Sprechen/Schreiben**   *TB, S. 77*

Festigung *if*-Satz Typ 1

a) Mit oder ohne Hilfe von *Copymaster 16* (vgl. TM S. 76) tragen S noch einmal alle Ideen zusammen, die das Taschengeld aufbessern oder Geld für eine Klassenfahrt zusammenbringen können, und wägen sie unter Verwendung des *if*-Satzes Typ 1 gegeneinander ab.

b) • S gestalten ein Poster, auf dem sie für ihre beste Idee werben. Die Ergebnisse werden im Portfolio abgeheftet.

     • Leistungsstarke S schreiben darüber hinaus einen Text, der speziell auf sie zugeschnitten ist und zum Ausdruck bringt, welche Idee für sie die beste ist, wofür sie zusätzlich Geld benötigen, wo und wann sie ihre Idee realisieren werden.

TB A9 Why do people sell things?   **Sprechen**   *TB, S. 78*

• L überzeugt sich, dass S die Aufgabenstellung verstanden haben, dann überlegen S in Partnerarbeit, was Leute dazu veranlasst/veranlassen könnte, bestimmte Dinge zu verkaufen, und tauschen ihre Erfahrungen aus.

• Anschließend tragen die Paare ihre Ergebnisse im Klassengespräch zusammen.

TB A10 Buying and selling   **Schreiben/Sprechen**   *TB, S. 78*

a) S ordnen die Äußerungen in schriftlicher Partnerarbeit dem Käufer/Verkäufer zu und ergänzen sie durch bereits aus Klasse 5/6 bekannte Wendungen.

     Mögliche Lösungen:

     Buyer: What size are they?/I think I'll take it./Does it work?/Oh, that's too expensive./How much is it?/Do you have any ...?/What do you want for that?

     Have you got anything special ...?/I'm looking for .../How much is/are the ...?/That's cheap/expensive./Here's £5./No, that's all, thank you.

     Seller: It's £9./What do you think about this?/OK. Let's say £8./Sorry, I don't have any ... but I have some .../Special offer./Is that OK?

     Can I help you?/What can I do for you?/Here you are./And here's your change./Anything else?

b) In Partnerarbeit wird ein Verkaufsgespräch auf einem Flohmarkt nachgestaltet. Nach Möglichkeit, damit es authentisch wirkt, sollten Realien eingesetzt werden, um mehr über Aussehen, Farbe, Alter, Preis etc. aussagen bzw. erfragen zu können.

c) Zusatzaufgabe: S zeichnen ihr Gespräch zu Hause auf Kassette oder Video auf. Anhand dieser Dokumente wird der beste Verkäufer/die beste Verkäuferin der Klasse ermittelt.

PB A7 How much is the blue vase ...?   **Schreiben/Sprechen**   *PB, S. 55*

• S überlegen zunächst allein, wie die Äußerungen zu vervollständigen sind und tragen sie mit Bleistift ein.

• In Partnerarbeit werden die Einträge verglichen, dann wird das Gespräch mit verteilten Rollen geführt.

Mögliche Lösungen: *help, much, window, one, get, careful, break, How much, old, much, cheaper, offer, birthday, expensive, what, of, 's, What, Here's, Here*

TB A11 Money   **Hören**   *TB, S. 79*

Das Lied von Simply Red sollte nicht zerredet werden. S hören es von der CD, lesen mit und werden verstehen, worum es geht. Die emotionale Wirkung von Text und Musik stehen im Vordergrund und bilden einen sinnvollen Abschluss des Themas.

Medium	Nummer	Seite	Titel	Fertigkeit	Zusatzinfo
TB	B1	80	Can you remember …?	Sprechen	Wiederholung Landeskunde (London)
TB/CD	B2	80	The London Marathon	Hören/Sprechen	Hörverstehen; Landeskunde
TB	B3	81	Ready for the Marathon	Lesen	Landeskunde; Leseverstehen
PB	B1	56	The wrong numbers or the right numbers?	Lesen/Sprechen	Zahlenangaben; Textverständnis
TB	B4	81	Get the numbers right!	Schreiben/Sprechen	Zahlenangaben; Textverständnis
PB	B2	56	When will I finish?	Lesen/Schreiben	Wiederholung/ Festigung if-Satz Typ 1
TB	B5	82	The right start	Sprechen	Festigung if-Satz Typ 1; Textverständnis
TB	B6	82	An e-mail to Rosemary	Lesen/Schreiben/ Sprechen	Leseverstehen
TB	B7	82	After the marathon	Sprechen	comparison of adverbs
TB	lif 11	129	Steigerung von Adverbien		
PB	B3	57	Quickly, carefully, hard and fast	Schreiben	comparison of adverbs
TB	PP	83	Charities	Lesen/Sprechen	Landeskunde
PB	B4	57	Charity poster	Schreiben	Festigung if-Satz Typ 1; Textproduktion
TB	B8	83	What can we do to help?	Sprechen/Schreiben	Textproduktion
TB	Optional	84	Oliver Twist	Lesen	Leseverstehen

Die grau unterlegten Felder stellen das Pflichtpensum dar, die weißen die Kür.

Teil B: • Eine Wohltätigkeitsveranstaltung beschreiben
      Sich über Wohltätigkeitsvereine informieren

In Großbritannien und den USA ist das *fund raising*, das Geldverdienen für einen guten
Zweck mittels Sponsoren, z. B. bei Sportaktivitäten, weit verbreitet. Die Sportler/Schulkinder
bemühen sich im Vorfeld, Sponsoren zu finden, die bereit sind, etwa für jeden gelaufenen/
geschwommenen Kilometer einen bestimmten Betrag zu zahlen. Am Tag des Wettkampfs
sind die Sponsoren eingeladen und verfolgen die Leistungen ihrer Kandidaten. Neuerdings
fangen auch in Deutschland Organisationen an, nach diesem Prinzip Spenden zu sammeln, wie
z. B. „Deutsche Multiple Sklerose Gesellschaft" und „Weißer Ring".
Oxfam (Oxford Committee for Family Relief) und andere *charity shops*, die in allen größeren
Städten Secondhandware anbieten, sind in Großbritannien sehr verbreitet. Einerseits
kommt der Erlös Menschen in Not zugute, andererseits sind die Läden durch ihre günstigen
Preise (Kleidung, Spielzeug, Bücher) zu einer zuverlässigen Einkaufsquelle für einkommens-
schwache Familien geworden.
Im Vorfeld von *Theme 6B* informieren S sich, welche gemeinnützigen Organisationen in ihrer
Stadt oder Region tätig sind. Auskunft darüber gibt es bei Caritas, Innere Mission, Malthe-
ser Hilfsdienst, Heilsarmee etc. oder im örtlichen Telefonbuch.

TB B1   Can you remember …?   **Sprechen**   *TB, S. 80*
 • Bevor in TB B2 vom *London Marathon* die Rede ist, wird das Wissen der S über London
   (u. a. *Theme 3B*) reaktiviert.
 • S erarbeiten die Zuordnung in Einzelarbeit, greifen ggf. auf TB S. 44/45 zurück.
Lösungen: *1. Buckingham Palace 2. Tower Bridge 3. Madame Tussaud's 4. the Thames
5. Covent Garden 6. Hyde Park 7. the Science Museum 8. the Tube*

TB B2   The London Marathon   **Hören/Sprechen**   *TB, S. 80*
Der Hörtext lautet:
*Radio speaker: In about 30 seconds more than 30,000 London Marathon runners will be on their
way. This is their route this year – you still have time to come and watch.*
*All runners set off from Greenwich. They pass the famous ship, the Cutty Sark. Then they run on
to Tower Bridge. When they have crossed Tower Bridge, they run towards the Isle of Dogs and
pass Canary Wharf Tower, one of Europe's tallest buildings. Then they run back along Narrow
Street. Now they run past the Tower of London and on past St. Paul's Cathedral and down to
the Houses of Parliament. They run into The Mall and finish outside Buckingham Palace. Now
I think they're ready. Yes … off they go!*

 • Einführendes Klassengespräch: *Who of you has heard of the London Marathon? When does
   it take place? (Sunday in April) How long is the race? (26 miles)*
 • Stilles Lesen des einführenden Textes. S fertigen Notizen zu folgenden Fragen an, die an
   der Tafel festgehalten werden: *What? When? How long? Where? Why? How many people?* *Tafel*
 • S geben kurze Zusammenfassung des gelesenen Textes.
 • Anhören des Textes von der CD und Verfolgen der Route auf der Karte. S nennen Statio-
   nen, die die Marathonläufer passieren, evtl. ist dafür ein zweiter Hörvorgang vonnöten.
Lösungen: *Greenwich–the Cutty Sark–Tower Bridge–Isle of Dogs–Canary Wharf Tower–Narrow
Street–Tower of London–St. Paul's Cathedral–the Houses of Parliament–The Mall–Buckingham
Palace*

> Erweiterung:
> Falls *Theme 6B* zur Zeit des *London Marathon* (Mitte April) durchgenommen wird, gestal-
> ten S ein Poster mit aktuellen Bildern, Zahlen und Informationen.

TB B3   Ready for the Marathon   **Lesen/Sprechen**   *TB, S. 81*
 • Zunächst stilles Lesen des Textes, S ergänzen ihre Notizen aus TB B2.
 • Im Klassengespräch erfolgt ein kurzer Austausch über die Länge der einzelnen Strecken
   und die Läufer, die diese in Angriff nehmen.
 • Da der Text viele Zahlen enthält, bietet es sich an, den Text laut zu lesen (siehe *tip* in der
   Randspalte, TB S. 81).

PB B1   The wrong numbers or the right …?   Lesen/Sprechen *PB, S. 56*
Die Aussagen werden mündlich richtig gestellt.
Lösungen: *1. four hours, twenty-seven minutes and eleven seconds 2. right 3. thirty-two thousand five hundred 4. No, it's the same. 5. No, they're the same.*

TB B4   Get the numbers right!   Schreiben/Sprechen *TB, S. 81*
• S übernehmen die Tabelle in ihr Heft und erarbeiten die Informationen in Partnerarbeit.
• Im Klassengespräch werden die Eintragungen verglichen und die Zahlen gefestigt.
Lösungen:
when?: 9.00 (start of women's race), 9.25 (start of wheelchair race), 9.30 (start of men's race/start of Mass Race)
how many?: 30,000 (runners), 2,500 (children in Mini Marathon)
how long?: 2.8 (miles; Mini Marathon), 26 (miles), 42.195 (kilometres)
how fast?: 2:06:05 (men's world record), 2:21:06 (women's world record)

> Erweiterung:
> In einer sportbegeisterten Klasse erstellen S ein Poster über weltweit stattfindende Marathonläufe. Informationen schöpfen sie aus Zeitschriften, Radio, Fernsehen und Internet, die Informationen werden ins Englische übertragen.

PB B2   When will I finish?   Lesen/Schreiben *PB, S. 56*
Wiederholung/Festigung *if*-Satz Typ 1
• S ergänzen zunächst die jeweiligen Startzeiten, vgl. TB S. 81, neben den Zeichnungen.
• S errechnen die Ankunftszeiten und tragen sie ebenfalls ein.
• Vergleich der Zeiten mit einem Partner/einer Partnerin.
• Mündliche Kontrolle im Klassengespräch mithilfe von *if*-Satz Typ 1, in leistungsschwachen Klassen schreibt L das Muster zur Stütze an die Tafel: *If … does his/her best time,* *Tafel*
  he/she will finish at …
Lösungen: *Lucy Jones: 14:56:25; Jamie McIver: 13:37:38; Peter Kranach: 11:49:40; Alice O'Neill: 12:24:50; David Archer: 12:30:20; Robert Matthews: 11:52:20; Susan Dauntsey: 13:28:17; Karen Davies: 14:07:25*

TB B5   The right start   Sprechen *TB, S. 82*
Wiederholung/Festigung *if*-Satz Typ 1
S bereiten in Stillarbeit, wahlweise mündlich oder schriftlich, drei Sätze vor, die Ergebnisse werden im Plenum zusammengetragen.
Mögliche Lösungen:
If you are a woman and fit, you can start at 9 o'clock from the Blue Start in Blackheath.
If you are a man and fit, you can start at 9.30 from the Blue Start in Blackheath.
If you want to dress up for the Marathon, you must start at 9.30 from the Red Start in Greenwich Park.
If you are in a wheelchair, you can start at 9.25 from the Blue Start in Blackheath.

TB B6   An e-mail to Rosemary   Lesen/Schreiben/Sprechen *TB, S. 82*
• S lesen die E-Mail jede/r für sich.
• Anfertigen von Notizen zu den Impulsen: *Who? What? Why? Other information?*
• S erhalten kurze Vorbereitungszeit für das monologische Sprechen.
• Mit Stoppuhr und Bleistift folgen die Partner ihren gegenseitigen Äußerungen und erkunden, wie viele Informationen in 30 Sekunden übermittelt werden konnten.

TB B7   After the marathon   Sprechen *TB, S. 82*
Bewusstmachung *comparison of adverbs*
• S lesen die einzelnen Aussagen in Stillarbeit und beantworten die fünf Fragen im Klassengespräch, ohne dass L sie auf das neue grammatische Pensum, *comparison of adverbs*, hinweist. Die fünf Antworten werden an der Tafel festgehalten. *Tafel*

- Im Anschluss lenkt L die Aufmerksamkeit der Kinder auf die grammatische Struktur der Sätze an der Tafel: Wie werden Tätigkeiten ausgeführt: schnell(er), gründlich(er), ... Da S sowohl mit den Regeln zur Adverbbildung als auch der Steigerung von Adjektiven vertraut sind, stellt das Pensum keine besondere Schwierigkeit dar.   *Tafel*
- S lesen *lif* 11 und fassen die Regeln zur Bildung zusammen.   *TB, S. 129*
- L stellt Fragen zu Gegebenheiten in der Klasse, z. B. *Who runs faster than ...? Who runs fastest? Who trains harder than ...? Who trains hardest in your class? Who speaks English well/better than .../best of all? Who does things more carefully than ...?* S antworten und stellen nach kurzer Zeit selbst solche Fragen.

Lösungen:
Karim collected the money more quickly than Roy.
Karim explained the rules more carefully than Roy.
Karim trained harder than Roy.
Karim ran faster than Roy.
Karim suffered more terribly than Roy.

PB B3   Quickly, carefully, hard and fast   Schreiben   *PB, S. 57*

Festigung *comparison of adverbs*
- L wiederholt zunächst die Möglichkeit des Vergleichs mit *as ... as*.
- Sie ordnen die Satzteile in Einzelarbeit und schreiben die Äußerungen auf.

Lösungen:
1. Roy didn't collect the money from his sponsors as quickly as Karim.
2. Karim collected the sponsor money more quickly than Roy.
3. Karim trained harder for the marathon than Roy.
4. Roy didn't train as hard as Karim.
5. Roy didn't explain the rules of sponsoring as carefully as Karim.
6. Roy didn't run as fast as Karim.

TB PP   Charities   Lesen/Sprechen   *TB, S. 83*

- Stilles Lesen des Textes durch S ohne Vorentlastung. S nutzen die ihnen bekannten Möglichkeiten, die Bedeutung unbekannter Wörter zu erschließen (vgl. TM S. 38).
- Klassengespräch über das Gelesene: *Have YOU ever heard of Red Nose Day? What do people do on this day? Do you think it's a good idea? What other ideas for raising money are mentioned in the text? Who would YOU collect money for?*

PB B4   Charity poster   Schreiben   *PB, S. 57*

Festigung *if*-Satz Typ 1
- S wählen jeweils ein Thema aus und bearbeiten es in Stillarbeit.
- Zu jedem der sechs Themen werden auf einem großen Stück Packpapier die Minitexte und Bildvorschläge gesammelt. Dies stellt eine gute Vorbereitung auf TB B8 dar.

Mögliche Lösungen:
If you have a large garden, let us know./Horse in a large garden with old trees.
If you have clothes you don't need anymore, you will make many people happy./Happy people trying clothes on.
If you have cans of food, we can feed hungry children./Cook in kitchen preparing food.
If you give us a pound, we can help to build wells (neu!) *in India./Happy people drinking water.*
If you give us a pound, we can buy medicine./Doctors taking care of children.
If you have old clothes which are still good, we can give them to homeless children, who will be happy./Children with sad eyes wearing old clothes.

TB B8   What can we do to help?   Sprechen/Schreiben   *TB, S. 83*

Diese Aufgabe kann ohne Schwierigkeiten in die Regie der S gegeben werden. In einem Klassengespräch bringen S ihre Ideen und Meinungen ein. Jedoch sollten nicht nur Poster gestaltet, sondern sollte in Verbindung mit einer Organisation/einem oder mehreren Sponsoren (Firmen in der näheren Umgebung der Schule) tatsächlich ein konkretes Hilfsprojekt in Angriff genommen werden. U. U. ist ein gemeinsames Unternehmen mit der Parallelklasse/den Parallelklassen sinnvoll und erfolgreich.

TB Optional   Oliver Twist   **Lesen**   *TB, S. 84*

Der berühmte Roman von Charles Dickens (1812–1870) ist ein typisches Beispiel für dessen Stil. Seine Charakterdarstellung zeichnet sich durch Fantasie, Humor und Feinsinn aus. Sein besonderes Gefühl für die Armen und Hilflosen ist allen seinen Werken zu Eigen. Besonders bekannt geworden sind neben *Oliver Twist* die Romane *Nicholas Nickleby, A Christmas Carol* und *David Copperfield*.

S ist der Name Oliver Twist sicher schon begegnet, denn Auszüge sind in Lesebüchern zu finden, und Verfilmungen werden an Feiertagen im Fernsehen gesendet. Das Musical *Oliver* feiert in London seit Jahren große Erfolge.

- S trainieren ihr Leseverstehen, das durch das Bild wesentlich erleichtert wird, und geben in groben Zügen die Handlung des Romans wieder.
- S holen Informationen über Charles Dickens und Details/Figuren des Romans ein (Bücherei, Internet, Eltern/Geschwister, …), halten Minireferate (zwei bis drei Minuten) und erkennen, dass Spuren von *Oliver Twist* und Charles Dickens bis in unsere Zeit reichen (Popgruppen *Artful Dodger* und *Uriah Heep*; Zauberer David Copperfield).

> Erweiterung:
> L besorgt eine der Verfilmungen von *Oliver Twist* (Videothek, Internet-Buchhandlungen!) und schaut sie mit der Lerngruppe.

Medium	Nummer	Seite	Titel	Fertigkeit	Zusatzinfo
Folie 14			Who is YOUR star?	Sprechen	Einstieg ins *Theme*
TB	A1	86	What do you think?	Sprechen	*pre-reading activity*
TB	A2	86	Brock Burnet	Lesen/Schreiben	Leseverstehen; Textverständnis
PB	A1	58	Is this the true Brock?	Lesen/Sprechen	Textverständnis
PB	A2	58	The truth about Brock Burnet	Lesen/Schreiben	Textverständnis
Folie 15			The signs of the zodiac	Sprechen	Sternzeichen
copy 17			YOUR horoscope	Sprechen/Lesen/ Schreiben	Sternzeichen
PB	A3	59	Positive or negative?	Sprechen/Lesen/ Schreiben	Charakterisierung von Personen
TB	A3	86	YOUR favourite star	Lesen/Schreiben	Portfolio
PB	A4	60	Who am I?	Schreiben/Sprechen	Textproduktion; Rätsel
TB/CD	A4	87	Radio Junior Europe Saturday Roadshow	Hören/Schreiben/ Sprechen	Hörverstehen
TB	A5	87	Their plans for the afternoon	Lesen/Sprechen	*present progressive for the future*
TB	lif 12	132	Present progressive for the future		
PB	A5	60	Vera's birthday party	Lesen/Sprechen	*present progressive for the future*
TB/CD	A6	88	Happy birthday, Anwar	Hören/Lesen	Lese-/Hörverstehen
PB/CD	A6	61	With love from me to you	Hören/Schreiben	Hörverstehen
TB	A7	88	A request programme	Lesen/Sprechen/ Schreiben	Projekt
TB	PP	89	The BBC World Service	Lesen	Landeskunde
PB	A7	61	World Service puzzle	Lesen/Schreiben	Wortschatzfestigung
TB	A8	89	Learning English with the BBC World Service	Hören/Lesen/ Sprechen	Landeskunde/ Hörverstehen

Die grau unterlegten Felder stellen das Pflichtpensum dar, die weißen die Kür.

Theme 7: Sight and sound

Teil A: • Über Lieblingsstars sprechen
Pläne machen
Musikwünsche im Radio äußern

Eine besondere Hinführung zum Thema ist nicht notwendig, da S an der Film-, Fernseh- und Popwelt in der Regel sehr interessiert sind. Diese wird ihnen in den Medien täglich präsentiert, und mit ihren „Heldinnen" und „Helden" identifizieren sie sich gern. Diesem altersgemäßen Verlangen nach Idolen kommt der Medienmarkt mit einer Vielzahl verschiedener Jugendzeitschriften nach, die die Teenager wöchentlich kaufen und in denen über das Leben der Stars berichtet wird.

Der Einstieg in das *Theme* erfolgt über Folie 14. S sprechen über ihre Lieblingsstars und sammeln Wortschatz zu diesem Bereich (auch in Vorbereitung auf TB A3, TB S. 86).

TB A1 What do you think?	**Sprechen**	*TB, S. 86*

• L oder S bringen Jugendzeitschriften mit. L: *Which of the German magazines for teenagers do YOU (sometimes, usually, often, always, never) read? Why do you read them? Who are your favourite stars? What do they do? Are they singers/musicians, actors/actresses, sports people …?* Wenn möglich, wird ein Gespräch über den übertriebenen Starkult und die Hintergründe geführt (u. U. auf Deutsch).
• L kündigt das Lesen eines Beitrags über Brock Burnet, den in Großbritannien sehr beliebten männlichen Star der Fernsehserie *Sweet Valley High* an: *Have you ever heard the name Brock Burnet? In your textbook you'll find an article about him from SHOUT magazine, a British magazine for teenagers. What would you like to find out/know about Brock Burnet?* Um S zu Äußerungen anzuregen, kann noch einmal Folie 14 herangezogen werden. Auch Anfänge von Äußerungen können an der Tafel vorgegeben werden, z. B.: *I'd like to find out if (he is …), how (old he is), where (he started his career), what (his hobbies are)* … *Tafel*

TB A2 Brock Burnet **Lesen/Sprechen/Schreiben** *TB, S. 86*
• S lesen den Text in Stillarbeit, legen im Heft ein *fact sheet* an und tragen die Fakten über Brock Burnet dort ein, ggf. nachdem sie den Text ein zweites Mal gelesen haben.
• Klassengespräch: *Did you get all the information about Brock Burnet you wanted?* S1: *I didn't find out how old he is/if he has a girlfriend/how he became an actor/* …
Mögliche Lösung:
Full name: Brock Burnet
Place of residence: sunny California
Hobbies: animals, sports, cooking, chocolate
Favourite sports: working out in a fitness studio, riding horses, water-skiing, skiing
Pets: two dogs and a fish

PB A1 Is this the true Brock? **Lesen/Sprechen** *PB, S. 58*
S markieren die *odd ones out* in Stillarbeit, die Begründung erfolgt im Unterrichtsgespräch.
Lösung:
'hamster' is the odd one out because Brock has two dogs and a fish but no hamster.
'doing the washing-up' is the odd one out because Brock likes the other three things in the list.
'an older brother' is the odd one out because Brock hasn't got an older brother.
'plays football' is the odd one out because Brock rides horses, water-skis, skis and works out.
'lazy' is the odd one out because Brock is a positive, honest and warm person.

PB A2 The truth about Brock Burnet **Lesen/Schreiben** *PB, S. 58*
• Erarbeitung in Einzelarbeit, Vergleiche der Ergebnisse im Plenum.
Lösungen: *Sentences 2, 4, 5 and 7 are false. 2. He has an older sister and a younger brother. 4. Brock's first acting job was in an advert for telephones. 5. He loves cooking for girls. 7. Brock finds it a bit strange and sometimes a bit frightening that all the girls run after him.*

Erweiterungen: Sternzeichen und Horoskope
- TB A2 nennt Brocks Sternzeichen Waage. S sind sicherlich daran interessiert, ihr eigenes Sternzeichen auf Englisch zu kennen, dafür wird Folie 15 eingesetzt. Klassengespräch: *Do you believe in horoscopes?*
- Mit *Copymaster 17* haben S die Möglicheit, Horoskope für Freunde zu verfassen (allein oder in Partnerarbeit). Weniger kreative S schöpfen ihre Ideen aus (Jugend-)Zeitschriften *(Be nice to a boy or girl who looks sad at school. You will soon have a new friend./You will make a lot of money this week/month and you will help a very good friend./Someone wants to meet you. Don't be shy and you will find a very special boy or girl)*.

PB A3   Positive or negative?   **Sprechen/Lesen/Schreiben**   *PB, S. 59*

a) In Partnerarbeit werden die Adjektive in die Listen eingeordnet.
Mögliche Lösung:
positive: honest, warm, cute, romantic, beautiful, great, fit
negative: frightening
both: strange

b) Vervollständigen der Sätze in Einzelarbeit, Ergebniskontrolle im Plenum.
Mögliche Lösung: *fit, warm, frightening, romantic, great, cute, strange, honest*

c) S nehmen das *Dictionary* E-D (TB ab S. 168) oder D-E (TB ab S. 193) zur Hilfe.
Mögliche Lösungen:
positive: brave, careful, cheerful, fair, friendly, funny, nice, patient, polite, sweet, wonderful
negative: boring, lazy, sad, silly, stupid, violent

Erweiterung:
S schreiben ein Adjektiv, das sie ihrer Meinung nach charakterisiert, groß und deutlich lesbar auf ein DIN-A4-Blatt, das sie verdeckt vor sich auf den Tisch legen. L sammelt sechs Blätter ein und ruft sechs beliebige andere S nach vorne, die die Blätter hochhalten. Der Rest der Lerngruppe stellt Vermutungen an, welchen sechs S die Blätter zuzuordnen sind. Anschließend selbes Vorgehen mit sechs weiteren Blättern.

TB A3   YOUR favourite star   **Lesen/Schreiben**   *TB, S. 86*

S einigen sich in Kleingruppen auf einen Star und besprechen ihr Vorgehen *(What do we want to find out? Where can we look for information? What kind of information do we have? (texts, photographs) How do we want to present our information?)*. Die entstandenen Poster werden im Klassenraum ausgehängt, die Texte zudem im Portfolio abgeheftet.

PB A4   Who am I?   **Schreiben/Sprechen**   *PB, S. 60*

a) Da S für diese Teilaufgabe ggf. recherchieren müssen, eignet sie sich als Hausaufgabe.

b) In der Folgestunde versuchen S in Partnerarbeit herauszufinden, in welche Rolle der/die jeweils andere geschlüpft ist. Ein oder zwei der rätselhaften Vorstellungen können auch vor der Klasse vorgetragen und gemeinsam gelöst werden.

TB A4   Radio Junior Europe Saturday ...   **Hören/Schreiben/Sprechen**   *TB, S. 87*

Der Hörtext lautet:

Tony Denims: *Hi, folks! It's Tony Denims here this week with your favourite Saturday Roadshow. And we're out in Portobello Road this morning, talking to some interesting people and listening to some great music! And right next to me is my first guest, Susan Johnson! Hallo, Susan.*

Susan: *Hallo, Tony.*

Tony: *And I see you have a friend with you.*

Charlie: *Yes, I'm Charlie Macintosh.*

Tony: *Let's find out something about you first, Susan. Do you listen to the Saturday Roadshow every week?*

Susan:	Well, I try to. Sometimes I tape it. I love the music.
Tony:	Great! What kind of music do you like?
Susan:	Oh, all kinds, hip-hop, raps, house …
Tony:	And you, Charlie?
Charlie:	I love techno and reggae.
Tony:	And stars. You must have a favourite star, Susan.
Susan:	Well, first of all, there's Sabrina. I think she's a fantastic singer. And she's at my school. Then I like to watch "Sweet Valley High" and "Neighbours". I really love Ben Barker. Oh, and then Brock Burnet.
Tony:	OK, Susan. Is there anyone you'd both like to say hello to on the programme?
Charlie:	Well, we'd both like to say "hi" to Vera Gulbenkian. It's her birthday. I hope she's listening.
Susan:	Yes, and then there's our great friend Karim Khan. He's playing in an important football match later this afternoon. Hope you win, Karim. I know you're listening!
Tony:	Great, great. Thanks for talking to me. Listeners, when you want to say "hi" to someone, just phone in or write a postcard to me, Tony Denims, Saturday Road-show at RJE. Now it's almost 9.30 and you're listening to RJE Saturday Roadshow out here in Portobello Road. Over to the studio for some music …

- Um das Zuhören effektiver zu machen, schreibt L Stichpunkte an die Tafel, die S in ihr Heft übernehmen und während des Hörens ergänzen. *Tafel*
  Who is speaking?
  Place:
  Guests:
  Information about Susan:
  Information about Charlie:
  Information about Vera:
  Information about Karim:
  L unterbricht das Anhören durch zwei Pausen oder spielt den Text zweimal vor.
- S tauschen die gesammelten Informationen aus und ergänzen ggf. ihre Einträge.

TB A5   Their plans for the afternoon   Lesen/Sprechen   TB, S. 87
Bewusstmachung *present progressive for the future*
- L formuliert Beispielsätze zum *present progressive* in der bisher bekannten Funktion mit Bezugnahme auf die Klasse, z. B.: *… is just reading in his/her textbook. … is just opening his schoolbag. A loud lorry is just passing by our school. Can you hear it?* S geben die Funktion dieser Äußerungen an: Es wird ausgedrückt, was gerade geschieht oder getan wird.
- S erhalten den Auftrag, *lif* 12 zu studieren und den Inhalt in eigenen Worten zu formulieren: Das *present progressive* wird auch verwendet, um ein zukünftiges Geschehen und Pläne auszudrücken. L zieht das Fazit: Das Englische ist eine sehr ökonomische Sprache, da ein und dieselbe Struktur sehr unterschiedliche Funktionen erfüllen kann. *TB, S. 132*
- Klassengespräch: *What are you doing this afternoon/at the weekend/next week …?* S formulieren Äußerungen im *present progressive* ohne schriftliche Vorlage oder Muster! Einige Beispiele werden im Heft unter der Redeabsicht ‚Über Zukünftiges sprechen, Pläne machen' notiert.

a) S arbeiten in schriftlicher Einzelarbeit.
   Lösungen: *Charlie is playing disc jockey at Vera's party. Susan is going to Vera's birthday party. Tony Denims is interviewing a famous basketball player. Vera's guests are playing party games. Vera's mother is picking up a friend from the station. David is helping his parents in Superstore.*

b) S machen in Partnerarbeit Angaben zu zukünftigen Aktivitäten. Dies kann abgekürzt werden, wenn S in der Phase der Bewusstmachung (siehe oben) bereits entsprechende Aussagen gemacht haben.

c) • S nennen zukünftige Aktivitäten, die kostspieliger sind, Erarbeitung ebenfalls in Partnerarbeit (*I'm going to the disco/cinema/a concert with … next Saturday/week/… I'm visiting my uncle in California next summer./…*).
   • Im Plenum geben S anschließend wieder, was sie von den Plänen des Partners/der Partnerin erfahren haben (*Niklas is going to the disco/cinema/a concert with … next Saturday/week/… Helena is visiting her uncle in California next summer./…*).

PB A5   Vera's birthday party   **Lesen/Sprechen**   *PB, S. 60*

- S bringen die Satzteile in Einzelarbeit in die richtige Reihenfolge. Da dies eine Aufgabe ist, die ein hohes Maß an kognitiver Arbeit erfordert, und da viele S Probleme haben, sich die Reihenfolge der Satzteile zu merken, hält L die S an, die korrekten Sätze aufzuschreiben. Evtl. werden ein oder zwei Beispiele mit großen Wortkarten an der Tafel demonstriert.
- S lesen die Äußerungen vor, vergleichen und korrigieren, falls erforderlich.

Mögliche Lösungen:

1. *Vera is getting ready for her birthday party this evening.*
2. *Fortunately Vera's mother is helping her with the food.*
3. *They are going to the supermarket to buy some bread and cheese.*
4. *Susan is bringing a few friends with her.*
5. *The disc jockey is choosing some techno and reggae music to play at the party.*
6. *At seven o'clock he is arriving to set up his equipment.*
7. *Vera is looking forward to her party.*
8. *She is wearing her new jeans and sweatshirt tonight.*

TB A6   Happy birthday, Anwar   **Hören/Lesen**   *TB, S. 88*

- Anhören des Textes bei geschlossenem TB.
- S geben an, was sie verstanden haben, um welche Art von Programm es sich handelt.
- Nochmaliges Anhören des Textes und Mitlesen im TB.
- Fragen zum Textverständnis: *What kind of programme is it? (Tony Campbell's request programme on the BBC.) Who is listening to the BBC World Service and where? (Karim and Sheree are listening to the BBC World Service in London, and their cousin Anwar is listening at the same time from Bombay, India.) Who is the request for? Why? (It's for Anwar from Karim and Sheree. It's Anwar's 18th birthday today.) What did Karim and Sheree choose for Anwar? (Anything by Ravi Shankar with his famous sitar.)*

PB A6   With love from me to you   **Schreiben/Hören**   *PB, S. 61*

a) S füllen den Lückentext in Partnerarbeit aus.

b) Der Hörtext lautet:

Tony Denims: Here's a request from Carl in Frankfurt. He says he has the best Mum in the world. She has a really busy life but she always has time for him and his sister. She's got a great sense of humour and she's a wonderful cook – she makes really good pizzas. It's her birthday tomorrow and she'd like to hear anything by Sting. (…)
Well, it's nearly the end of the programme. There's just time for one more request. Trudi sent me this e-mail from Copenhagen. She wants to thank her teacher Mr Green who's helped her to pass all her exams at school. She'd never have done it without him. He likes classical music so she's asked for a piece by Mozart.

- Anhören der CD und Vergleichen der Eintragungen mit dem Text.

TB A7   A request programme   **Projekt**   *TB, S. 88*

Durch TB A4, TB A6 und PB A6 sind S mit dem Sprachmaterial für Radiowunschsendungen vertraut. In diesem kleinen Projekt dürfen sie nun Radio spielen.

- S bilden Arbeitsgruppen und wählen jeweils einen ‚Moderator'.
- Während der eine, größere Teil der Klasse die Musikwünsche auf Papier vorbereitet (Schritte wie im TB angegeben), sammelt L mit den ‚Moderatoren' die für sie wichtigen Redemittel aus TB A4, TB A6 und PB A6 *(Welcome to …/You're listening to …/Here's a request from …/And now we have a request for … in … from …/Thanks for listening to …).*
- Die fertigen Radiogrüße präsentieren S entweder live oder nehmen sie auf und spielen sie dann vor. In letzterem Fall sollte jeder Gruppe ein Kassettenrekorder zur Verfügung stehen, ggf. werden S gebeten, Geräte von zu Hause mitzubringen.

> Erweiterung:
> Eine Nachfrage bei der Schulleitung, die Grüße in einer Pause über die Lautsprecheranlage senden zu dürfen, wird sicherlich nicht abgelehnt und kann als *Radio Junior Request Programme* eine feste Einrichtung für eine Pause pro Woche werden.

TB PP   The BBC World Service   **Lesen**   *TB, S. 89*
S lesen den Text in Stillarbeit und geben den Inhalt wieder, nur in ausgesprochen leistungsstarken Lerngruppen sollte dies auf Englisch erfolgen.

PB A7   World Service puzzle   **Lesen/Schreiben**   *PB, S. 61*
S lösen das Rätsel in Still- oder Freiarbeit, bei Schwierigkeiten greifen sie auf *People and places*, TB S. 89, zurück.
Lösungen: *1. pioneer 2. cable 3. Worldwide 4. satellite 5. drama 6. model 7. radio 8. documentary 9. viewer 10. thirty 11. newsreader*

TB A8   Learning English with the BBC ...   **Lesen/Hören**   *TB, S. 89*
Ob S sich im Internet ein Programm auswählen können, hängt von den technischen Möglichkeiten in der Schule oder zu Hause ab. Folgende Alternativen sind denkbar:
• L oder ein/e S suchen den *BBC World Service* im Internet auf und drucken das Radioprogramm aus, das kopiert oder auf Folie der gesamten Lerngruppe zur Verfügung   *Folie*
  gestellt wird. Weiteres Vorgehen wie im TB beschrieben.
• L bringt ein Radiogerät mit in den Unterricht und sucht gemeinsam mit S den Sender (Frequenzen siehe TB). S versuchen, so viel wie möglich von der gerade laufenden Sendung zu verstehen und wiederzugeben.
• S suchen zu Hause jede/r für sich den Sender, weiteres Verfahren wie oben.
• L präsentiert den Mitschnitt einer Sendung auf *BBC World Service*, den er/sie zu Hause vorgenommen hat, S geben wieder, was sie verstanden haben.

Medium	Nummer	Seite	Titel	Fertigkeit	Zusatzinfo
TB	B1	90f.	Sabrina and the Gatecrashers	Sprechen/Lesen	Comic
TB	B2	91	Guess who's speaking	Lesen/Sprechen	Textverständnis; *reported speech* (R)
PB	B1	62	I just called to say	Lesen/Schreiben	*prepositions* (R)
PB	B2	62	Word square	Lesen	Wortschatzfestigung
PB	B3	62f.	Music words	Schreiben	Wortschatzfestigung
TB	B3	92f.	What's on in London?	Lesen/Sprechen	Landeskunde
PB	B4	63	A day out	Schreiben, Sprechen	*present progressive for the future* (R)
TB	B4	94	Two pictures from the Tate Gallery	Sprechen	Fächerübergreifendes Arbeiten mit dem Fach Kunst möglich
PB	B5	64	Opposites	Lesen/Sprechen	Wortschatzfestigung
TB	B5	95	Picture exhibition	Schreiben/Lesen	Portfolio
PB	B6	64f.	Pictures that tell stories	Sprechen	Textproduktion
TB	B6	95	Prints and patterns	Lesen/Gestalten	Fächerübergreifendes Arbeiten mit dem Fach Kunst möglich
TB	Optional	96	Optical illusions	Sprechen	

Die grau unterlegten Felder stellen das Pflichtpensum dar, die weißen die Kür.

Teil B: • Veranstaltungskalender lesen
      Einen Titel finden
      Gemälde beschreiben

TB B1   Sabrina and the Gatecrashers   Sprechen/Lesen   *TB, S. 90f.*

- S bringen Fotos ihrer Lieblingspopgruppen mit und stellen sie vor: *My favourite group are ... They're from ... Their names are ... They are ... years old. They make a kind of (reggae/hip-hop/heavy metal ...) music. Their greatest hit/s is/are ... I like them because ...* Bilder und kleine Texte zu den Gruppen werden auf einem großen Poster gesammelt.
- Überleitung zum Comic im TB: *Do you remember who Susan's favourite group is? (Sabrina and the Gatecrashers)*
- S lesen den Comic, beantworten im Anschluss Fragen zum Textverständnis mündlich: *What have Sabrina and her group just come back from? (a very successful concert in Reading) What are her plans? (She hopes they can have a bit of a break now.) What are Fred's plans? (He has signed them up for a new gig next weekend.) What's the problem with the roadies? (Half of them have gone home.) Who can help? (the Gatecrashers' London Fan Club)*
- Klassengespräch: *Would you like to be a member of a pop group? Are you a member of a fan club? What do you do there? ...*

TB B2   Guess who's speaking   Lesen/Sprechen   *TB, S. 91*

Wiederholung *reported speech*

- Bevor die Sätze vervollständigt werden, ist an die Umwandlung der Personal- und Possessivpronomen zu erinnern. Klassengespräch: L: *How old are you, ...?* S1: *I'm ... (years old).* L: *He/She says (that) he/she's ... (years old).* (an eine/n andere/n S gewandt) *Where do you live?* S2: *I live in ...* L: *He/She says (that) he/she lives in ...* Danach übernehmen S die Wiedergabe in indirekter Rede, nach ein paar weiteren Sätzen auch die Fragen.
- Erarbeitung der Lösungen im Unterrichtsgespräch.

Lösungen:

Hank says (that) half of the roadies have gone home.
Fred says (that) they still have to pay a lot of money for the new instruments.
Susan says (that) at least they've got free tickets for the show.
Sabrina says (that) they are recording a new album next month.
Fred says (that) they are starting their rehearsal in half an hour.
Susan says (that) they are helping Sabrina and her band at their gig this weekend.
Sabrina says (that) they are doing exams at school almost every day next week.

PB B1   I just called to say   Lesen/Schreiben   *PB, S. 62*

S ergänzen die Präpositionen in Einzelarbeit, zur Ergebniskontrolle lesen sie die Sätze vor.
Lösungen: *X, until, at, on, at, on, X, in*

PB B2   Word square   Lesen   *PB, S. 62*

Wortschatzfestigung: Wortfeld *music*
S arbeiten zunächst jede/r für sich und vergleichen/ergänzen ihre Ergebnisse anschließend in Partnerarbeit.
Lösungen:

→ : *ticket, album, hit, rehearsal, solo, tour, guitar, disco, show, drum, single, concert, techno*
↓ : *sing, roadie, instrument, gig, fan club, recording*
↘ : *band, amp, rap*

Erweiterungen:

- Um den Wortschatz zum Wortfeld *music* übersichtlich zu notieren und so die Behaltensleistung zu fördern, erstellen S in Partnerarbeit eine *mind map*. Sie beginnen mit den 22 Wörtern aus PB B2, ergänzen aber weitere. Folgende Unter-/Oberbegriffe sind denkbar: *instruments, kinds of music, people in the world of music, equipment* etc. S vergleichen und ergänzen ihre *mind maps* in Gruppen oder im Plenum.

- S erarbeiten Rätsel zum Wortfeld *music*: Eine Gruppe umschreibt einen Begriff, die andere Gruppe muss ihn erraten.

PB B3   Music words   **Schreiben**   *PB, S. 62f.*

Wortschatzfestigung: Wortfeld *music*

S ergänzen die in PB B2 gefundenen Wörter in Einzel- oder Partnerarbeit, die Ergebnisse werden im Unterrichtsgespräch vorgetragen und verglichen.

Lösungen: *single, album, recording, concert, show/gig, ticket, band, rehearsal, fan club, disco, tour, gig/show, roadie, instrument, drum, guitar, sing, solo, amp, hit, techno, rap*

TB B3   What's on in London?   **Lesen/Sprechen**   *TB, S. 92f.*

- S überfliegen die Texte in Stillarbeit und finden die Antworten auf acht der 16 Fragen. Ein/e S übernimmt die Rolle von L, tritt vor die Klasse, stellt die 16 Fragen und ruft die Ergebnisse ab, die anderen S bemühen sich um zügige und umfassende Antworten.
- Alternative: S werden in fünf Gruppen beauftragt, die Texte zu je einer der fünf Überschriften zu lesen: *film and theatre, exhibitions, music, sports, shopping.* Danach finden sich S in fünf neuen Gruppen zusammen mit je einem Vertreter der fünf Bereiche. Sie befragen sich nun gegenseitig und bitten um Empfehlungen für Veranstaltungen, Ausstellungen etc. S1: *I'd like to buy some children's books. Where should I go?* S2: *There's the Children's Bookshop in Fortis Green Road. It's open Monday to Saturday from …*

Lösungen:
1. *0171 887 8000*
2. *Croydon Clocktower*
3. *National Maritime Museum*
4. *Oxford Street*
5. *Tate Gallery*
6. *£15 for adults, £10 for children*
7. *Monday to Saturday from 9.15 am to 5.45 pm*
8. *new and second-hand video games and consoles*
9. *at the Children's Bookshop on Saturday mornings and during the school holidays*
10. *concert with the* Lighthouse Family
11. *£6*
12. *Friday, Saturday and Tuesday at 7.30 pm at Wimbledon Stadium*
13. *No, you can't. It's closed on a Sunday morning, it doesn't open until 2.30.*
14. *seven*
15. *Egypt*
16. *the musical* Oliver

> Erweiterung:
> Das Lesen von Veranstaltungskalendern ist für die eigene Information wichtig, kann aber ebenso für Ratschläge für andere Personen hilfreich sein. Nach der Bearbeitung von TB B3 sollte ein Transfer auf die Heimatregion erfolgen. S erstellen einen Veranstaltungskalender für englischsprachige Gäste und geben Empfehlungen für einen vorgegebenen Zeitraum zum Besuch von Veranstaltungen, Ausstellungen etc. Die nötigen Informationen erhalten S aus der Lokalzeitung und den Veranstaltungskalendern des Heimatortes.

PB B4   A day out   **Schreiben/Sprechen**   *PB, S. 63*

Festigung *present progressive for the future*

a) S planen ihren Tag in Einzelarbeit mithilfe TB B3, S. 92/93.

b) In Partnerarbeit informieren sie sich gegenseitig über ihre Pläne.

c) Erarbeitung ebenfalls in Partnerarbeit.

TB B4   Two pictures from the Tate Gallery   **Sprechen**   *TB, S. 94*

Diese Aufgabe kann, wie auch TB B6, gemeinsam mit dem Kunstlehrer bearbeitet werden.

a)/b) Die beiden Teilaufgaben werden im Unterrichtsgespräch erarbeitet.

c) Die Begründung erfolgt schriftlich in der Hausaufgabe. Kreative S denken sich weitere Titel aus.

d) S ordnen den Bildern in Partnerarbeit mögliche Adjektive zu.

PB B5   Opposites   Lesen/Sprechen   *PB, S. 64*

Wortschatzfestigung: *adjectives*

S ordnen die Oppositionspaare in Einzelarbeit zu, Ergebniskontrolle in Partnerarbeit.

Lösungen: *cool–warm, dangerous–safe, sunny–cloudy, black–white, friendly–unfriendly, exciting–boring, empty–full, cold–hot, soft–hard, strong–weak, beautiful–ugly, happy–sad, strange–normal*

> Erweiterung:
> Das Einprägen der Adjektivpaare kann spielerisch in Gruppenarbeit geschehen. Ein/e S nennt ein Adjektiv *(safe)*. Der/die S, der zuerst das Gegenteil sagt *(dangerous)*, bekommt einen Punkt und nennt nun das nächste Adjektiv.
> Alternativ fungiert ein/e S als L und gibt jeweils ein Adjektiv vor.
> Die Punkte werden von S selbst notiert. Der Wettstreit kann auch schriftlich durchgeführt werden (nur die Wörter erhalten die volle Punktzahl, die auch richtig geschrieben wurden!) und trägt so auch zur Festigung der Schreibung der Wörter bei.

TB B5   Picture exhibition   Schreiben/Lesen   *TB, S. 95*

a) S beschreiben zunächst ein von L mitgebrachtes Bild, um die Redemittel einzuschleifen. Das Erstellen des eigenen Textes sollte allerdings in Ruhe zu Hause erledigt werden.

b) In der Folgestunde lesen S ihre Texte der Klasse vor und zeigen dazu jeweils drei oder mehr Bilder. Bild und Text werden ins Portfolio eingeheftet.

PB B6   Pictures that tell stories   Sprechen   *PB, S. 64f.*

a) In Partnerarbeit sind die Aufgaben leichter zu bewältigen. L stellt Wörterbücher bereit. Mögliche Lösung: *There are 16 people in the picture. They are in a strange house. Some are going downstairs, some are going upstairs. Two people are sitting at a table and having a meal. A man and a woman are leaving the house. Some people are carrying something. …*

b) S sollten nicht gleich die Lösung anschauen, sondern versuchen, die vier Gesichter zu erkennen.

TB B6   Prints and patterns   Lesen/Gestalten   *TB, S. 95*

Hier bietet sich fächerübergreifendes Arbeiten mit dem Kunstunterricht an.

• S wählen eine Technik aus und gestalten ein Muster/ein Bild. Ihre Erklärungen zu den Arbeitstechniken und -verfahren halten sie schriftlich fest, da die Ausstellung der Arbeiten auch Erläuterungen enthalten sollte.

• Da S derartige Aktivitäten, die sie ganzheitlich fordern, in der Regel sehr gern ausführen, sollten sie nicht einer Streichung aus Zeitnot zum Opfer fallen, denn auch hierbei sind S in der Fremdsprache tätig.

TB Optional   Optical illusions   Sprechen   *TB, S. 96*

Durch folgende kleine Tafelskizze mit der Frage *Which of the lines is longer?* werden S mit   *Tafel*
dem Begriff *optical illusions* vertraut gemacht.

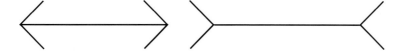

Die drei Bilder im TB werden im Klassengespräch besprochen. Dabei können Adjektive noch einmal wiederholt werden mit der Frage: *Which of the following adjectives would you use to describe the pictures? (ugly, interesting, funny, fantastic, fascinating, beautiful, nice, boring, dark, exciting, modern, monstrous, terrible, cool, sad, great)*

Medium	Nummer	Seite	Titel	Fertigkeit	Zusatzinfo
TB	A1	98	Getting ready to go	Hören/Lesen/Sprechen	Hör-/Leseverstehen; Textverständnis
TB	lif 13	134	one, ones		
PB	A1	66	A list of lists	Schreiben	Textverständnis; *going to-future* (R)
Folie 16			Our next school trip	Sprechen	
TB	A2	98	Yours and mine	Lesen/Sprechen	*possessive pronouns*
TB	lif 14	135	Possessivpronomen		
TB	PP	99	United Kingdom – Focus on Scotland	Sprechen/Lesen	Landeskunde; Leseverstehen
PB	A2	66	Words and music	Lesen/Schreiben	Landeskunde; Textverständnis
TB	A3	100	What are they going to see?	Sprechen	Route der Klassenfahrt
PB	A3	67	Where is Wick?	Lesen/Sprechen/ Schreiben	Landeskunde
TB/CD	A4	101	Arriving at the youth hostel	Hören/Lesen	Hör-/Leseverstehen
PB	A4	68	Whose is it?	Schreiben/Sprechen	*possessive pronouns*
TB/CD	A5	101	Questions at the youth hostel	Schreiben/Hören/ Sprechen	Hörverstehen
PB/CD	A5	68	Please may I …?	Hören/Schreiben/ Sprechen	Textproduktion; Fragestellung

Die grau unterlegten Felder stellen das Pflichtpensum dar, die weißen die Kür.

Theme 8: A trip to Scotland

Teil A: • **Vermutungen äußern**
Um Erlaubnis bitten

Die Durchführung einer Klassenfahrt beschäftigt S und L über lange Zeit, da nicht nur das Ziel klug gewählt sein will, sondern auch Unterbringung, Verpflegung, mögliche Aktivitäten und nicht zuletzt die Finanzierung.

Die folgenden Adressen des Deutschen Jugendherbergswerks, der *Youth Hostels Association* in England/Wales *(YHA)* und der *Scottish Youth Hostels Association (SYHA)* können für die Vorbereitung und Durchführung des *Theme* nützlich sein.

DJH Service GmbH
Bismarckstraße 8
32756 Detmold
Tel.: (0 52 31) 74 01-0; Fax: (0 52 31) 74 01-74
Internet: www.djh.de; E-Mail: service@djh.de

YHA (England and Wales)
Trevelyan House
8 St Stephen's Hill
St Albans
Hertfordshire AL1 2DY
England
Tel.: +44 870 870 8808
Fax: +44 1727 844126
Internet: www.yha.org.uk/
E-Mail: customerservices@yha.org.uk

SYHA National Office (Scotland)
7 Glebe Crescent
Stirling FK8 2JA
Schottland
Tel.: + 44 1786 891400
Fax: + 44 1786 891333
Internet: www.syha.org.uk
E-Mail: info@syha.org.uk

TB A1   Getting ready to go　　　　　**Hören/Lesen/Sprechen**　　　*TB, S. 98*
Bewusstmachung *one, ones*
- S hören den Text bei geschlossenem TB und geben danach grob den Inhalt wieder.
- Bei geöffnetem TB lesen S die Höraufträge unter dem Text, hören dann den Text ein zweites Mal und beantworten die Fragen.
- L geht auf *remind* (an dieser Stelle neu!) und *remember* ein, schreibt folgende Beispiele an die Tafel und lässt S Vermutungen über den Unterschied anstellen:　　*Tafel*
  I hope I'll remember to feed the dog.　　*I must remind him to feed the dog before we go.*
  I remember sending her a postcard.　　*Remind me to send her a postcard.*
  (*remember*: sich erinnern; *remind*: jemanden an etwas erinnern)
- Noch einmal wird auf den Text Bezug genommen. S schauen sich die rechte Spalte an, beginnend mit Gillian: *I'm OK for walking shoes …* Im Klassengespräch finden S heraus, worauf sich *one, ones* beziehen. Dazu lesen sie *lif* 13 und übersetzen die folgenden Sätze:　*TB, S. 134*
  Welchen Pullover soll ich mitnehmen? Den schwarzen oder den blauen? *(Which jumper should I take? The black one or the blue one?)* Welche CDs sollen wir mitnehmen? – Nimm bitte die mit, die wir gestern gehört haben. *(Which CDs shall/should we take? – Please take the ones we listened to yesterday.)* Welche? – Die, die ich dir zum Geburtstag geschenkt habe. *(Which ones? – The ones I gave you for your birthday.)* Die Sätze werden an die Tafel oder auf Folie geschrieben, S übernehmen den Anschrieb ins Heft.　　*Tafel*

Mögliche Lösungen: *Susan might still have to buy some camera batteries. Gillian is taking her camera, a film, a pair of (blue) jeans, an umbrella, David's walking shoes and her Discman. Vera wants Susan to take the CDs she got for her birthday from Karim and Gillian.*

PB A1   A list of lists　　　　　　　**Schreiben**　　　　　　　*PB, S. 66*
Wiederholung/Festigung *going to-future*
a) S erstellen die Listen in Einzel- oder Partnerarbeit im Heft.
　Mögliche Lösungen: *Gillian: siehe Lösungen zu TB A1; Vera: two films, some new pens and an umbrella; Susan: camera, an umbrella, her black shoes, her Discman and the CDs she got for her birthday from Karim and Gillian*

b) • S schreiben Sätze nach dem vorgegebenem Muster, L fragt nach, was mit dem *going to-future* ausgedrückt wird: eine Absicht, ein geplantes Vorhaben. S kontrollieren ihre Äußerungen zunächst in Partnerarbeit, dann im Plenum.

• Sätze im Plural sind ebenso möglich (*Gillian, Vera and Susan are going to take … because they want to … when they are in Scotland.*).

Mögliche Lösungen:

Gillian is going to take her blue jeans because she wants to look nice when she is in Scotland.
Gillian is going to take David's walking shoes because she wants to go walking when she is in Scotland.
Vera is going to take some new pens because she wants to write a postcard to her cousin Cheryl when she is in Scotland.
Susan is going to take her Discman because she wants to listen to music when she is in Scotland.
Susan is going to take an umbrella because she wants to stay dry when she is in Scotland.

> **Erweiterung:**
> Mithilfe von Folie 16 *Our next school trip* äußern S sich zu unterschiedlichen Aspekten einer Klassenfahrt.

TB A2   Yours and mine   **Lesen/Sprechen**   *TB, S. 98*
Bewusstmachung *possessive pronouns*

a) • S finden die Stellen im Text, lesen sie laut vor und schreiben sie an die Tafel.   *Tafel*

• S übersetzen die Sätze und erkennen, dass beim Einsatz eines Possessivpronomens das Substantiv nicht wiederholt werden muss.

• S lesen *lif* 14 und geben die Funktion der Possessivpronomen in eigenen Worten   *TB, S. 135*
wieder.

Lösungen: *Mine is too small for me./David says he'll lend me his./Are you taking yours, too?*

b) • S schreiben die Sätze mit den Possessivpronomen vollständig neu.

• Um die neue grammatische Struktur weiter zu festigen, sammelt L einige Gegenstände von S ein, die ihren Besitzern wieder zukommen sollen. L demonstriert mögliche Fragen: *Is this cap yours, …?* S1: *No, it isn't.* L: *Annika, do you think it's Laura's?* S2: *No, I don't think it's hers. I think it's Christian's.* S1: *Yes, that's right. It's mine.* Danach übernimmt ein/e S die Rolle von L.

Lösungen: *1. That jacket's not hers. 2. Is this comb yours or is it his? 3. What are you doing with that bag? It's mine. 4. That's the boys' room and this is ours. 5. Those shoes are theirs.*

TB PP   United Kingdom – Focus on Scotland   **Sprechen/Lesen**   *TB, S. 99*

• L schreibt *SCOTLAND and the SCOTS* an die Tafel, um bei S Vorwissen zu aktivieren. S *Tafel* tragen zusammen, was sie über Schottland und die Schotten wissen: *the monster of Loch Ness/Nessie, Scottish people wear kilts, play the bagpipes, Scotch whisky, famous Scottish people: Sean Connery, …*

• S lesen den Text still mit folgenden Aufgaben: *Find out what you shouldn't do in Scotland. (Don't call a Scottish person English.) When did Scotland become part of Great Britain? (in 1707) What's different in Scotland from the rest of Britain? (Scotland has its own laws, bank notes and school system.) What inventions came from Scotland? (telephone and television)*

• Hinweis: Der Text kann für den Portfolio-Fragebogen im PB S. 73 genutzt werden, S lesen ihn und schätzen ihre Fertigkeiten im Lesen ein.

> **Zusatzinformationen: *Scotland***
> Touristische Informationen sowie eine Vielzahl von historischen, gesellschaftlichen, politischen und statistischen Links bietet die Internetadresse: www.visitscotland.com

> **Erweiterung:**
> Mit Materialien aus dem Internet (siehe oben) und/oder Reisebüro, mit Fotos, Ansichts- und Landkarten gestalten S eine Schottlandkarte mit kleinen Texten und Bildern zu Sehenswürdigkeiten, geografischen Besonderheiten, Industriezweigen, Produkten etc. und erweitern damit neben ihrem Wortschatz auch ihre Allgemeinbildung. Die Poster werden zumindest für die Dauer der Unterrichtseinheit im Klassenzimmer aufgehängt.

PB A2   Words and music   Lesen/Schreiben   *PB, S. 66*

S erarbeiten das Rätsel in Einzelarbeit mithilfe von TB S. 99 und S. 100.
Lösungen: *1. blue 2. Andrew 3. Glasgow 4. Parliament 5. Inverness 6. phone 7. England
8. Scottish* Lösungswort: *bagpipes*

TB A3   What are they going to see?   Sprechen   *TB, S. 100*

Zusatzaufgabe

- S studieren die Schottlandkarte. Arbeitsauftrag: *Look at the map of Scotland in your textbook and write down the names of major cities (Glasgow, Edinburgh, Aberdeen), rivers
  (Tweed, Forth, Spey), lakes (Loch Ness, Loch Lomond), mountains (Ben Nevis) and islands
  around Scotland (Skye, Mull, Outer Hebrides, Orkney Islands, Shetland Islands). The list of
  geographical names on page 207 of your textbook will help you to say the names.*
- S schauen die Route (gepunktete Linie) an und versprachlichen sie: *From London they are
  going to drive to Scotland, their first stop is going to be Edinburgh. The next stops on their trip
  are going to be Sterling, Perth, Dundee and Aberdeen. After that they are going to visit Inverness and Loch Ness, drive to Fort William, maybe climb Ben Nevis. Their last stop on the way
  back is going to be Glasgow. From there they are going to go back to London by train.*
- Klassengespräch: *What do you think they might see in the different places they are going to?*
  Ein Satzmuster wird angeschrieben, nach etwa vier Äußerungen wird es ausgewischt,
  S machen Äußerungen ohne schriftliche Vorlage.

Mögliche Lösungen: *In Edinburgh I think they may see men wearing kilts and playing the bagpipes outside the castle. Near Aberdeen they may see oil rigs* (neu in TB B5) *in the North Sea.
At Loch Ness they are going to look for the monster but I don't think they are going to see it. In
Fort William they are going to see Ben Nevis, the highest mountain in Scotland. I'm sure everywhere in Scotland they may see some sheep.*

PB A3   Where is Wick?   Lesen/Sprechen/Schreiben   *PB, S. 67*

a) S beantworten die Fragen in Partnerarbeit mithilfe von TB S. 100 und schreiben die Antworten in ihr Heft. Um die Eigennamen beim Abrufen der Ergebnisse im Plenum aus-
sprechen zu können, schlagen sie unter den *Geographical names* im TB S. 207 nach.
Lösungen: *1. Skye and Lewis 2. the Orkney Islands 3. Ben Nevis 4. Aberdeen
5. Inverness 6. Sterling 7. Berwick 8. Firth of Clyde 9. Loch Lomond 10. b) about 20 km*

b) Das Überprüfen der Ergebnisse erfolgt anschließend in Selbstkontrolle mithilfe des TB.

TB A4   Arriving at the youth hostel   Hören/Lesen   *TB, S. 101*

- S hören den Text ohne Hörauftrag bei geschlossenem TB und fassen ihn zusammen.
- Klassengespräch zu Erfahrungen mit Jugendherbergen, z. B.: *Have you ever stayed at a
  youth hostel? When was it? Where was it? Did you go with your family or with your class?
  How many beds were there in a room? Who booked the rooms for your trip? Did you have
  breakfast, lunch and an evening meal there? Did you have to fill in a registration form?*
- L: *OK. The children at the youth hostel in Edinburgh have to fill in a registration form. Let's
  have a look at it.* Ein/e S liest die Fakten (*name, address, date of birth, ...*) vor, ein/e ande-
  re/r mögliche Einträge. Dabei wird die Aussprache von Wörtern wie *birth, arrival, depar-
  ture, Youth Hostel Association* gesichert.
- Damit der Wortschatz zum Wortfeld *youth hostels* gefestigt wird, wird er in einer *mind
  map* fixiert, die nicht nur einzelne Wörter, sondern auch Redemittel, die typisch für die
  Situation sind, enthält (*Let's check in first./We booked a room .../We're leaving on .../How
  many nights are you staying here?/Could you fill in these forms, please?/ ...*).

PB A4   Whose is it?   Schreiben/Sprechen   *PB, S. 68*

Festigung *possessive pronouns*

- Bevor S die Aufgabe erarbeiten, formulieren sie einige Sätze zur Erinnerung an die
  Possessivpronomen. L: *Whose book is this?* S1: *It's mine.* L oder S: *Whose ... ?*
- S ergänzen die Äußerungen unter Rückgriff auf *lif* 14 in schriftlicher Einzelarbeit.   *TB, S. 135*
- S lesen die Einträge vor, L oder S schreiben die Antworten an die Tafel oder auf Folie.   *Tafel*

Lösungen: *ours, yours, hers, mine, yours, ours, theirs, mine, his*

TB A5   Questions at the youth hostel   Schreiben/Hören/Sprechen   TB, S. 101

Der Hörtext lautet:

Gillian:	*May we listen to music in our rooms?*
Warden:	*You may listen to music during the day, but please keep the volume down so that you don't disturb the other guests. From 8 pm onwards you can only listen to music if you use headphones. We have some families with young children staying here, too.*
Vera:	*What time is breakfast?*
Warden:	*Breakfast is between 7 and 8.30 am on weekdays, and between 7.30 and 9 am at weekends. At weekends you can have a cooked breakfast, and during the week there's a continental breakfast.*
Girl (a):	*Where are the toilets?*
Warden	*Oh, sorry, I forgot to mention that. The toilets are at the end of the corridor on the left. Opposite the toilets, on the right, is the door to the showers.*
Girl (b):	*Is there a television?*
Warden:	*Yes, there is. There's a television room downstairs, next to the dining hall. There's also a games room with a pool table in it. You can play board games, too. And we've got a collection of books in the room opposite the television room. You can either borrow books to read while you're here or swap books there.*
Susan:	*Are there any books about Edinburgh?*
Warden:	*We have a lot of information brochures about Edinburgh at the reception desk. You can also buy a guide-book there for £3.50.*

a) S übernehmen das Anmeldeformular in ihr Heft und füllen es aus.

b) S hören die kurzen Gespräche und notieren die fünf Fragen der Mädchen, ggf. stoppt L die CD jeweils.

c) S geben mündlich an, was die Jugendherbergsmutter auf die Fragen geantwortet. Dafür ist evtl. ein zweiter Hörvorgang erforderlich.

> Erweiterung:
> L stellt S den Hörtext in Kopie zur Verfügung, S gestalten die Dialoge nach und variieren und erweitern sie.
> Variante: Zwei Gruppen von S gestalten ein Dialogquiz. Die eine Gruppe stellt eine für die Situation typische Frage, die andere Gruppe reagiert mit einer passenden Antwort.

PB A5   Please may I ...?   Hören/Schreiben/Sprechen   PB, S. 68

a) Falls ein nochmaliges Hören des Textes aus TB A5 nicht erforderlich ist, formulieren S sofort ihre Fragen. Einige lesen sie vor, dabei wird besonders auf die Intonation geachtet. Mögliche Lösungen: *May I go into the kitchen when I'm hungry?/What is your cat's name?/ Where is the bathroom?/Could I call my parents, please?/Do you speak German?/Could I have a glass of water, please?*

b) In Partnerarbeit werden die Fragen gestellt und beantwortet. Einige der Mini-Dialoge werden anschließend im Plenum präsentiert.

Medium	Nummer	Seite	Titel	Fertigkeit	Zusatzinfo
TB/CD	B1	102	Different Englishes	Hören	Hörverstehen
TB	B2	102	English as a world language	Lesen/Schreiben/ Sprechen	Leseverstehen; Textverständnis
copy 18			A map of the world	Sprechen	*English as a world language*
PB	B1	69	World atlas	Lesen/Schreiben	*English as a world language*
TB/CD	B3	103	A day in Edinburgh	Hören/Sprechen	Hörverstehen
PB/CD	B2	70	A city tour	Hören/Schreiben/ Sprechen	Hörverstehen
TB	B4	103	Scotland's thistle	Lesen/Schreiben Sprechen	Landeskunde
TB	B5	104	Highlights of the rest of the trip	Lesen/Schreiben/ Sprechen	Textproduktion
copy 19			A Scotland game	Sprechen	Brettspiel entwickeln
PB	B3	71	That reminds me of when I was in Scotland	Lesen/Schreiben	Textverständnis; Textproduktion
PB	B4	71	I'll be in Scotland before you	Sprechen/Schreiben	Textproduktion
TB	B6	105	The UK Quiz	Lesen/Sprechen/ Schreiben	Landeskunde
TB/CD	Optional	106	Flower of Scotland	Lesen/Hören	Schottisches Lied
PB	Portfolio	72f.		Hören/Sprechen/Lesen/ Schreiben/Lern- und Arbeitstechniken	Selbsteinschätzung

Die grau unterlegten Felder stellen das Pflichtpensum dar, die weißen die Kür.

Teil B: • Informationen darstellen
Vorlieben äußern und begründen

Zu den Grunderfahrungen sprachlich-kommunikativer Tätigkeit gehört ganz sicher die, dass Menschen – selbst wenn sie sich der gleichen Sprache bedienen – keineswegs immer und überall gleich sprechen. Dabei interessieren hier weniger die individuell bedingten als vielmehr solche Unterschiede, die bei Sprechern einer bestimmten Region gegenüber solchen einer anderen Gegend vorkommen. Zu Beginn von *Theme 8B* werden S mit regionalen Varianten des *British English* konfrontiert.

Wenn Englisch in der internationalen Kommunikation als *lingua franca* zum Einsatz kommt, begegnet man jedoch weit mehr Varianten dieser Sprache, die zu einem Großteil durch die jeweilige Muttersprache der Sprecher entstehen. Auch auf diese *varieties* werden S vorbereitet. Das ist heute bei der weltweiten Verbreitung des Englischen dringend geboten, denn dem *British Standard English* begegnet man selbst in Großbritannien nur noch selten.

TB B1 Different Englishes	**Hören**	*TB, S. 102*

a) • S hören die vier Vorstellungen bei geschlossenem TB von der CD und notieren, wo sie herkommen: *North Wales, Belfast/Northern Ireland, Aberdeen/Scotland, Newcastle/ England.*
   • S finden die genannten Städte/Länder auf der Karte auf dem hinteren Innendeckel des TB.

b) Beim zweiten Hören achten S auf die Unterschiede zwischen den Varianten und geben an, welcher Akzent ihnen am besten gefällt, welcher für sie schwer zu verstehen war.

c) Die Frage, in welchen anderen Ländern ebenfalls Englisch gesprochen wird, leitet unmittelbar zu TB B2 über. Die Ergebnisse werden an der Tafel oder auf Folie gesammelt.   *Tafel*

TB B2 English as a world language	**Lesen/Sprechen**	*TB, S. 102*

• S lesen den Text ohne weitere Hinführung möglichst zügig.
• Um eine intensive Beschäftigung zu gewährleisten, beantworten S die Fragen zum Text schriftlich.
• Im Klassengespräch reaktivieren S ihre Geografiekenntnisse und zeigen die im Text genannten Länder an einer Weltkarte (Alternative: siehe Erweiterung). In den Antworten auf die Fragen 4 und 5 wird deutlich, ob S die Unterschiede zwischen Englisch als erster und zweiter Sprache bzw. als Fremdsprache erkannt haben.

Mögliche Lösungen: *1. about 350 million people (in Britain, North America, Australia, New Zealand and other countries) 2. India, Pakistan, Zimbabwe, Hong Kong and Trinidad 3. in government, business and schools 4.–6.* individuelle Lösungen

copy
18

> **Erweiterung:**
> Wenn keine Wandkarte der Welt zur Verfügung steht, kann *Copymaster 18* eingesetzt werden, der viele Einsatzmöglichkeiten bietet: S beschriften mithilfe von Lexika/dem Internet die Länder/Hauptstädte/Nationalitäten/… auf Englisch und/oder markieren die Länder, in denen Englisch als erste oder zweite Sprache gesprochen wird.

Zusatzinformationen: *English as a world language*
• *World languages and their numbers of speakers:*

Chinese: 800 million	Arabic: 160 million
English: 400 million	Portuguese: 160 million
Spanish: 290 million	Bengali: 155 million
Russian: 275 million	German: 130 million
Hindustani: 250 million	Japanese: 120 million

• *Some other interesting facts about the English language:*
  – *There are more than 500,000 words in the Oxford English Dictionary. Compare that with the vocabulary of German (about 200,000) and French (about 100,000)!*
  – *80% of all information in the world's computers is in English.*
  – *English is just one of over 2,700 languages in the world today.*
  – *80% of all English vocabulary comes from other languages.*

PB B1   World atlas   **Lesen/Schreiben**   PB, S. 69

Für diese Aufgabe sollten S ihre Atlanten bereitliegen haben. Alternativ können eine Wand-
karte oder nochmals *Copymaster 18* herangezogen werden.

a) S erarbeiten die Teilaufgabe mithilfe von TB B2 in Partnerarbeit. Da die Arbeit recht zeit-
aufwendig ist und der Recherche bedarf, kann sie auch als Hausaufgabe gestellt werden.
Lösungen:
*English as a first language: Exeter (England), Dublin (Republic of Ireland), Nashville (USA),
New Orleans (USA), Sydney (Australia), Toronto (Canada), Wellington (New Zealand)*
*English as a second language: Colombo (Sri Lanka), Madras (India), Lahore (Pakistan), Port
of Spain (Trinidad), Harare (Zimbabwe)*
City/language: Lublin/Polish, Oslo/Norwegian, Shanghai/Chinese

b) In Partnerarbeit ergänzen S mithilfe des Atlas weitere Städte/Sprachen in der Tabelle.

TB B3   A day in Edinburgh   **Hören/Sprechen**   TB, S. 103

Der Hörtext lautet:

Gillian: *Edinburgh Castle is really amazing. There is loads to see there and it is very
interesting. We saw the Scottish Crown Jewels as part of an exhibition there. They
were really impressive. Edinburgh Castle is very old – the first people lived there in
about 800 BC, maybe even before that. We saw a cannon there, that was used in the
15th century. At the castle there are guards who wear tartan trousers. They look very
different from the guards at the Tower of London or Buckingham Palace.*
*From the castle rock, you can see most of Edinburgh. In the summer there is a big
international arts festival in Edinburgh and there are fireworks at the castle. Did you
know that about 1 million people visit Edinburgh Castle every year?*

Vera: *The Queen used to sail around the world on the Royal Yacht Britannia. The yacht
carried the Queen and the Royal Family on a total of 968 official trips. Britannia was
launched in 1953 and finished her last journey on the 5th of May, 1998, when she
arrived in Edinburgh. Now the yacht is open for visitors. We found out about
Britannia's history – where she has been, and who has been on board. We saw the
Queen's bedroom and the State Dining Room. They were really fantastic. We also saw
lots of pictures in the Royal Family Picture Gallery, and learned about life on board
Britannia for the staff – there were 300 of them! For a state visit, the Royal Family
needed five tonnes of luggage! The Engine Room was really interesting, too. Did you
know that the Britannia was built in Scotland, too? It was built in Glasgow.*

Susan: *The Museum of Scotland was really interesting. There, we found out about Scotland's
history from its beginnings through to the 20th century. We learned about famous
kings and queens of Scotland, about Scottish inventors like Alexander Graham Bell
and John Logie Baird. Do you know what they invented?*
*I thought the Twentieth Century part was the best. There was everything there – tele-
visions, pens, teddy bears and even a tartan band that the Queen Mother wore. That
was really beautiful.*
*The other parts of the museum were interesting, too, though. We found out about life
in Scotland before it was part of Great Britain. I don't think life was very easy in the
18th century. I'm glad I live now and not then. I found out why we have seen so many
thistles in Scotland. It's a special symbol here because of a Viking attack a long, long
time ago …*

- Hinweis: *Alexander Graham Bell invented the telephone and John Logie Baird invented the
television.*
- Aufgrund der Illustrationen im TB wissen S bereits vor dem ersten Hören, welches
Mädchen welche Sehenswürdigkeit besucht hat. L teilt die Lerngruppe in drei Gruppen,
die sich auf je eines der Mädchen konzentrieren und beim Hören, vermutlich zweimaliges, Details zu den drei Zielen notieren.
- Anschließend informieren sich die drei Gruppen im Plenum gegenseitig über ihre Ergebnisse.

Zusatzinformationen: *Edinburgh International Festival* und *Edinburgh Festival Fringe*
Edinburgh International Festival: www.eif.co.uk
Edinburgh Festival Fringe: www.edfringe.com

PB B2   A city tour   **Hören/Schreiben/Sprechen**   *PB, S. 70*

- S hören alle drei Texte noch einmal von der CD. Dabei vergleichen sie den Hörtext mit den Stichpunkten und unterstreichen zunächst die falschen Informationen, ggf. in arbeitsteiliger Gruppenarbeit wie in TB B4.
- In einem weiteren Schritt korrigieren S die Aussagen mündlich im Klassengespräch.

Lösungen:

Edinburgh Castle: fantastic ➔ *amazing; 1800 BC* ➔ *800 BC; 50th century* ➔ *15th century; tartan kilts* ➔ *tartan trousers; in winter* ➔ *in summer*

The Royal Yacht Britannia: 986 ➔ *968; 1893* ➔ *1953; the Queen's kitchen* ➔ *the Queen's bedroom; 15 tonnes of luggage* ➔ *5 tonnes of luggage*

The Museum of Scotland: Alexander Graham Ross ➔ *Alexander Graham Bell; 19th century best* ➔ *20th century best; telephones* ➔ *televisions; life easy in 18th century* ➔ *life not easy in 18th century; English attack* ➔ *Viking attack*

TB B4   Scotland's thistle   **Lesen/Schreiben/Sprechen**   *TB, S. 103*

a) S erarbeiten die richtige Reihenfolge der Sätze in Stillarbeit, Kontrolle im Plenum.

Lösungen: *It was a dark night and the Scots were asleep in the castle. The Vikings wanted to surprise the Scots and take over their castle while they were sleeping. The Vikings took off their shoes because they didn't want to make any noise. The Vikings stood on the thistles growing in the fields. The Scots heard the Vikings scream when they stood on the thistles, and woke up. The Scots scared the Vikings away and the castle was saved.*

b) S informieren sich und geben Auskunft darüber, welches spezielle Symbol, Wappen o. Ä. ihre Stadt oder eine Stadt ihrer Wahl hat. Die empfohlene Gruppenarbeit braucht etwas Zeit, da u. U. ein Besuch auf dem Verkehrsamt, im Museum, im Rathaus, im Internet o. Ä. nötig ist. S fassen die Informationen in einem Text zusammen, den sie – unterstützt durch Fotos oder Zeichnungen – der Klasse vorstellen.

Diese Informationen in englischer Sprache sind eventuell für das Verkehrsamt der Stadt von Interesse, wenn Englisch sprechende Gäste die Stadt besuchen.

TB B5   Highlights of the rest of the trip   **Lesen/Schreiben/Sprechen**   *TB, S. 104*

a) • S erarbeiten die Texte in Einzelarbeit, ggf. als schriftliche Hausaufgabe.
- Zu jedem der vier Notizzettel tragen zwei S ihre Texte vor, die von der Klasse kommentiert werden. Folgende Kriterien sollten berücksichtigt werden: abwechslungsreiche Satzanfänge, komplexe Sätze, inhaltliche Vielfalt und Wortwahl.

Mögliche Lösungen:

We spent Tuesday and Wednesday in Stirling. We visited the castle and Wallace Monument, a monument built for William Wallace, who is a Scottish hero. He lived in the 13th century and fought to free Scotland. There is also a film about William Wallace – Braveheart. We didn't see it, but maybe we can go and see it when we're back in London.

Thursday was a sunny day but it was very cold! We took the train to Aberdeen. There we saw many fishing boats and we talked to a fisherman. His name was Bob White. He says he has to get up early in the morning because he goes out in his boat. I'm glad I'm not a fisherman (or a fisherwoman!). There is a fish market in Aberdeen every day, that's where they sell fresh fish. We also saw some oil rigs in the North Sea. Oil rig workers have a dangerous job. They have to live on the rig for weeks. Well, I'm also glad I'm not an oil rig worker!

On Saturday we took the bus to Loch Ness. We also visited Urquhart Castle, which is my favourite castle because it looks very old. There were high mountains everywhere, it was incredible. And Loch Ness is very deep! We visited the Loch Ness Monster Centre, but we didn't see Nessie!

On Sunday we took the bus to Fort William. From Fort William you can see Ben Nevis, the highest mountain in Britain, it's 1343 m high. But we didn't climb it, we just took photos. I think mountains are amazing.

And on Tuesday we took the train to Glasgow. Glasgow is the biggest city in Scotland. We saw the Kelvingrove Art Galleries, which are in a really beautiful building. We looked at lots of paintings there. After that we went on the underground. It's really small, not like London at all. The people here in Scotland are very friendly.

b) • S äußern und begründen ihre Vorlieben im Klassengespräch.

> **Erweiterung:**
> S verfügen nun über viele Informationen über Schottland, die spielerisch gefestigt und überprüft werden können. Eine Möglichkeit ist es, S eigene Spiele gestalten zu lassen, z. B. Quartett, Würfelspiel.
> *Copymaster 19* bietet eine Schottlandkarte, die zum Spielfeld ausgestaltet werden kann. Die Ausgestaltung bleibt S überlassen (Spiel-/Aufgabenfelder, farbige Kennzeichnung, Legende, Liste von Aufgaben, …). Die zu bewältigenden Aufgaben sollten sprachlicher und nichtsprachlicher Art sein (z. B. fünf schottische Städte benennen, das schottische Nationalemblem, die Distel, zeichnen, den Anfang eines Liedes summen/singen, …).

PB B3   That reminds me of when I was …   Lesen/Schreiben   *PB, S. 71*
S arbeiten in Einzelarbeit und greifen auf die Informationen in TB A4 und TB B5 zurück.

PB B4   I'll be in Scotland before you   Sprechen   *PB, S. 71*
- Die Paare verständigen sich zunächst, welche Stationen/Ziele/Sehenswürdigkeiten sie in den acht Tagen besuchen möchten und fixieren diese in Stichworten.
- L achtet darauf, dass S beim Ausformulieren der Stichpunkte das *going to-future* (vgl. *lif*)   *TB, S. 136*
  verwenden und in ihren Texten Entscheidungen für und gegen den Besuch einer Stadt/Sehenswürdigkeit mit einbeziehen, um einen lebendigen Text zu erhalten.
- An einem Beispiel, das auf Folie geschrieben ist, beraten L und S, was einen guten Text   *Folie*
  ausmacht, welche Fehler vermieden werden müssen etc. Danach prüfen S ihre Texte noch einmal und übertragen sie in ordentlicher Schrift ins Heft bzw. Portfolio.   *Portfolio*

TB B6   The UK Quiz   Lesen/Sprechen   *TB, S. 105*
a) Dieses Landeskunde-Quiz bildet einen schönen Abschluss zum Schuljahresende und vermittelt S ein Bild ihrer Kenntnisse. S beantworten die Fragen in Einzel- oder Partnerarbeit.
Lösung: *1. b) 2. a) 3. c) 4. a) 5. b) 6. c) 7. b) 8. b) 9. a), c) 10. b) 11. c) 12. b)*

b) Das Abrufen der Gruppenergebnisse wird als Wettbewerb gestaltet.

> **Erweiterung:**
> S erarbeiten ein ähnliches Quiz mit leichteren Fragen zu Großbritannien für die 6. Klassen und hängen es im Schulhaus aus. Für vollständig richtige Lösungen, die bis zu einem bestimmten Termin abgegeben werden, werden kleine Preise (Lektüren o. Ä.) ausgelobt.

TB Optional   Flower of Scotland   Hören   *TB, S. 106*
S lesen den einführenden Text jede/r für sich und hören dann das Lied von der CD. Es bildet den emotionalen Abschluss des *Theme* und sollte nicht zerredet werden.

PB Portfolio   Gesamtbewertung   *PB, S. 72f.*
Der vierseitige Fragebogen dient der Selbsteinschätzung der S zum Abschluss des Schuljahres. Es gilt, den Stand der Kenntnisse in den vier Fertigkeiten Hören, Sprechen, Lesen, Schreiben sowie den Lern- und Arbeitstechniken Vokabellernen, Texte verstehen und Grammatik einzuschätzen.
- S füllen die vier Seiten in Ruhe zu Hause aus und vergleichen ihre Ergebnisse anschließend mit denen nach *Theme 4*, PB S. 44/45.
  Ein Erfahrungsaustausch in der Folgestunde über die Ergebnisse ist wünschenswert. L fragt nach, auf welchen Gebieten S noch Schwächen und Defizite haben, um ihnen Gelegenheit zu geben, in den bevorstehenden Ferien mithilfe zusätzlicher Übungen und Aufgaben daran zu arbeiten (Leseempfehlungen, Lektüren, Hörkassetten o. Ä.).

Woche	Theme	Sprechabsichten	Grammatische Strukturen
1	**Introduction:** **Back to Bayswater** Textbook pages 10–12 Practicebook Portfolio 1–4 Folie 1 Copymaster 1, 2	Aktivierung des Vorwissens aus den ersten beiden Lernjahren: über Lehrwerkfiguren und Ereignisse sprechen	
2	**Theme 1: Eating out** **Theme 1A:** Eating out Textbook A1–A5 Practicebook A1–A5 Folie 2	Ein Restaurant auswählen Eine Speisekarte lesen und Essen bestellen Jemanden zum Essen einladen	Revision: *much* und *many*
3	**Theme 1A:** Eating out Textbook A6–A10 Practicebook A6–A11 Copymaster 3	Berichten, was man schon getan hat	Bestätigungsfragen indirekte Rede Revision: *present perfect*
4	**Theme 1B:** Karim's curry party Textbook B1–B5 Practicebook B1–B4 Copymaster 4, 5	Über das Kochen sprechen Zutaten auswählen Ein Rezept lesen Über fremde Essgewohnheiten reden	Revision: *some* und *any* und ihre Zusammensetzungen
5	**Theme 1B:** Karim's curry party Textbook B6–B7 Practicebook B5 Test 1 **Optional 1:** Fish and chips Textbook Optional	Über eigene Essgewohnheiten reden	
6	**Theme 2: How fit are you?** **Theme 2A:** Sports freak or couch potato? Textbook A1 Practicebook A1 Folie 3 Copymaster 6, 7		

Jahresplan

Woche	Theme	Sprechabsichten	Grammatische Strukturen
7	**Theme 2A:** Sports freak or couch potato? Textbook A2–A5 Practicebook A2–A5 Folie 4 Copymaster 8	Lebensgewohnheiten beschreiben Verhaltensweisen beschreiben Über Sportarten reden Über Idole sprechen	Adverbien der Art und Weise Revision: Steigerung von Adjektiven
8	**Theme 2A:** Sports freak or couch potato? Textbook A6–A8 Practicebook A6–A8	Über Sportarten reden Sagen, welche Fähigkeiten jemand haben muss, um etwas zu tun	Revision: Formen von *be* Revision: Steigerung von Adjektiven Revision: *must, don't have to*
9	**Theme 2B:** The story of Christy Brown Textbook B1–B5 Practicebook B1–B3 Copymaster 9 Test 2	Über Behinderungen und Behinderten-sport sprechen Sagen, was jemand konnte und wozu er/sie nicht in der Lage war	*to be able to*
	Optional 2: Kieran Textbook Optional		
10	**Theme 3: Going public** **Theme 3A:** The Notting Hill Carnival Textbook A1–A5 Practicebook A1–A5 Folie 5 Copymaster 10	Veranstaltungen kommentieren Genau sagen, wer jemand ist	Relativsätze Revision: *present progressive*
11	**Theme 3A:** The Notting Hill Carnival Textbook A6–A7 Practicebook A6–A8 Folie 6 Copymaster 11	Über Vor- und Nachteile von Großveranstaltungen sprechen Einen Ratschlag erteilen	*past progressive*
12	**Theme 3A:** The Notting Hill Carnival Textbook A8 Practicebook A9 **Theme 3B:** London for teenagers Textbook B1–B3 Practicebook B1–B2 Folie 7	Sightseeing in London planen Meinungen äußern und begründen	

Woche	Theme	Sprechabsichten	Grammatische Strukturen
13	**Theme 3B:** London for teenagers Textbook PP–B5 Practicebook B3–B5 Test 3	Jemanden förmlich um etwas bitten Sich förmlich bei jemandem bedanken Eine Grußformel in einem Brief aus- drücken Heimatort beschreiben	
	Optional 3: The skating ramp Textbook Optional		
14	**Theme 4: No man is an island** **Theme 4A:** Problems and helplines Textbook A1–A4 Practicebook A1–A2 Folie 8 Copymaster 12	Persönliche Probleme beschreiben Verständnis äußern Ratschläge geben Antworten bewerten	
15	**Theme 4A:** Problems and helplines Textbook A5–A9 Practicebook A3–A6	Sorgen/Befürchtungen äußern Verständnis äußern Ratschläge geben Antworten bewerten	each other Revision: *simple past*
16	**Theme 4B:** Robinson Crusoe Textbook B1–B5 Practicebook B1–B5 Folie 9 Copymaster 13	Ein Interview führen Einen Zeitungsbericht schreiben Über Einsamkeit reden Fragen, wie jemand etwas gemacht hat Fragen, was jemandem gefallen/nicht gefallen hat	*past perfect* Revision: *past participle*
17	**Theme 4B:** Robinson Crusoe Textbook B6–B7 Practicebook B6–B8 Copymaster 14 Test 4	Familie und Zuhause beschreiben	
	Optional 4: Split between two houses Textbook Optional Practicebook Portfolio		
18	**Theme 5: Learning from the past** **Theme 5A:** Museums and inventions Textbook A1–A3 Practicebook A1–A4 Folie 10	Ein Museum beschreiben Vermutungen äußern Über besondere Interessen sprechen	

Woche	Theme	Sprechabsichten	Grammatische Strukturen
19	**Theme 5A:** Museums and inventions Textbook A4–A5 Practicebook A5–A7 **Theme 5B:** School magazines Textbook B1 Practicebook B1–B2	Über Erfindungen sprechen Die Wichtigkeit von etwas ausdrücken	
20	**Theme 5B:** School magazines Textbook B2–B5 Practicebook B3–B5 Copymaster 15	Ideen sammeln	Reflexivpronomen
21	**Theme 5B:** School magazines Textbook B6–B9 Practicebook B6 Folie 11 Test 5	Über alternative Technologien reden	
	Optional 5: Levi's invention Textbook Optional		
22	**Theme 6: Cash in hand** **Theme 6A:** Money problems Textbook A1–A4 Practicebook A1–A4 Folie 12 Copymaster 16	Einen Vorschlag machen Auf einen Vorschlag reagieren Vorschläge diskutieren Über Taschengeld sprechen Über Möglichkeiten des Geld-dienens reden	*if*-Satz Typ 1
23	**Theme 6A:** Money problems Textbook A5–A11 Practicebook A5–A7 Folie 13	Kaufen und Verkaufen Einen Preis aushandeln Einen Einwand machen	Revision: *will-future*
24	**Theme 6B:** The London Marathon Textbook B1–B6 Practicebook B1–B2	Eine Wohltätigkeitsveranstaltung beschreiben	

Woche	Theme	Sprechabsichten	Grammatische Strukturen
25	**Theme 6B:** The London Marathon Textbook B7–B8 Practicebook B3–B4 Test 6 **Optional 6:** Oliver Twist Textbook Optional	Sich über Wohltätigkeitsvereine informieren	Steigerung von Adverbien
26	**Theme 7: Sight and sound** **Theme 7A:** TV stars Textbook A1–A2 Practicebook A1–A2 Folie 14, 15 Copymaster 17	Über Lieblingsstars sprechen	
27	**Theme 7A:** TV stars Textbook A3–A7 Practicebook A3–A6	Über Lieblingsstars sprechen Pläne machen	*Present progressive for the future*
28	**Theme 7A:** TV stars Textbook PP–A8 Practicebook A7 **Theme 7B:** What's on? Textbook B1–B2 Practicebook B1–B3	Musikwünsche im Radio äußern	
29	**Theme 7B:** What's on? Textbook B3–B6 Practicebook B4–B6 Test 7 **Optional 7:** Optical illusions Textbook Optional	Einen Veranstaltungskalender lesen Einen Titel finden Gefallen ausdrücken und begründen Missfallen ausdrücken und begründen Ein Bild beschreiben	
30	**Theme 8: A trip to Scotland** **Theme 8A:** Class trip to Scotland Textbook A1–PP Practicebook A1–A2 Folie 16	Fragen, ob jemand alles Notwendige dabei hat Jemanden darum bitten, einen an etwas zu erinnern	*one, ones* Possessivpronomen *(mine, yours, …)* Revision: *going to-future*

Jahresplan

Woche	Theme	Sprechabsichten	Grammatische Strukturen
31	**Theme 8A:** Class trip to Scotland Textbook A3–A5 Practicebook A3–A5	Um Erlaubnis bitten Vermutungen äußern Über ein Zimmerbuchung sprechen	*may*
32	**Theme 8B:** Different Englishes Textbook B1–B5 Practicebook B1–B2 Copymaster 18	Informationen darstellen	
33	**Theme 8B:** Different Englishes Textbook B6 Practicebook B3–B4 Copymaster 19 Test 8	Vorlieben äußern und begründen	
	Optional 8: Flower of Scotland Textbook Optional Practicebook Portfolio		

Identity card

First name:
Family name:
Address:

Age:
Height:
Colour of eyes:
Brothers/sisters:

Hobbies:

What don't you like?

Identity card

First name:
Family name:
Address:

Age:
Height:
Colour of eyes:
Brothers/sisters:

Hobbies:

What don't you like?

Identity card

First name:
Family name:
Address:

Age:
Height:
Colour of eyes:
Brothers/sisters:

Hobbies:

What don't you like?

Identity card

First name:
Family name:
Address:

Age:
Height:
Colour of eyes:
Brothers/sisters:

Hobbies:

What don't you like?

ISBN 3-425-09103-4

Pets   **A**

Find out about your partner's pet and answer his/her questions.

YOU want to know

- if he/she has a pet
- what it is
- its colour, name and age.

Pets   **B**

Find out about your partner's pet and answer his/her questions.

YOU want to know

- if he/she has a pet
- if not, if he/she would like to have one
- which zoo animals he/she likes best
- when he/she was at the zoo the last time.

Holidays   **A**

Find out about your partner's holidays and answer his/her questions.

You want to know

- where he/she stayed
- how long he/she stayed there
- what the weather was like
- what he/she did
- what he/she didn't like there
- if he/she wants to go there again.

Holidays   **B**

Find out about your partner's holidays and answer his/her questions.

YOU want to know

- if he/she stayed at home
- if not, where he/she spent his/her holidays
- when he/she went there
- when he/she came back home
- what the weather was like
- what he/she didn't like there.

Music   **A**

Find out about your partner's favourite kinds of music and answer his/her questions.

YOU want to know

- if he/she collects music CDs
- what kind of music he/she prefers
- if he/she would like to go to an open air concert with you next month
- if he/she plays an instrument.

Music   **B**

Find out about your partner's favourite kinds of music and answer his/her questions.

YOU want to know

- if he/she plays the piano
- what kind of music he/she likes best
- if he/she has ever been to an open air concert
- if yes, when and where it was.

School   **A**

Find out about your partner's likes and dislikes and answer his/her questions.

YOU want to know

- what his/her favourite subjects are
- if he/she is new at this school
- if he/she likes his/her class teacher
- if he/she would be interested in a sports club at school.

School   **B**

Find out about your partner's likes and dislikes and answer his/her questions.

YOU want to know

- if English is his/her favourite subject
- how long he/she has been at this school
- if he/she knows his/her class teacher well
- if he/she would be interested in a theatre group at school.

Question tags, question tags

You weren't at school last week,
_____ ?

Fruit is good for you,
_____ ?

Charlie loves horse-riding,
_____ ?

You don't like tea,
_____ ?

Your meal doesn't look very filling,
_____ ?

You like ice-cream,
_____ ?

Peter can speak English well,
_____ ?

Tom wasn't at home yesterday,
_____ ?

Gillian was frightened about the tiger,
_____ ?

Beans are vegetables,
_____ ?

Peter doesn't look very healthy,
_____ ?

He can't play the piano,
_____ ?

Vera is a football talent,
_____ ?

Karim cooks meals for his friends,
_____ ?

Gillian's mum forgot to buy milk,
_____ ?

Can you find other examples? Then write them down here.

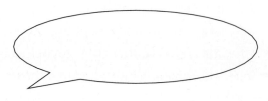

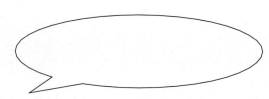

ISBN 3-425-09103-4

Diesterweg

A questionnaire about eating and cooking habits

Write down more questions and ask five people in your class. Take notes and report the results to the class, e.g.: *Three of the five people don't do any cooking ...*

• How often a week do you eat junk food?

• How often a week do you eat vegetarian food?

• Do you like cooking?

• Who does the cooking in your family?

• How often a week do you make breakfast for your family?

_____

_____

_____

_____

_____

_____

_____

_____

_____

Results:

_____

_____

_____

Diesterweg

Where are these things?

A

B

ISBN 3-425-09103-4

How fit are you?

Read the following exercises and write down how fit you *think* you are (use a green pen). Then do the exercises and write down how fit you *really* are (now use a red pen). Is there a difference?

1   Jump up and down for 30 seconds. Then read the text about India on page 21 in your textbook to a partner. Are you
☐ out of breath?   ☐ only a bit out of breath?   ☐ not out of breath?

2   Step on and off a chair 10 times quickly. How do you feel?
☐ out of breath   ☐ only a bit out of breath   ☐ not out of breath

3   Touch your left foot with your right hand. Then touch your right foot with your left hand. Do this 8 times quickly. How do you feel?
☐ out of breath   ☐ only a bit out of breath   ☐ not out of breath

4   How many press-ups against the wall can you do?
☐ 0–5   ☐ 6–10   ☐ 11–15   ☐ 16–20   ☐ 21+

5   Lift your chair up in the air 5 times. Are you
☐ out of breath?   ☐ only a bit out of breath?   ☐ not out of breath?

6   Bend down. But keep your legs straight! Can you touch the floor?
☐ yes   ☐ almost   ☐ no

Diesterweg

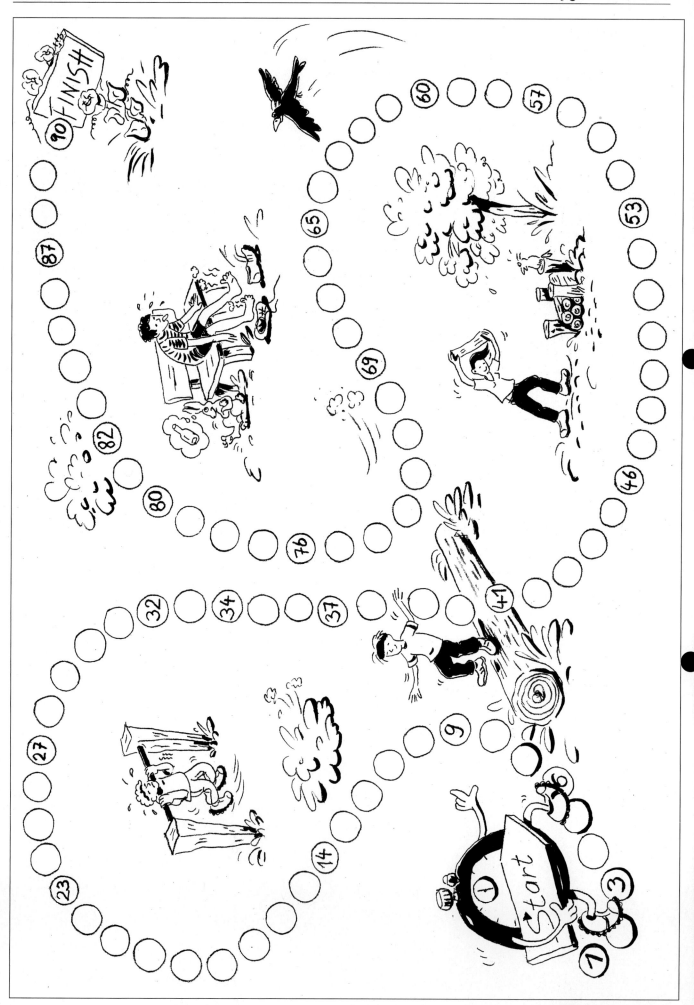

ISBN 3-425-09103-4

What a day!

Play in groups of 2–4 people. Throw the dice, then move your counter. When you get onto one of the numbered fields, look at this list. If your answers are wrong, you must miss a turn. Enjoy the game!

(dice = Würfel, throw a dice = würfeln, counter = Spielfigur, miss a turn = aussetzen)

1. You're ready to start, but your friends are late so you have to wait. Talk about your hobbies for 30 seconds.
3. Your friends have arrived. They say they couldn't phone you because they didn't have your phone number. Give them your phone number.
6. What are the 7 days of the week? And spell two of them, please.
9. You meet a young family on the way. Talk about babies and young children for 30 seconds.
14. This is a lovely walk through the forest. You feel like running. Throw the dice twice.
23. Now you're out of breath. Sit down and relax. And miss a turn!
27. There's a nice snack bar on the way but it's closed! Go on only if you get a 3.
32. What are the 12 months of the year? And spell one of them, please.
34. You find a bird that has fallen from its nest. Let's see if you can sing as nicely as a bird. Sing an English song!
37. Some girls ask you what time it is. Tell them the time!
41. Doesn't time fly when you're having fun! What's today's date?
46. Time for lunch! Enjoy your food but miss two turns.
53. You've eaten too much for lunch and can't move. Miss a turn.
57. You see a funny animal on the way but you don't know what it is. Name 7 animals.
60. You meet a friend on the way. Tell him/her about your last weekend.
65. Touch your left foot with your right hand. Then touch your right foot with your left hand. Do this 10 times.
69. You've lost your way and you don't know where you are. Name 5 towns or cities in Great Britain.
76. Where's your pullover? Go back to 67 to look for it.
80. You want to go for a swim, but the water is very cold. So you walk quickly to get warm again. Go to 84.
82. Your feet hurt from the quick walking. Miss a turn.
87. The player to your right gives you three new words from *Theme 1*, which you have to spell.
90. Say and write the forms of three irregular verbs which the other players choose for you.

Diesterweg

get up before 8 o'clock	tidy my room	play computer games
ride a bicycle	play football	play tennis
sit in front of the TV	eat salad and fresh fruit	go to dancing lessons
sing songs	draw pictures	go swimming
run up and down the stairs	go to the cinema	play minigolf on the computer
make breakfast	do the washing-up	get out of bed
go shopping	do gym exercises	go to bed
go to the library	do press-ups	eat crisps and burgers
learn new words and phrases	explain things	
go to school	play with friends	

never	quickly	never	quickly
usually	happily	usually	happily
sometimes	carefully	sometimes	carefully
always	badly	always	badly
often	well	often	well
terribly	slowly	terribly	slowly
funnily	lazily	funnily	lazily
fast	unhappily	fast	unhappily
fairly	healthily	fairly	healthily

ISBN 3-425-09103-4

Diesterweg

The story of Christy Brown

Put the passages of the text in the correct order and number them.

☐ Later, he wrote more books and articles and won many prizes as a writer. Christy died in 1981 and eight years later, his life story was made into a film called "My Left Foot".

☐ His mother was a very strong woman and she decided to help him. She had a very busy life because there were younger children in the family and there were no modern machines to help her with the housework. But she always found time – and patience – to help Christy to learn his alphabet and to write with his left foot.

☐ Christy Brown was born in Dublin in 1932. His family was very large and he had 22 brothers and sisters. They didn't have much money – they lived in a small house and Christy's father worked as a bricklayer to earn enough to feed his large family.

☐ Later, they built a little house in the garden for him where he could write his stories, read and draw. But Christy was never able to go to school.

☐ Christy was a few months old when his mother noticed that he could not move properly. It became clear that Christy was handicapped. He was unable to feed himself or put on his clothes. He could not walk and the only part of his body that he could control was his left foot. He could not talk because he was unable to control his tongue. But he was not deaf.

☐ One day, an American doctor visited him. She worked in a clinic for children and young people like Christy. He went to this clinic and learnt how to control his body a little. His family always helped him and he wrote about them in his book "My Left Foot", which made more money than his father earned in a year in his job as a bricklayer. It was a bestseller.

☐ Christy was a very intelligent child and he started to draw pictures, too. People bought his pictures. His brothers made him a box on wheels so that he was able to play with them in the streets.

Put the words into the right order and re-write the sentences about Christy Brown.

1. in • family • Christy's • Dublin • lived

_____

2. clothes • unable • feed • put on • his • himself • and • was • he • to • to

_____

3. had • work • of • to • his • a lot • do • mother • but • patient • was • she

_____

4. in • write • garden • was • house • a • the • in • little • Christy • able • stories • his • to

_____

5. family • about • later • wrote • his • a • he • novel • and • a lot of • and • money • made • his • life

_____

Notting Hill Carnival – who or which?

At Notting Hill Carnival there is usually a poster ☐ tells you what's going on.

There are often small children ☐ have lost their parents.

Every year there are many tourists ☐ enjoy the Carnival.

There are clowns ☐ make people laugh.

There are many people ☐ dance to the music.

There are stalls ☐ sell soft drinks.

There are floats ☐ are brightly coloured.

If you're lucky, you can see a woman ☐ carries a basket with fresh fruit on her head.

There are singers and dancers ☐ wear fantastic costumes.

There are many bands ☐ play steel band music.

There are people ☐ wave to the singers and dancers in the streets.

And sometimes you can see a man ☐ runs away with a handbag.

Use these relative pronouns in the right places.

which	which	which	which	who	who
who	who	who	who	who	who

ISBN 3-425-09103-4

we were sunbathing in the garden	I was waiting for the bus	I/… fell over and broke my/… leg
I was sleeping in my bed	my parents were visiting friends	a dancer began to cry
a woman was listening to a band	my friend was talking to a policeman	fire came out of a window
my father was sitting at his desk	my mother was walking through the park	a ball hit me/…
the cat was watching the hole	we went jogging in the park	it jumped up at me/…
we were laughing and shouting	my aunt was buying a ticket at the station	a mouse came out of its hole
a thief was running away with a handbag	I wasn't expecting anything nice to happen	a child lost his/her parents
a tourist was taking a photo of the parrot	we were looking at the river	a loud knock frightened me/…
we were talking to our friends	a monster swam towards us	my/… video equipment was stolen
I was watching a big dog	a man snatched my/… handbag	a pickpocket stole my/… purse
my brother was watching the float	I/… lost my/… watch	I/… fell out of bed
we were watching a thriller on TV	a ghost came through the door	I/… met …
I was doing my homework	it began to rain	the bed collapsed
Peter was writing on the board	the parrot flew away	the sun came out
the teacher was telling us a nice story	I met you, so it was great	the telephone rang loudly
we were listening to a CD in class	the teacher came in	a policewoman suddenly stood in front of me/…

Diesterweg

When do YOU feel like this?

These words can help you:

angry • frightened • bored • interested • unhappy • sad • lonely • excited •
frustrated • horrified • happy • silly

ISBN 3-425-09103-4

Irregular verbs

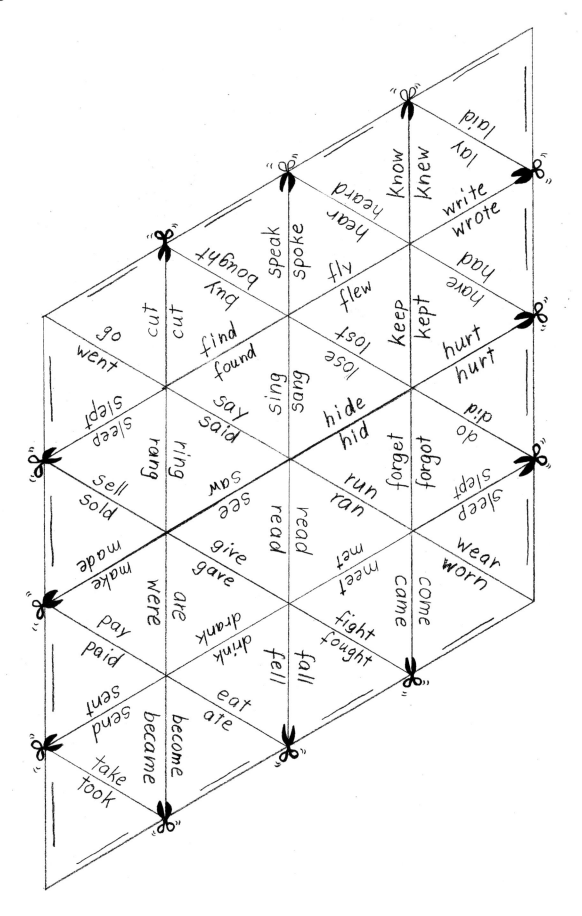

Poems, poems, poems

This is how you can write a poem.

Step 1 – Write down your topic, e.g.:　　　*At home*
Step 2 – Write down two adjectives:　　　*warm and exciting*
Step 3 – Write down three verbs:　　　*work, eat, sleep*
Step 4 – What is special about the topic?　*my brother, good fun*
Step 5 – Write down your topic again:　　*At home*

Here is another example.

At home

nice and warm

help, talk, play

The best place in the world

At home!

Write your poems here.

_____　　_____

_____　　_____

_____　　_____

_____　　_____

You can also write about other topics: school, sports, love, friends, London, …

ISBN 3-425-09103-4

Diesterweg

Riddles, riddles, riddles

Riddle	Answer
It comes and comes but never will arrive.	Driver.
Which word can you put in front of -dresser, -dryer, -brush and -cut?	Because 7 8 9.
What time is it when ten men are running after five chicken?	To go to the second-hand shop.
Why was 6 afraid of 7?	Tomorrow.
Add a letter to PLACE to make a building.	When it is read.
How would you get your purse back if it fell into a river?	A clock.
Add a letter to DIVER to make a job.	Hot – because you can catch a cold.
When is a green book not green?	Palace.
What has a face and hands but can't speak?	Hair.
Which is faster – hot or cold?	I don't know but it certainly would look funny.

Riddle	Answer
What is red, blue and purple all over?	She wanted to see a butterfly.
Why did the woman throw butter out of the window?	Flight.
Why did the man with one hand go into town?	You would get it back wet.
Why did the computer get some cheese?	Work.
Find an animal in CONGRATULATE.	To give it to the mouse.
Change a letter in MOUSE to make a building.	The letter A.
Which word can you put in front of -book, -shop, -man, -day?	Ten after five.
Add a letter to LIGHT to make a trip in a plane.	House.
Change a letter in MONEY to make something very sweet.	Rat.
What is in the middle of Italy?	Honey.

Diesterweg

Money

What I spend my money on

How I could save money

What I'd like to buy

How I could earn money

ISBN 3-425-09103-4

Diesterweg

CAPRICORN
23 December — 20 January
['kæprɪkɔːn]

_____
_____
_____

AQUARIUS
21 January — 19 February
[ə'kweərɪəs]

_____
_____
_____

PISCES
20 February — 20 March
['paɪsiːz]

_____
_____
_____

ARIES
21 March — 20 April
['eəriːz]

_____
_____
_____

TAURUS
21 April — 21 May
['tɔːrəs]

_____
_____
_____

GEMINI
22 May — 21 June
['dʒemɪnaɪ]

_____
_____
_____

CANCER
22 June — 23 July
['kænsə]

_____
_____
_____

LEO
24 July — 23 Aug.
['liːəʊ]

_____
_____
_____

VIRGO
24 August — 23 September
['vɜːgəʊ]

_____
_____
_____

LIBRA
24 September — 23 October
['laɪbrə]

_____
_____
_____

SCORPIO
24 October — 22 November
['skɔːpɪəʊ]

_____
_____
_____

SAGITTARIUS
23 November — 22 December
['sædʒɪˌteərɪəs]

_____
_____
_____

Diesterweg

A map of the world

Zimbabwe

USA

Trinidad

Australia

Canada

Sweden

China

Germany

Great Britain

Sri Lanka

India

Republic of Ireland

New Zealand

Norway

Pakistan

Poland

Diesterweg

A Scotland game

Name: _____

Year: _____

Date: _____

Days | Lessons

This is	what I must do	what I can do	what I need				what I do with it			com-pleted?	my score/mark
			TB	PB	CD/Cass.	and	present to the class	record	hand in		

ISBN 3-425-09103-4

Diesterweg

Name: _Helena_

Year: _7_

Date: _25.10._

This is	what I must do	what I can do	TB	PB	CD/ Cass.	and	present to the class	record	hand in	com- pleted?	my score/ mark
					what I need			*what I do with it*			
TB 3/B1	✓		✓			group	✓				
PB 3/B1	✓			✓							
PB 3/B2		✓		✓							
TB 3/B2		✓	✓			partner					
TB 3/B3a	✓		✓				✓				
TB 3/B3b		✓	✓						✓		
TB 3/B3c	✓		✓		✓		✓				
TB 3/PP	✓		✓								
PB 3/B3	✓								✓		

HV-Text zum Vorlesen für Lehrer/in:
Charlie, Susan and Vera have got a good idea for the last day of their school holidays. They want to go out for lunch somewhere. Charlie wants to go to an Italian restaurant because his family often goes there. They always have very good pizzas. But Susan and Vera want to have fish and chips. They love fish and chips. It's not very expensive and you can have it as a take-away. In the end the friends choose to go to a fish and chips shop. They get their food there, and then they sit in the park with their lunch. They enjoy the sun and have a lot of fun.

Lösungen:

1. 1. for the last day of their school holidays. 2. for lunch. 3. Charlie. 4. Good pizzas. 5. No. 6. it's not very expensive. 7. a fish and chips shop. 8. in the park.
2. many; many; much; much; much; many; many; much; many; much
3. Individuelle Lösungen.
4. He has tried vegetarian food and he liked it. He has tried sweet carrot halva but he didn't like it. He hasn't tried cheese fondue./She has tried pizza and she liked it. She has tried chicken salad but she didn't like it. She hasn't tried melon salad./They have tried tuna salad but they didn't like it. They have tried fish and chips and they liked it. They haven't tried snake.
5. 1. Hong Bin Ku. 2. Chinese food. 3. Between 11 am and 3 pm. 4. Over 100 different dishes/very cheap. 5. Yes. 6. Nothing, it's free. 7. Two.
6. 1. aren't they? 2. don't you? 3. do I? 4. doesn't he? 5. didn't he? 6. could he? 7. were you? 8. doesn't it? 9. wasn't it?
7. Mögliche Lösung: Are you ready to order?/What would you like?/Would you like some bread with your soup?/Anything to drink?/And would you like a dessert?/That's £11.20, please./Thank you very much.

1. 1. for the last day of their school holidays. 2. for lunch. 3. Charlie. 4. Good pizzas. 5. No. 6. it's not very expensive. 7. a fish and chips shop. 8. in the park.
2. many; many; much; much; much; many; many; much; many; much
3. Individuelle Lösungen.
4. He has tried vegetarian food and he liked it. He has tried sweet carrot halva but he didn't like it. He hasn't tried cheese fondue./She has tried pizza and she liked it. She has tried chicken salad but she didn't like it. She hasn't tried melon salad./They have tried tuna salad but they didn't like it. They have tried fish and chips and they liked it. They haven't tried snake.
5. 1. Hong Bin Ku. 2. Chinese food. 3. Between 11 am and 3 pm. 4. Over 100 different dishes/very cheap. 5. Yes. 6. Nothing, it's free. 7. Two.
6. 1. aren't they? 2. don't you? 3. do I? 4. doesn't he? 5. didn't he? 6. could he? 7. were you? 8. doesn't it? 9. didn't you?
7. Mögliche Lösung: Are you ready to order?/What would you like?/Would you like some bread with your soup?/Anything to drink?/And would you like a dessert?/That's £11.20, please./Thank you very much.

Mögliche Erweiterungen:
– TB A1 als HV einsetzen und Fragen dazu stellen.
– Write about your favourite meal.
– Write a letter to a penfriend and tell him/her about your favourite restaurant or your favourite food.
– Copymaster 3: *Question tags, Question tags*
– *jumbled sentences* wie in PB B5
– What do you know about India? (*mind map* oder Text)

ISBN 3-425-09103-4

Diesterweg

1 ★ Eating out

Listen to the text and tick (✔) the right answers.

1. Charlie, Susan and Vera have got a good idea …
   - ☐ for the first day of their Christmas holidays.
   - ☐ for the last day of their Christmas holidays.
   - ☐ for the last day of their school holidays.

2. They want to go …
   - ☐ to a concert.
   - ☐ for a walk in the park.
   - ☐ for lunch.

3. Who would like to go to an Italian restaurant?
   - ☐ Charlie.
   - ☐ Vera.
   - ☐ Susan.

4. What does the Italian restaurant have?
   - ☐ Nice music.
   - ☐ Good pizzas.
   - ☐ Friendly waiters.

5. Would Susan and Vera like to go to the Italian restaurant?
   - ☐ Yes.
   - ☐ No.
   - ☐ They don't know.

6. They like fish and chips because …
   - ☐ it's very hot.
   - ☐ you have lots of tomatoes with it.
   - ☐ it's not very expensive.

7. In the end they go to …
   - ☐ Burger Queen.
   - ☐ Pizza World.
   - ☐ a fish and chips shop.

8. The friends enjoy their lunch …
   - ☐ at the restaurant.
   - ☐ in the park.
   - ☐ at school.

2 ★ What's in the fridge?

Complete the sentences with 'much' or 'many'.

There are _____ things in my kitchen. Let's look into the fridge first: There are _____

eggs, but there's not _____ milk. Do you want to know how _____ cheese there is?

Not _____ ! In the cupboard there are _____ cups and plates and _____

knives, forks and spoons, but not _____ sugar. You will find _____ biscuits in it,

too, but not _____ ketchup. And you love sausages with ketchup, don't you?

3 ★ YOUR salad

What do you put in YOUR favourite salad?

_____

_____

_____

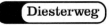

4 ⭐ Have they ever tried ...? And did they like it?

Complete the sentences.

✔ vegetarian food ☺
✔ sweet carrot halva ☹
– cheese fondue

He has tried vegetarian food and he _____

He has tried sweet carrot halva but he didn't _____

He hasn't tried _____

✔ pizza ☺
✔ chicken salad ☹
– melon salad

_____

_____

_____

_____

✔ fish and chips ☺
✔ tuna salad ☹
– snake

_____

_____

_____

_____

5 ⭐ A Chinese restaurant

Read the text and answer the questions.

1. What is the name of the restaurant?

_____

2. What kind of food does this restaurant have?

_____

3. When can you eat the lunch special?

_____

4. What's special about the lunch?

_____

> ## Hong Bin Ku
>
> ### RESTAURANT
> • AUTHENTIC CHINESE FOOD •
> Fully licensed • Air-conditioned
> Open Sun – Thu 11am – 11pm, Fri + Sat 11am – 1am
>
> ### LUNCH SPECIAL
> Over 100 different dishes to choose from
> Including daily specials • From £1.80
> Between 11am & 3pm • 7 days a week
> Free soup and dessert with every main dish after 7pm
>
> **17 Wardour Street**   **20 Rupert Street**
> **London W1**   **London W1**
> **Tel: 0207-734 3586**   **Tel: 0207-437 8899**

5. Can you get a lunch special on Sundays, too? _____

6. How much do you pay for a dessert after 7 pm? _____

7. How many Hong Bin Ku restaurants are there in London? _____

ISBN 3-425-09103-4

6 ⭐ This exercise is easy, isn't it?

Fill in the missing question tags, please.

1. Vegetables are good for you, _____ they?

2. You like milk, _____ you?

3. I don't look very healthy, _____ I?

4. Charlie loves playing football, _____ he?

5. His father forgot to go shopping, _____ he?

6. Peter couldn't speak French well, _____ he?

7. You weren't at school yesterday, _____ you?

8. It looks like rain, _____ it?

9. This exercise was very easy, _____ it?

could/couldn't

are/aren't   did/didn't

was/wasn't

were/weren't

do/don't

does/doesn't

7 ⭐ In a restaurant

What does the waiter say?

Waiter: *Are you* _____

Guest: Yes, I am.

Waiter: *What* _____

Guest: I'd like the onion soup and the chicken curry with rice, please.

Waiter: *Would you* _____

Guest: No, thank you. No bread with the soup.

Waiter: *Anything* _____

Guest: Yes, I'll have a lemonade, please.

Waiter: _____

Guest: No, thank you. I'm not that hungry. – *(later)* – The bill, please.

Waiter: _____

Guest: Here's £12. Keep the change.   **Waiter:** _____

1 ★ ★ Eating out

Listen to the text and tick (✔) the right answers.

1. Charlie, Susan and Vera have got a good idea …
   - ☐ for the first day of their Christmas holidays.
   - ☐ for the last day of their Christmas holidays.
   - ☐ for the last day of their school holidays.

2. They want to go …
   - ☐ to a concert.
   - ☐ for a walk in the park.
   - ☐ for lunch.

3. Who would like to go to an Italian restaurant?
   - ☐ Charlie.
   - ☐ Vera.
   - ☐ Susan.

4. What does the Italian restaurant have?
   - ☐ Nice music.
   - ☐ Good pizzas.
   - ☐ Friendly waiters.

5. Would Susan and Vera like to go to the Italian restaurant?
   - ☐ Yes.
   - ☐ No.
   - ☐ They don't know.

6. They like fish and chips because …
   - ☐ it's very hot.
   - ☐ you have lots of tomatoes with it.
   - ☐ it's not very expensive.

7. In the end they go to …
   - ☐ Burger Queen.
   - ☐ Pizza World.
   - ☐ a fish and chips shop.

8. The friends enjoy their lunch …
   - ☐ at the restaurant.
   - ☐ in the park.
   - ☐ at school.

2 ★ ★ What's in the fridge?

Complete the sentences with 'much' or 'many'.

There are _____ things in my kitchen. Let's look into the fridge first: There are _____

eggs, but there's not _____ milk. Do you want to know how _____ cheese there is?

Not _____ ! In the cupboard there are _____ cups and plates and _____

knives, forks and spoons, but not _____ sugar. You will find _____ biscuits in it,

too, but not _____ ketchup. And you love sausages with ketchup, don't you?

3 ★ ★ And what's in YOUR kitchen?

Write five sentences about YOUR kitchen.

_____

_____

_____

ISBN 3-425-09103-4

Diesterweg

4 **Have they ever tried ...? And did they like it?**

Complete the sentences.

✔ vegetarian food ☺
✔ sweet carrot halva ☹
– cheese fondue

He has tried vegetarian food and he _____

He has tried sweet carrot halva but he _____

He hasn't _____

_____

_____

✔ pizza ☺
✔ chicken salad ☹
– melon salad

_____

_____

✔ tuna salad ☹
✔ fish and chips ☺
– snake

_____

_____

_____

5 ★ ★ **A Chinese restaurant**

Read the text and answer the questions.

1. What is the name of the restaurant?

_____

2. What kind of food does this restaurant have?

_____

3. When can you eat the lunch special?

_____

4. What's special about the lunch?

_____

Hong Bin Ku
RESTAURANT
• AUTHENTIC CHINESE FOOD •
Fully licensed • Air-conditioned
Open Sun – Thu 11am – 11pm, Fri + Sat 11am – 1am
LUNCH SPECIAL
Over 100 different dishes to choose from
Including daily specials • From £1.80
Between 11am & 3pm • 7 days a week
Free soup and dessert with every main dish after 7pm

17 Wardour Street	**20 Rupert Street**
London W1	**London W1**
Tel: 0207-734 3586	**Tel: 0207-437 8899**

5. Can you get a lunch special on Sundays, too? _____

6. How much do you pay for a dessert after 7 pm? _____

7. How many Hong Bin Ku restaurants are there in London? _____

6 ★ ★ **This exercise is easy, isn't it?**

Fill in the missing question tags, please.

1. Vegetables are good for you, _____ ?

2. You like milk, _____ ?

3. I don't look very healthy, _____ ?

4. Charlie loves playing football, _____ ?

5. His father forgot to go shopping, _____ ?

6. Peter couldn't speak French well, _____ ?

7. You weren't at school yesterday, _____ ?

8. It looks like rain, _____ ?

9. You did your homework yesterday afternoon, _____ ?

7 ★ ★ **In a restaurant**

What does the waiter say?

Waiter: _____

Guest: Yes, I am.

Waiter: _____

Guest: I'd like the onion soup and the chicken curry with rice, please.

Waiter: _____

Guest: No, thank you. No bread with the soup.

Waiter: _____

Guest: Yes, I'll have a lemonade, please.

Waiter: _____

Guest: No, thank you. I'm not that hungry. – *(later)* – The bill, please.

Waiter: _____

Guest: Here's £12. Keep the change.   **Waiter:** _____

ISBN 3-425-09103-4

Diesterweg

HV-Text zum Vorlesen für Lehrer/in:
1. Stand straight with your feet together. 2. Touch your feet. 3. Lift your right arm above your head and move it to the left. 4. Pull up your right leg. 5. Touch your left foot with your right hand. 6. Stand straight and hold your arms straight above your head.

Lösungen:

1. 4–1–2–6–5–3 (von links oben nach rechts unten)
2. name: Mitchell Butler; age: 22; family: very active, his father was an American football player, his mum is a sports teacher; sport: basketball, wanted to run the 100 metres when he was little; titles: "the best young player of the year"; other information: always tells jokes, makes the team laugh, last season he scored 729 points, had a lot of energy as a kid, basketball stopped him from being bad
3. 1. How old are you? 2. Do you train regularly? 3. When did you start your sports career? 4. How many hours do you train every week? 5. Do you get out of breath quickly? 6. Have you got any hobbies? 7. What do you like best about your kind of sport? 8. Do you always enjoy the hard work?
4. 1. happy 2. quickly, slow 3. well, good 4. easy, easily 5. lazy, healthy, rarely, beautifully
5. a) young–younger–youngest; cheap–cheaper–cheapest; nice–nicer–nicest; interesting–more interesting–most interesting; brilliant–more brilliant–most brilliant; big–bigger–biggest; careful–more careful–most careful; good–better–best; bad–worse–worst
   b) Individuelle Lösungen.
6. wasn't able to; wasn't able to; wasn't able to; was able to; was able to; were able to; was able to; was able to

1. 4–1–2–6–5–3 (von links oben nach rechts unten)
2. name: Mitchell Butler; age: 22; family: very active, his father was an American football player, his mum is a sports teacher; sport: basketball, wanted to run the 100 metres when he was little; titles: "the best young player of the year"; other information: always tells jokes, makes the team laugh, last season he scored 729 points, had a lot of energy as a kid, basketball stopped him from being bad
3. 1. How old are you? 2. Do you train regularly? 3. When did you start your sports career? 4. How many hours do you train every week? 5. Do you get out of breath quickly? 6. Have you got any hobbies? 7. What do you like best about your kind of sport? 8. Do you always enjoy the hard work?
4. 1. happy 2. quickly, slow 3. well, good 4. easy, easily 5. lazy, healthy, rarely, beautifully
5. a) tall–taller–tallest; young–younger–youngest; expensive–more expensive–most expensive; cheap–cheaper–cheapest; nice–nicer–nicest; interesting–more interesting–most interesting; much–more–most; good–better–best; careful–more careful–most careful; bad–worse–worst; big–bigger–biggest
   b) Individuelle Lösungen.
6. wasn't able to; wasn't able to; wasn't able to; was able to; was able to; were able to; was able to; was able to

Mögliche Erweiterungen:
– Write about your favourite sportsperson.
– Write about your favourite singer, band, actor or actress.
– Which kinds of sports do you like or don't you like? Write six sentences.
  (ggf. unterstützt durch Folie 3: *Fit for fun*)
– Folie 4: *Who is it? – An interview*
– Copymaster 9: *The life of Christy Brown*

1 ⭐ Do you know your warm-up exercises?

Number the six exercises in the order you hear them.

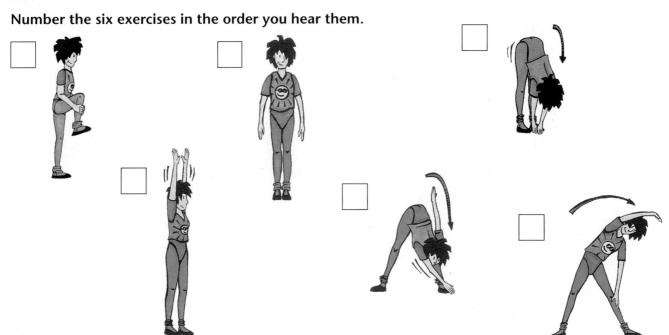

2 ⭐ Sports hero of the week – Mitchell Butler

Basketball has a new star to take the place of Michael Jordan. And his name? Mitchell Butler! Sports reporters across America have voted the 22-year-old "the best young player of the year". And his team likes him a lot, too: "You know, Mitchell is great. He always tells jokes and helps make the team laugh". He also helps the team win. Last season he scored 729 points. Mitchell comes from a very active family. His father was an American football player and his mum is a sports teacher. "When I was little, I wanted to run the 100 metres but I got taller and taller, and then someone said I should play basketball. I started and loved it. My mum was happy because I always had a lot of energy as a kid and basketball stopped me from being bad. Well, most of the time!"

Find out this information from the text.

name: _____

age: _____

family: _____

_____

sport: _____

titles: _____

other information: _____

_____

ISBN 3-425-09103-4

Diesterweg

3 ⭐ **Your interview**

The words in the questions are in the wrong order. Put them into the right order and re-write the eight questions.

1. _____

(are – old – how – you – ?) "I'm much older than I look."

2. _____

(do – regularly – train – you – ?) "Yes, every morning before work."

3. _____

(you – career – start – when – your – sports – did – ?) "When I was 17."

4. _____

(every – many – week – do – hours – how – train – you – ?) "About 15."

5. _____

(get – of – quickly – breath – you – out – do?) "No, I don't. I'm very fit."

6. _____

(hobbies – any – got – have – you – ?) "I watch TV and I love burgers but I know they're not healthy."

7. _____

(of – do – about – like – best – you – your – kind – sport – what – ?) "I look younger than I am!"

8. _____

(work – hard – the – enjoy – always – you – do ?) "I love it. It's good fun."

4 ⭐ **Adjective or adverb?**

Choose the correct word.

1. David is _____ (happy/happily) because he can go inline-skating.

2. Susan can run _____ (quick/quickly) but Vera is a _____ runner (slow/slowly).

3. Charlie plays football _____ (good/well), and he is also a _____ (good/well) swimmer.

4. This recipe for a chicken curry is very _____ (easy/easily). You can make it very

_____ (easy/easily).

5. Tim's brother Jack is very _____ (lazy/lazily). He doesn't eat _____

(healthy/healthily) things, so he _____ (rare/rarely) moves. He is a couch potato, but he

sings _____ (beautiful/beautifully).

5 ⭐ Can you compare?

a) Fill in the correct forms of these adjectives, please.

tall	taller	tallest
expensive	more expensive	most expensive
young		
cheap		
nice		
interesting		
brilliant		
big		
careful		
good		
bad		

b) Now compare these four things or people with each other. Choose one of the forms from a).

1. My grandmother is _____ than my grandfather.

2. I think a Discman is _____ than a Walkman.

3. My maths teacher is _____ than my German teacher.

4. A good book is always _____ than a boring talkshow on TV.

6 ⭐ Christy Brown

Fill in the missing forms of 'be able to'. | was able to | | wasn't able to | | were able to |

In 1932, when Christy Brown was very young, his mother noticed that he _____

move properly. He _____ put on his clothes and he _____

talk but he _____ hear. And he _____ control his left foot,

too. When his brothers _____ make him a box on wheels, he

_____ play with them in the streets. And years later, when he went to a special

clinic, he _____ control his body a little and wrote a book about his family.

ISBN 3-425-09103-4

Diesterweg

1 Do you know your warm-up exercises?

Number the six exercises in the order you hear them.

2 Sports hero of the week – Mitchell Butler

Basketball has a new star to take the place of Michael Jordan. And his name? Mitchell Butler! Sports reporters across America have voted the 22-year-old "the best young player of the year". And his team likes him a lot, too: "You know, Mitchell is great. He always tells jokes and helps make the team laugh". He also helps the team win. Last season he scored 729 points. Mitchell comes from a very active family. His father was an American football player and his mum is a sports teacher. "When I was little, I wanted to run the 100 metres but I got taller and taller, and then someone said I should play basketball. I started and loved it. My mum was happy because I always had a lot of energy as a kid and basketball stopped me from being bad. Well, most of the time!"

Find out this information from the text.

name: _____

age: _____

family: _____

_____

sport: _____

titles: _____

other information: _____

_____

Diesterweg

3 ⭐ ⭐ Your interview

Ask eight questions to find out interesting facts about the sportsman.

Frage ihn,

– wie alt er ist

– ob er regelmäßig trainiert

– wann er mit seiner Sportkarriere begonnen hat

– wie viele Stunden er pro Woche trainiert

– ob er schnell außer Atem gerät

– ob er Hobbys hat

– was ihm an seiner Sportart am besten gefällt

– ob ihm die harte Arbeit immer Spaß macht.

_____

_____

_____

_____

_____

_____

_____

_____

_____

_____

4 ⭐ ⭐ Adjective or adverb?

Decide if you need the adjective or the adverb.

1. David is _____ (happy) because he can go inline-skating.

2. Susan can run _____ (quick) but Vera is a _____ runner (slow).

3. Charlie plays football _____ (good), and he is also a _____ (good) swimmer.

4. This recipe for a chicken curry is very _____ (easy). You can make it very

_____ (easy).

5. Tim's brother Jack is very _____ (lazy). He doesn't eat _____

(healthy) things, so he _____ (rare) moves. He is a couch potato, but he sings

_____ (beautiful).

ISBN 3-425-09103-4

5 ★★ Can you compare?

a) Fill in the correct forms of these adjectives, please.

		tallest
young		
expensive		
	cheaper	
nice		
		most interesting
much		
	better	
careful		
		worst
big		

b) Now compare four things or people with each other.

_____

_____

_____

_____

6 ★★ Christy Brown

Fill in the missing forms of 'be able to' or 'not be able to'.

In 1932, when Christy Brown was very young, his mother noticed that he _____

move properly. He _____ put on his clothes and he _____

talk but he _____ hear. And he _____ control his left foot,

too. When his brothers _____ make him a box on wheels, he

_____ play with them in the streets. And years later, when he went to a special

clinic, he _____ control his body a little and wrote a book about his family.

HV-Text zum Vorlesen für Lehrer/in:
We have an Old Town Festival every year in summer. In the morning there's a flea market. You can buy a lot of interesting things there: books, comics, computer games and CDs. In the afternoon there are three bands that play loud music on the market place. You can see some magicians and jugglers, too. People put up a lot of stalls where you can buy fantastic food – hot dogs, burgers, cakes and other sweets. If it's dry, people sit and drink and eat outside, and they dance, too! If it rains, they can sit in big tents. I like it, because I can always stay up late.

Lösungen:

1. 1. autumn ➔ summer 2. all day ➔ in the morning 3. ten ➔ three 4. jugglers and floats ➔ jugglers and magicians 5. right 6. right
2. 1. carnival 2. bands 3. jugglers 4. tourists 5. floats 6. dancers 7. clowns 8. poster 9. stalls
3. 1. While I was having lunch with my brother, our cat caught a mouse. 2. While I was waiting for the bus into town, a young girl asked me the way to the bookshop. 3. While I was trying on a pair of trousers in a shop, it started to rain. 4. While it was raining, I met a friend and we went and had an ice-cream together. 5. While we were eating our ice-creams, the rain stopped. 6. While I was waiting for the bus back home, an old lady asked me the way to the post office. 7. And while my parents and I were having dinner, my brother came home with a broken bicycle helmet. What an afternoon!
4. make–made–made; have–had–had; cut–cut–cut; mean–meant–meant; think–thought–thought; try–tried–tried; steal–stole–stolen; hit–hit–hit; take–took–taken; beat–beat–beaten
5. 1. At the Tower. 2. see jugglers and clowns. 3. Tower Bridge. 4. In summer. 5. At Madame Tussaud's. 6. Hyde Park
6. St. Stephen's Gardens ➔ Chepstow Road ➔ Talbot Road ➔ Moorhouse Road ➔ Artesian Road ➔ Ledbury Road

1. 1. autumn ➔ summer 2. all day ➔ in the morning 3. ten ➔ three 4. jugglers and floats ➔ jugglers and magicians 5. right 6. right
2. 1. carnival 2. bands 3. jugglers 4. tourists 5. floats 6. dancers 7. clowns 8. poster 9. stalls
3. 1. While I was waiting for the bus into town, a young girl asked me the way to the bookshop. 2. While I was trying on a pair of trousers in a shop, it started to rain. 3. While it was raining, I met a friend and we went and had an ice-cream together. 4. While we were eating our ice-creams, the rain stopped. 5. While I was waiting for the bus back home, an old lady asked me the way to the post office. 6. And while my parents and I were having dinner, my brother came home with a broken bicycle helmet. What an afternoon!
4. make–made–made; have–had–had; cut–cut–cut; mean–meant–meant; think–thought–thought; try–tried–tried; steal–stole–stolen; hit–hit–hit; take–took–taken; beat–beat–beaten
5. St. Stephen's Gardens ➔ Chepstow Road ➔ Talbot Road ➔ Moorhouse Road ➔ Artesian Road ➔ Ledbury Road
6. Individuelle Lösungen.

Mögliche Erweiterungen:
– gekürzte Version von TB A1 als Lückentext.
– Copymaster 10: *Who or which?*
– Write a letter to the London Tourist Office and ask them for information about London's tourist attractions. (Arbeitsauftrag ggf. eingrenzen, z. B.: Ask them for information about the opening times of the London Dungeon/Tower of London/…)
– Say why you would or wouldn't like to visit the Notting Hill Carnival next August.

ISBN 3-425-09103-4

1 ★ The Old Town Festival

Right or wrong? Listen to the text and correct the wrong sentences.

1. We have an Old Town Festival every year in autumn.

_____

2. There's a flea market all day.

_____

3. In the afternoon there are ten bands that play loud music.

_____

4. You can see some jugglers and floats.

_____

5. People put up a lot of stalls where you can buy fantastic food.

_____

6. If it rains, people can sit and drink and eat in big tents.

_____

2 ★ Carnival crossword

1. Colourful summer event in Notting Hill.
2. Groups that play music.
3. People who can play with ten balls at a time.
4. People who take photos and enjoy the Carnival.
5. Everybody likes to look at them. They are brightly coloured.
6. People who dance to the music.
7. People who make other people laugh.
8. A large piece of paper that shows you what's on.
9. Places where you can buy food or soft drinks.

3 ⭐ What happened while ...?

What did Emma tell her friend Sally about her afternoon? Fill in the past progressive or the simple past of the verbs.

1. While I was having lunch with my brother, our cat

_____ (catch) a mouse.

2. While I _____ (wait) for the bus into town, a young girl asked me the way to the bookshop.

3. While I _____ (try) on a pair of trousers in a shop, it started to rain.

4. While it _____ (rain), I met a friend and we went and had an ice-cream together.

5. While we were eating our ice-creams, the rain _____ (stop).

6. While I was waiting for the bus back home, an old lady _____ (ask) me the way to the post office.

7. And while my parents and I _____ (have) dinner, my brother came home with a broken bicycle helmet. What an afternoon!

4 ⭐ Irregular verbs

Fill in the correct forms of these irregular verbs, please.

infinitive	simple past (second form)	past participle (third form)
make		
	had	
		cut
mean		
	thought	
		tried
steal		
	hit	
		taken
beat		

ISBN 3-425-09103-4

Diesterweg

5 ★ London quiz

Tick (✔) the right answers.

1. Where can you see the Crown Jewels?
   ☐ At Buckingham Palace.   ☐ At the Tower.   ☐ At St. Paul's Cathedral.

2. At Covent Garden you can …
   ☐ see the Queen's horses.   ☐ see jugglers and clowns.   ☐ learn about life in cyberspace.

3. Which of the bridges in London can open?
   ☐ London Bridge.   ☐ Westminster Bridge.   ☐ Tower Bridge.

4. When can you visit Buckingham Palace?
   ☐ In winter.   ☐ In summer.   ☐ When the flag is flying on the Palace.

5. Where can you meet lots of famous people who can't speak?
   ☐ At London Dungeon.   ☐ At Madame Tussaud's.   ☐ At the Royal National Theatre.

6. Speaker's Corner is in
   ☐ Kensington Gardens.
   ☐ Regent's Park.
   ☐ Hyde Park.

6 ★ The way home

How did Karim take the lost girl home? Read the text. Then take a pencil and follow their way on the map.

The little girl was at the Carnival with her big brother. She was lost but Karim found her. He took the little girl home to her parents. They started from Karim's stall outside his house in St. Stephen's Gardens. They walked to Chepstow Road and turned left. They went down Chepstow Road until they got to Talbot Road and turned right. They took the third street on the left: Moorhouse Road. In Moorhouse Road they passed the school and came to Artesian Road. They turned right into Artesian Road and then left into Ledbury Road. The little girl's house was on the right.

1 ⭐ ⭐ **The Old Town Festival**

Right or wrong? Listen to the text and correct the wrong sentences.

1. We have an Old Town Festival every year in autumn.

_____

2. There's a flea market all day.

_____

3. In the afternoon there are ten bands that play loud music.

_____

4. You can see some jugglers and floats.

_____

5. People put up a lot of stalls where they sell fantastic food.

_____

6. If it rains, people can sit and drink and eat in big tents.

_____

2 ⭐ ⭐ **Carnival crossword**

1. Colourful summer event in Notting Hill.
2. Groups that play music.
3. People who can play with ten balls at a time.
4. People who take photos and enjoy the Carnival.
5. Everybody likes to look at them. They are brightly coloured.
6. People who dance to the music.
7. People who make other people laugh.
8. A large piece of paper that shows you what's on.
9. Places where you can buy food or soft drinks.

ISBN 3-425-09103-4

Diesterweg

3 ★★ What happened while ...?

What did Emma tell her friend Sally? Use the past progressive or simple past of the verbs.

1. While I _____ (wait)

for the bus into town, a young girl _____
(ask) me the way to the bookshop.

2. While I _____ (try)
on a pair of blue trousers in a shop, it started to rain.

3. While it _____ (rain), I _____ (meet) a friend from
school and we went and had an ice-cream together.

4. While we _____ (eat) our ice-creams, the rain

_____ (stop).

5. While I _____ (wait) for the bus back home, an old lady

_____ (ask) me the way to the post office.

6. And while my parents and I _____ (have) dinner, my brother

_____ (come) home with a broken bicycle helmet. What an afternoon!

4 ★★ Irregular verbs

Fill in the correct forms of these irregular verbs, please.

infinitive	simple past (second form)	past participle (third form)
make		
	had	
		cut
mean		
	thought	
		tried
steal		
	hit	
		taken
beat		

Diesterweg

5 ★ ★ Can you help Karim?

**How did Karim take the lost girl home?
Read the text. Then take a pencil
and follow their way on the map.**

The little girl was at the Carnival
with her big brother. She was
lost but Karim found her. He
took the little girl home to her
parents. They started from
Karim's stall outside his house in
St. Stephen's Gardens. They walked
to Chepstow Road and turned left.
They went down Chepstow Road until
they got to Talbot Road and turned right.
They took the third street on the left:
Moorhouse Road. In Moorhouse Road
they passed the school and came to
Artesian Road. They turned right into
Artesian Road and then left into Ledbury
Road. The little girl's house was on the right.

6 ★ ★ Tourists in YOUR area

**What sight or interesting place would you show tourists
in your area? Write a short guide for tourists. You should tell them**
- **the name of the sight**   - **where it is**   - **how they can get there**
- **what they can see there**   - **when they can visit it**   - **something about its history.**

_____

_____

_____

_____

_____

_____

_____

ISBN 3-425-09103-4

Diesterweg

HV-Text zum Vorlesen für Lehrer/in:
Mum: 7943399.
Sally: Hello, this is Sally. Is Emma there?
Mum: Just a minute. I'll get her.
Emma: Hello?
Sally: Hi, it's Sally. Do you have some time? I need to talk to you. I have a problem with my dad again.
Emma: What's the matter?
Sally: He says I can't wear my new shoes. He doesn't like them. That's not fair! I bought them with my own money.
Emma: When do you want to wear them, Sally?
Sally: To the disco at the weekend.
Emma: Well, wear some old shoes when you leave your house and take the new shoes with you in a bag. You can put them on later. Your dad will never know.
Sally: Very clever! Thank you very much, Emma.
Emma: No problem! Right, now you can help me, too, Sally. You know I hate my hair. It is too curly and I wish it was straight. What can I do?
Sally: I think your hair is pretty but if you don't like it, why don't you wear it short?
Emma: Yes, that's a good idea. Perhaps I'll try it. Thanks a lot! And bye for now.
Sally: Bye, Emma.

Lösungen:

1. 1. problems at home. 2. with her dad. 3. her new shoes to the disco. 4. her new shoes with her own money. 5. put her new shoes on at the disco. 6. too curly.
2. 1. Brenda. 2. She wants a cat. 3. Her mum. 4. She is too busy to look after the cat. Cats smell. 5. She would feed it and play with it and clean the cat's toilet.
3. moved, started, were, waited, knew, had, walked, talked, heard, found, got, called, put, answered, rang, ran, stood, shouted, was, found, helped
4. After I had gone swimming, I visited my grandmother. After I had visited my grandmother, I helped Dad in the garden. After I had helped Dad in the garden, I did my homework. After I had done my homework, I watched a video. After I had watched a video, I called my best friend. After I had called my best friend, I went to bed.
5. 3–11–6–2–5–7–9–10–4–1–8
6. Individuelle Lösungen.

1. 1. problems at home. 2. with her dad. 3. her new shoes to the disco. 4. her new shoes with her own money. 5. put her new shoes on at the disco. 6. too curly.
2. a) 1. She wants a cat but her mother doesn't want a cat in the house. 2. She is too busy to look after the cat. Cats smell. 3. She has always wanted a cat. All her friends have a pet. She'd love to play with it. b) Individuelle Lösungen.
3. moved, started, were, waited, knew, had, walked, talked, heard, found, wasn't, got, called, put, answered, rang, ran, stood, shouted, was, found, helped
4. After I had gone swimming, I visited my grandmother. After I had visited my grandmother, I helped Dad in the garden. After I had helped Dad in the garden, I did my homework. After I had done my homework, I watched a video. After I had watched a video, I called my best friend. After I had called my best friend, I went to bed.
5. 3–11–6–2–5–7–9–10–4–1–8
6. Individuelle Lösungen.

Mögliche Erweiterungen:
– Freies Schreiben: Briefe zu wirklichen/fiktiven häuslichen Problemen.
– Probleme skizzieren, S geben schriftlich Ratschläge (vgl. TB A4)
– Folie 8: *Alone on a high mountain*
– Folie 9: *Creative use of things*
– Have you ever been lonely or homesick? Describe the situation.
– "Home is where you make it." Discuss. (What is home for you? Where do you feel at home? How important is home to you?)
– What would you take with you to a desert island? And why? Write six sentences.

1 ⭐ Sally's problem

Listen to the two girls Emma and Sally and tick (✔) the right answers.

1. Emma and Sally talk about …
   - ☐ problems at school.
   - ☐ plans for the weekend.
   - ☐ problems at home.

2. Sally has a problem …
   - ☐ with her dad.
   - ☐ with her mum.
   - ☐ with her boyfriend.

3. Sally wants to wear …
   - ☐ her new dress to the disco.
   - ☐ her new shoes to the disco.
   - ☐ her new skirt to the disco.

4. Sally bought …
   - ☐ her new shoes with her own money.
   - ☐ her new dress with her own money.
   - ☐ her new shoes with her dad's money.

5. Emma says Sally should …
   - ☐ wear her old dress at the disco.
   - ☐ wear her old shoes at the disco.
   - ☐ put her new shoes on at the disco.

6. Emma hates her hair because it's …
   - ☐ too curly.
   - ☐ too straight.
   - ☐ too short.

2 ⭐ Brenda's problem

Read the letter and answer the questions.

> Mum says: No cat!
> All my friends have a pet. I've always wanted a cat. But my mother doesn't want a cat in the house. She says she is too busy to look after it. I've told her that I will feed it and clean the cat's toilet. A cat can stay alone in the house. I'd love to play with it. Mum says cats smell. What do you think? Can you help me?
>
> Brenda, 12

1. Who has a problem? _____

2. What does Brenda want? _____

3. Who is against it? _____

4. What are the reasons? _____

_____

5. What would Brenda do for the cat? _____

_____

ISBN 3-425-09103-4

Diesterweg

3 Charlotte's problem

Write down the simple past tense forms of the verbs in brackets.

When Charlotte and her parents _____ (move) to a new town, some girls from her street

_____ (start) to pick on Charlotte. They _____ (be) at the same school, and they

_____ (wait) for Charlotte after school because they _____ (know) she _____ (have)

no one to walk home with. They _____ (walk) behind her and _____ (talk) about her

all the time, and Charlotte _____ (hear) everything. Soon the girls _____ (find) out

that her mother wasn't at home when Charlotte _____ (get) back from school. So they

_____ (call) her and _____ (put) the phone down when she _____ (answer).

Or they _____ (ring) the doorbell and _____ (run) away. Or they just _____ (stand)

outside the house and _____ (shout). Charlotte _____ (be) really frightened. But when

her parents _____ (find) out about everything, they _____ (help) Charlotte. The girls

have stopped now but Charlotte is still scared.

4 What did you do after that?

**Make sentences with the past perfect and
the simple past.**

After I had tidied my room, I went swimming. After

I had gone swimming, _____

_____

_____

_____

_____

_____

_____

_____

tidy my room

go swimming

visit grandmother

help Dad in the garden

do my homework

watch a video

call my best friend

go to bed

5 ⭐ Robinson is mixed up

Put the right numbers into the boxes.

☐ His ship sank in a storm in the Caribbean on 30th September, 1659.

☐ Robinson arrived in York on 11th June, 1687. He was back in England. Home, sweet home!

☐ One day, some cannibals came to the island.

☐ Robinson left London on a ship to the Caribbean on 1st September, 1659.

☐ He lived alone for many years.

☐ They had a prisoner with them and Robinson rescued him.

☐ Robinson taught Man Friday to speak English, and Man Friday showed Robinson how to use plants as medicine.

☐ 19th December, 1686. An English ship sailed by and rescued them.

☐ Robinson swam to an island and survived.

☐ Robinson left his parents in York on 1st September, 1651 and took a ship to London.

☐ Robinson called him Man Friday because he had found him on a Friday.

6 ⭐ Friends

**Which words come to your mind when you think of 'friends'?
Write down 15 words.**

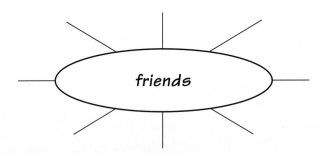

ISBN 3-425-09103-4

Diesterweg

1 ★ ★ **Sally's problem**

Listen to the two girls Emma and Sally and tick (✔) the right answers.

1. Emma and Sally talk about …
   ☐ problems at school.
   ☐ plans for the weekend.
   ☐ problems at home.

2. Sally has a problem …
   ☐ with her dad.
   ☐ with her mum.
   ☐ with her boyfriend.

3. Sally wants to wear …
   ☐ her new dress to the disco.
   ☐ her new shoes to the disco.
   ☐ her new skirt to the disco.

4. Sally bought …
   ☐ her new shoes with her own money.
   ☐ her new dress with her own money.
   ☐ her new shoes with her dad's money.

5. Emma says Sally should …
   ☐ wear her old dress at the disco.
   ☐ wear her old shoes at the disco.
   ☐ put her new shoes on at the disco.

6. Emma hates her hair because it's …
   ☐ too curly.
   ☐ too straight.
   ☐ too short.

2 ★ ★ **Brenda's problem**

a) Read the letter and answer the questions.

> Mum says: No cat!
> All my friends have a pet. I've always wanted a cat. But my mother doesn't want a cat in the house. She says she is too busy to look after it. I've told her that I will feed it and clean the cat's toilet. A cat can stay alone in the house. I'd love to play with it. Mum says cats smell. What do you think? Can you help me?
>
> Brenda, 12

1. What's Brenda's problem?

_____

2. What are her mother's reasons against a cat?

_____

3. Why does Brenda want a cat?

_____

b) What advice would you give Brenda? Write three sentences.

_____

_____

_____

3 ★ ★ Charlotte's problem

Write down the simple past tense forms of the verbs in brackets.

When Charlotte and her parents _____ (move) to a new town, some girls from her street _____ (start) to pick on Charlotte. They _____ (be) at the same school, and they _____ (wait) for Charlotte after school because they _____ (know) she _____ (have) no one to walk home with. They _____ (walk) behind her and _____ (talk) about her all the time, and Charlotte _____ (hear) everything. Soon the girls _____ (find) out that her mother _____ (not be) at home when Charlotte _____ (get) back from school. So they _____ (call) her and _____ (put) the phone down when she _____ (answer). Or they _____ (ring) the doorbell and _____ (run) away. Or they just _____ (stand) outside the house and _____ (shout). Charlotte _____ (be) really frightened. But when her parents _____ (find) out about everything, they _____ (help) Charlotte. The girls have stopped now but Charlotte is still scared.

4 ★ ★ What did you do after that?

Make sentences with the past perfect and the simple past.

After I had tidied my room, _____

_____

tidy my room

go swimming

visit grandmother

help Dad in the garden

do my homework

watch a video

call my best friend

go to bed

5 ★ ★ Robinson is mixed up

Put the right numbers into the boxes.

☐ His ship sank in a storm in the Caribbean on 30th September, 1659.

☐ Robinson arrived in York on 11th June, 1687. He was back in England. Home, sweet home!

☐ One day, some cannibals came to the island.

☐ Robinson left London on a ship to the Caribbean on 1st September, 1659.

☐ He lived alone for many years.

☐ They had a prisoner with them and Robinson rescued him.

☐ Robinson taught Man Friday to speak English, and Man Friday showed Robinson how to use plants as medicine.

☐ 19th December, 1686. An English ship sailed by and rescued them.

☐ Robinson swam to an island and survived.

☐ Robinson left his parents in York on 1st September, 1651 and took a ship to London.

☐ Robinson called him Man Friday because he had found him on a Friday.

6 ★ ★ A problem shared with Jane

Two people made these notes for their letters for the problem page of a youth magazine. Choose ONE and write a letter. Remember to write a beginning and an end.

problem: party
• parents say no – too young
• friends go – don't understand
• talk about parties at school
• feel terrible – sit at home

problem: pocket money
• father pays for house – no money left
• get only £2 a week
• friends: £6
• hamburgers, sweets, magazines

Dear Jane, _____

_____

_____

_____

_____

_____

HV-Text zum Vorlesen für Lehrer/in:
The London Toy and Model Museum is the place for fans of toys and models. Here you can see model trains, ships, spaceships and planes. They also have modern Japanese toys, and teddy bears from all over the world. My sister loves the teddies but I like the computer games room best. It's open every day from 10 am–5.30 pm.

Lösungen:

1. 1. In London. 2. The Toy and Model Museum. 3. Model trains, ships, spaceships, planes, Japanese toys, teddy bears from all over the world. 4. Every day from 10 am–5.30 pm. 5. The computer games room.
2. 1. yourself 2. herself 3. themselves 4. ourselves 5. himself 6. myself
3. Individuelle Lösungen.
4. 6–3–4–2–1–5 (von links oben nach rechts unten)
5. Individuelle Lösungen.
6. a) 3–2–1
   b) 2–1–3
7. Individuelle Lösungen.

1. 1. In London. 2. The Toy and Model Museum. 3. Model trains, ships, spaceships, planes, Japanese toys, teddy bears from all over the world. 4. Every day from 10 am–5.30 pm. 5. The computer games room.
2. 1. yourself 2. herself 3. themselves 4. ourselves 5. himself 6. myself 7. themselves
3. Individuelle Lösungen.
4. 6–3–4–2–1–5 (von links oben nach rechts unten)
5. Individuelle Lösungen.
6. Individuelle Lösungen.
7. Individuelle Lösungen.

Mögliche Erweiterungen:
– Have you ever been to a museum? Write six sentences about your visit.
– Imagine a day without electricity.
  • Write what happened *(simple past)*.
  • Write what will happen *(will-future)*.
  • Write what is going to happen *(going to-future)*.
  • Write what would happen *(conditional I)*.
– Suggest at least four ways how we can save electricity at home.

ISBN 3-425-09103-4

1 ⭐ A museum for children

Listen and answer the questions.

1. Where is the museum? _____

2. What kind of museum is it? _____

3. What can you see in the museum? _____

_____

4. When is the museum open? _____

5. What does the speaker like best? _____

2 ⭐ Do it yourself

Fill the gaps with the correct reflexive pronouns.

themselves	himself	yourself	ourselves	myself	herself

1. I know it's difficult. But you must write that letter _____ . I can't help you.

2. This article is really good. Did your sister write it _____ ?

3. The pupils were able to work out the riddles _____ .

4. Let's introduce _____ to our readers in the next issue of our magazine.

5. I think your brother thinks too much of _____ .

6. I'm going to talk to him _____ .

3 ⭐ Electricity words

When do you use electricity at home?

– when I listen to the radio _____

_____

_____

_____

_____

Diesterweg

4 ⭐ Inventions

Match the texts with the pictures (put the right numbers in the boxes).

1. Sir Rowland Hill made an invention that you have to put on a letter. You can buy it at a post office.
2. Alexander Fleming made an important invention that helps people when they are ill.
3. The German engineer Karl Benz invented something that moves on four wheels.
4. Laszlo Biro's invention was something to write with. People often use his name to talk about it.
5. Thomas Alva Edison made an invention that helps you to see in the dark.
6. The invention of Whitcomb L. Judson helps you to close trousers, skirts and anoraks.

5 ⭐ What do you think of these inventions?

Are the inventions on this page important/not important/helpful/…? Choose eight of them and write down what you think.

Example: I think the ballpoint is a helpful invention.

1. _____

2. _____

3. _____

4. _____

5. _____

6. _____

7. _____

8. _____

ISBN 3-425-09103-4

6 ⭐ Bottle garden

Like all living things, plants need water. They get their water from the rain or when someone waters them. Here you can make a garden you will never have to water. You will need a large glass bottle or a jar with a top, small stones, charcoal (Holzkohle), some damp soil (feuchte Erde) and some small plants.

a) Read the texts and put them in the right order.

☐ Put the top on the bottle and leave it in a warm, light place. The plants will take the water from the soil through their roots. They will breathe out damp air so the soil stays damp.

☐ Carefully plant a few small plants and then sprinkle them with water. To make the planting easier you can fix a spoon to a stick.

☐ Put the glass bottle or jar on its side. Put in small stones, then charcoal and damp soil.

b) And now match the texts with the pictures. Put the right numbers in the boxes.

 ☐

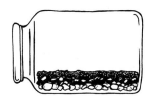 ☐

 ☐

7 ⭐ YOUR favourite museum

Write about a museum you know.

My favourite museum is the _____ in _____

You can see _____

_____

The most interesting thing(s) is/are _____

The museum is open _____ and is closed _____

I can get there by bus/by bike/ _____

 **Diesterweg**

1 ⭐⭐ A museum for children

Listen and answer the questions.

1. Where is the museum?_____

2. What kind of museum is it?_____

3. What can you see in the museum?_____

_____

4. When is the museum open?_____

5. What does the speaker like best?_____

2 ⭐⭐ Do it yourself

Fill the gaps with the correct reflexive pronouns.

1. I know it's difficult. But you must write that letter _____ . I can't help you.

2. This article is really good. Did your sister write it _____ ?

3. The pupils were able to work out the riddles _____ .

4. Let's introduce _____ to our readers in the next issue of our magazine.

5. I think your brother thinks too much of _____ .

6. I'm going to talk to him _____ .

7. Some people always have to talk about _____ .

3 ⭐⭐ Electricity words

When do you use electricity at home?

_____

_____

_____

_____

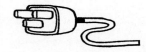

ISBN 3-425-09103-4

Diesterweg

4 ★ ★ Inventions

Match the texts with the pictures (put the right numbers in the boxes).

1. Sir Rowland Hill made an invention that you have to put on a letter. You can buy it at a post office.
2. Alexander Fleming made an important invention that helps people when they are ill.
3. The German engineer Karl Benz invented something that moves on four wheels.
4. Laszlo Biro's invention was something to write with. People often use his name to talk about it.
5. Thomas Alva Edison made an invention that helps you to see in the dark.
6. The invention of Whitcomb L. Judson helps you to close trousers, skirts and anoraks.

5 ★ ★ What do you think of these inventions?

Are the inventions on this page important/not important/helpful/…? Choose eight of them and write down what you think. And say why!

Example: I think penicillin is a helpful invention because it helps people to become healthy again.

1. _____

2. _____

3. _____

4. _____

5. _____

6. _____

7. _____

8. _____

Diesterweg

6 ★ ★ Museums in YOUR area

Write about a museum you know. The following questions can help you.

– What museums are there in your area? Which of these museums do you know well?
– Which museum do you like best?
– Why do you like it?
– What can you see/do/... there?
– Where is it?
– How can you get there?
– Is it expensive to get in? How much is a ticket for children/adults?
– Any other information?

_____

_____

_____

_____

_____

_____

_____

_____

7 ★ ★ YOUR choice!

Choose exercise a) or b).

a) Write about a useful invention you would like to have for the future.

b) Write about the museum of your dreams.

_____

_____

_____

_____

_____

_____

ISBN 3-425-09103-4

HV-Text zum Vorlesen für Lehrer/in:

Susan: Hi, Gillian! Hi, Vera! Wow, your car-boot sale looks fantastic! I'm looking for a birthday present for my brother Jack. He's interested in computers.

Gillian: What do you think about this old computer? It's still working but I want to sell it because I got a new one a month ago. It's only £35. Is that OK for you?

Susan: Well, it's a little bit more than I thought …

Gillian: OK. Let's say £30. What do you think?

Susan: Still quite expensive but I think I'll take it. I'll ask our parents to give some money, too. My brother will love it!

Gillian: Great! And here are some old computer magazines, too – for free!

Susan: Thank you very much.

Vera: Look! There's Roy. Hi, Roy! What are you looking for?

Roy: Hi! Well, I'm interested in music. Do you have any CDs?

Vera: Sorry, I don't have any CDs but I have some cassettes.

Roy: Let me see … Wow, this is really cool music. What do you want for these two cassettes?

Vera: Hmm, they are £1. And what about this music video? A special offer. Just £2.

Roy: No, thank you. I don't have a video player at home. I'll just take the two cassettes.

Lösungen:

1. What are they looking for? Susan: birthday present for her brother Jack; Roy: CDs
   What do they get? Susan: a computer and some old computer magazines; Roy: two cassettes
   How much do they pay? Susan: £30; Roy: £2
2. go, expensive, girls, idea, car-boot sale, Saturday, sell, toys, books, friends, will, trip
3. Individuelle Lösungen.
4. Individuelle Lösungen.
5. Individuelle Lösungen.
6. 1. If we don't get any homework today, I will go into town this afternoon. 2. If it is sunny tomorrow, we can all go swimming. 5. If I win a million in the lottery, I can buy myself my own computer. 6. If our school wins the football cup, there will be an article about us in the newspaper. 10. If I win a ticket to New York, I will take my best friend with me./Darüber hinaus individuelle Lösungen.
7. Individuelle Lösungen.

1. What are they looking for? Susan: birthday present for her brother Jack; Roy: CDs
   What do they get? Susan: a computer and some old computer magazines; Roy: two cassettes
   How much do they pay? Susan: £30; Roy: £2
2. go, expensive, girls, idea, car-boot sale, Saturday, sell, toys, books, friends, will, trip
3.–7. Individuelle Lösungen.

Mögliche Erweiterungen:
– What do you know about the London Marathon? (*mind map* oder Text)
– Write a dialogue. Ask a neighbour for a Saturday job./Ask an old lady if she needs help at home.
– What do YOU do to earn extra pocket money?
– Folie 12: *What happens if …*
– Folie 13: *What should I sell? What could I buy?*
– Copymaster 16: *Money*

1 ★ Wow, what a car-boot sale!

Listen to the dialogue and fill in the information.

	Susan	Roy
What are they looking for?		
What do they get?		
How much do they pay?		

2 ★ Wow, another car-boot sale!

Read the text and fill in what's missing.

At Gillian and Vera's school they plan to go on a class trip to France. Gillian and Vera would like to

_____ but it is very _____ . So the two _____ need

some extra money. They have a good _____ : They want to organize a _____

_____ . It will be next _____ , 6th June. They want to _____ a

lot of old things from their rooms like old _____ and _____ . Some

_____ were helpful and gave them some old things, too. If they sell enough, they

_____ earn the pocket money for their _____ to France.

| books   car-boot sale   expensive   friends   girls   go   idea   Saturday   sell   toys   trip   will |

3 ★ Sell, sell, sell!

Write down eight things in the car boot that you could buy or sell at a car-boot sale.

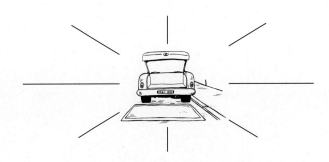

ISBN 3-425-09103-4

4 ★ The best ideas for making money

Your friend needs some extra money. What could you tell him/her? Here are some ideas.

Example: For some extra money you could …/Why don't you …?/What about …?

wash cars

repair bikes

sell things at a flea market

babysit

take a dog for a walk

sell ice-cream

help in the garden

clean windows

1. _____

2. _____

3. _____

4. _____

5. _____

6. _____

7. _____

8. _____

5 ★ The London Marathon

What do you remember about the London Marathon? Write your words in the lists.

verbs	nouns	adjectives
run	race	expensive

You can start with these words but try to find some more: ambulance, collect, important, race, pay, charity, different, expensive, wheelchair, run, …

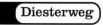

6 ★ What if ...?

Match the two parts of the sentences. You will have to find your own second half for five sentences.

1. If we don't get any homework today,

2. If it is sunny tomorrow,

3. If it begins to rain in ten minutes,

4. If I lose my pocket money,

5. If I win a million in the lottery,

6. If our school wins the football cup,

7. If I get a 6 in the next maths test,

8. If all my friends have green hair one day,

9. If no one comes to my birthday party,

10. If I win a ticket to New York,

there will be an article about us in the newspaper.

we can all go swimming.

I can buy myself my own computer.

I will go into town this afternoon.

I will take my best friend with me.

_____

_____

_____

_____

_____

7 ★ YOUR pocket money

Write a text about YOUR pocket money. These questions can help you:
- **How much do you get?**
- **How often/when do you get it?**
- **What do you buy with your pocket money?**
- **Do you save your money? What for?**

_____

_____

_____

_____

_____

_____

_____

ISBN 3-425-09103-4

Diesterweg

1 ⋆⋆ Wow, what a car-boot sale!

Listen to the dialogue and fill in the information.

	Susan	Roy
What are they looking for?		
What do they get?		
How much do they pay?		

2 ⋆⋆ Wow, another car-boot sale!

Read the text and fill in what's missing.

At Gillian and Vera's school they plan to go on a class trip to France. Gillian and Vera would like to

_____ but it is very _____ . So the two _____ need

some extra money. They have a good _____ : They want to organize a _____

_____ . It will be next _____ , 6th June. They want to _____ a

lot of old things from their rooms like old _____ and _____ . Some

_____ were helpful and gave them some old things, too. If they sell enough, they

_____ earn the pocket money for their _____ to France.

| books   car-boot sale   expensive   friends   girls   go   idea   Saturday   sell   toys   trip   will |

3 ⋆⋆ Sell, sell, sell!

Write down eight things in the car boot that you could buy or sell at a car-boot sale.

4 ⭐⭐ The best ideas for making money

Your friend needs some extra money. What could you tell him/her? Here are some ideas.

Example: For some extra money you could …/Why don't you …?/What about …?

wash cars

repair bikes

sell things at a flea market

babysit

take a dog for a walk

sell ice-cream

help in the garden

clean windows

1. _____

2. _____

3. _____

4. _____

5. _____

6. _____

7. _____

8. _____

5 ⭐⭐ The London Marathon

What do you remember about the London Marathon? Write your words in the lists.

verbs	nouns	adjectives

You can start with these words but try to find some more: ambulance, red nose, important, collect, race, pay, charity, different, expensive, wheelchair, run, …

ISBN 3-425-09103-4

6 ★ ★ What if ...?

Complete the second parts of the sentences.

1. If we don't get any homework today, _____

2. If it is sunny tomorrow, _____

3. If it begins to rain in ten minutes, _____

4. If I lose my pocket money, _____

5. If I win a million in the lottery, _____

6. If our school wins the football cup, _____

7. If I get a 6 in the next maths test, _____

8. If all my friends have green hair one day, _____

9. If I win a ticket to New York, _____

7 ★ ★ What can YOU do?

**What can YOU do to help other people? Think of institutions or people who need help
and write about your ideas. These questions can help you:**
- **Who needs help?**
- **How could you raise money?**
- **What help could you give that doesn't cost any money?**
- **How can your friends/family/... help?**

_____

_____

_____

_____

_____

_____

_____

Diesterweg

HV-Text zum Vorlesen für Lehrer/in:
"Hi, this is Lucy, Lucy Brand.
I'd like to say 'Happy birthday' to Ron. He lives in Cambridge and is 15 today.
See you tomorrow at your birthday party, Ron. I love you."

"My name is Thomas Miller. I want to say 'Hello' to my friends in Hendon.
Hi friends! – Yes, and we must win the football match on Sunday.
You know we are the champions!"

"This is Mrs Williams speaking.
Hello to all our friends. Our supermarket is 20 years old now.
We are very happy and would like to invite everyone to come and celebrate with us.
See you on Saturday between 10 am and 5 pm."

Lösungen:

1. Who are the messages for – and why? Message 1: for Ron, it's his 15th birthday; Message 2: for his friends in Hendon, important football match on Sunday; Message 3: for all their friends, their supermarket is 20 years old.
   Other information: Message 1: Lucy loves Ron, Ron lives in Cambridge, he'll have his birthday party tomorrow; Message 2: Thomas and his team are the champions; Message 3: they are very happy, would like to invite everyone to come and celebrate with them on Saturday between 10 am and 5 pm.
2. 1. dark 2. interesting 3. ugly 4. white 5. full 6. dangerous 7. strong 8. cloudy 9. hot 10. hard
3. Individuelle Lösungen.
4. a) Vera is listening to Tony Denims's show. Gillian is buying the new 'Gorillas' CD. Susan is cleaning the hamster cage. David is helping his dad in the shop. Karim is sending an e-mail to Anwar. Charlie is doing his homework.
   b) Individuelle Lösungen.
5. Mögliche Lösung: If Brock Burnet plays the role of James Bond, he will live in London and in Paris/ he will have two villas/he will have no time to cook/he will do no sports/he will make three films every year/he will earn a lot of money/he will be nervous/he will meet the woman of his dreams.
6. Mögliche Lösung: Justin Heart lives in Los Angeles, California. His birthday is on 20th March. His hobbies are cycling and swimming. His favourite food is sweet carrot halva and his favourite music is jazz. He has got one younger sister and his dream is to have his own movie company. His best subject at school was French.
7. Individuelle Lösungen.

1. Who are the messages for – and why? Message 1: for Ron, it's his 15th birthday; Message 2: for his friends in Hendon, important football match on Sunday; Message 3: for all their friends, their supermarket is 20 years old.
   Other information: Message 1: Lucy loves Ron, Ron lives in Cambridge, he'll have his birthday party tomorrow; Message 2: Thomas and his team are the champions; Message 3: they are very happy, would like to invite everyone to come and celebrate with them on Saturday between 10 am and 5 pm.
2. 1. dark 2. interesting 3. ugly 4. white 5. full 6. dangerous 7. strong 8. cloudy 9. hot 10. hard
3. Individuelle Lösungen.
4. a) Vera is listening to Tony Denims's show. Gillian is buying the new 'Gorillas' CD. Susan is cleaning the hamster cage. David is helping his dad in the shop. Karim is sending an e-mail to Anwar. Charlie is doing his homework.
   b) Individuelle Lösungen.
5. Mögliche Lösung: If Brock Burnet plays the role of James Bond, he will live in London and in Paris/ he will have two villas/he will have no time to cook/he will do no sports/he will make three films every year/he will earn a lot of money/he will be nervous/he will meet Patricia King, the woman of his dreams.
6. Mögliche Lösung: Justin Heart lives in Los Angeles, California. He was born on 20th March 1975. His hobbies are cycling and swimming. His favourite food is sweet carrot halva and his favourite music is jazz. He has got one younger sister and his dream is to have his own movie company. His best subject at school was French.
7. Individuelle Lösungen.

Mögliche Erweiterungen:
– Bildbeschreibung (L präsentiert Bild oder Gemälde über Folie oder als Kopie)
– Freies Schreiben: S erstellen Horoskope unter Verwendung des *will-future* (vgl. Copymaster 17: *YOUR horoscope*).
– Lückentext wie in PB A6.

ISBN 3-425-09103-4

1 ⭐ Radio messages

Listen to the messages and write down the information.

	Lucy	Thomas	Mrs Williams
Who are the messages for – and why?			
other information			

2 ⭐ Night and day

Write down the opposites.

1. light   – _____

2. boring   – _____

3. beautiful – _____

4. black   – _____

5. empty   – _____

6. safe   – _____

7. weak   – _____

8. sunny   – _____

9. cold   – _____

10. soft   – _____

3 ⭐ Free-time activities

Which words come to your mind when you think of 'free-time activities'?
Write down twelve words.

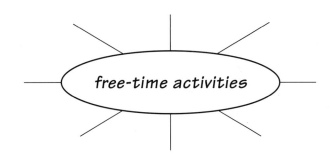

4 ★ What are they doing this afternoon?

a) What are the friends' plans for this afternoon?

Vera: listen to Tony Denims's show

Gillian: buy the new 'Gorrillas' CD

Susan: clean the hamster cage

David: help his dad in the shop

Karim: send an e-mail to Anwar

Charlie: do his homework

Vera is listening to Tony Denims's show.

b) And what are your plans for this afternoon? Write two sentences.

5 ★ How will his life change?

Brock Burnet must decide if he wants to play the role of James Bond. How will his life change if he plays the role? Write five sentences.

Home: live in London and Paris, have two villas
Free time: have no time to cook, do no sports
Job: make three films every year, earn a lot of money
His private life: be nervous, meet the woman of his dreams

If Brock Burnet plays the role of James Bond, he will

Diesterweg

6 ⭐ Justin Heart

Brock Burnet is just one of the stars of 'Sweet Valley High'. Here is some information about another star – Justin Heart. Use the information to write a text about him.

home: Los Angeles, California

best subject at school: French

dream: have his own movie company

family: one younger sister

birthday: 20th March

hobbies: cycling, swimming

favourite food: sweet carrot halva

favourite music: jazz

_____

_____

_____

_____

_____

_____

_____

_____

7 ⭐ YOUR radio message

Imagine you want to send a radio message. Write down what you want to say.

Your name: _____

Who is the message for? _____

Your message: _____

_____

_____

The music you want to have played: _____

1 ★ ★ **Radio messages**

Listen to the messages and write down the information.

	Lucy	Thomas	Mrs Williams
Who are the messages for – and why?			
other information			

2 ★ ★ **Night and day**

Write down the opposites.

1. light   – _____

2. boring   – _____

3. beautiful – _____

4. black   – _____

5. empty   – _____

6. safe   – _____

7. weak   – _____

8. sunny   – _____

9. cold   – _____

10. soft   – _____

3 ★ ★ **Free-time activities**

Which words come to your mind when you think of 'free-time activities'?
Write down 15 words.

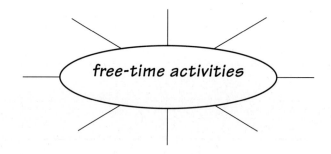

ISBN 3-425-09103-4

Diesterweg

4 ★ ★ What are they doing this afternoon?

a) What are the friends' plans for this afternoon?

Vera is listening to _____

_____

_____

_____

_____

_____

Vera: listen to Tony Denims's show

Gillian: buy the new 'Gorrillas' CD

Susan: clean the hamster cage

David: help his dad in the shop

Karim: send an e-mail to Anwar

Charlie: do his homework

b) And what are your plans for this afternoon?

_____

_____

5 ★ ★ How will his life change?

Brock Burnet must decide if he wants to play the role of James Bond. How will his life change if he plays the role? Write six sentences.

Home: London and Paris, two villas
Free time: no time to cook, no sports
Job: three films every year, a lot of money
Private life: nervous, Patricia King – the woman of his dreams

If Brock Burnet plays the role of James Bond, _____

_____

_____

_____

_____

6 ★ ★ Justin Heart

Brock Burnet is just one of the stars of 'Sweet Valley High'. Here is some information about another star – Justin Heart. Use the information to write a text about him.

Los Angeles, California

best subject at school: French

dream: have movie company

younger sister

20th March 1975

hobbies: cycling, swimming

favourite food: sweet carrot halva

favourite music: jazz

_____

_____

_____

_____

_____

_____

_____

_____

7 ★ ★ YOUR radio message

Imagine you want to send a radio message. Write down what you want to say.

Your name: _____

Who is the message for? _____

Your message: _____

_____

_____

The music you want to have played: _____

ISBN 3-425-09103-4

Diesterweg

HV-Text zum Vorlesen für Lehrer/in:

Karim: "Hello, is that you, David?"

David: "Yes, it's me."

Karim: "This is Karim. I must tell you something interesting. When I passed the youth club this afternoon, I saw a poster of the YHA."

David: "Of what?"

Karim: "Of the Youth Hostel Association. They offer a weekend at the Dover Youth Hostel with exciting activities."

David: "Exciting activities? Tell me more."

Karim: "Well you can go walking and bird-watching and you can visit Dover Castle. I would like to go there. What about you?"

David: "That sounds great! And it's just a weekend trip?"

Karim: "Yes, from Friday afternoon until Sunday afternoon."

David: "How much is it?"

Karim: "It costs £30."

David: "But that's not very much! We can help in my father's supermarket so we can earn the money. Then we could go to Dover next month. What do you think?"

Karim: "That's a good idea. You're right. We needn't ask our parents for the money. We can take a Saturday job."

David: "And perhaps we'll meet some nice girls there. All right then, I'll come with you."

Karim: "That's great. I'll ring the youth hostel and book the weekend. See you tomorrow."

David: "Bye, Karim."

Lösungen:

1. 1. Karim calls David. 2. at the youth club. 3. Youth Hostel Association. 4. walking. 5. Friday afternoon until Sunday afternoon. 6. £30.
2. 1. Gillian, Vera and Susan are going on a school trip to Scotland. 2. The girls are excited and they have lots of things to do. 3. Susan needs to check her camera batteries. 4. Gillian needs to get a new film for her camera. 5. Miss Anderson said they should take a raincoat. 6. They have to take a good pair of shoes for walking. 7. Gillian is going to take her Discman. 8. Susan hasn't decided yet which CDs to take.
3. 1. Between 6.30 am and 9 am. 2. You can eat cornflakes, toast, or the traditional English breakfast. 3. It's very cheap. 4. You must order it the day before. 5. Yes, there's a small kitchen which you can use.
4. 1. wrong 2. right 3. right 4. wrong 5. right 6. wrong 7. wrong
5. yours, Mine, Hers, hers, his, mine, his, ours, theirs
6. Individuelle Lösungen.

1. 1. at the youth club. 2. Youth Hostel Association. 3. bird-watching. 4. Friday afternoon until Sunday afternoon. 5. £30. 6. Help in David's dad's supermarket.
2. 1. Gillian, Vera and Susan are going on a school trip to Scotland. 2. None of them have been to Scotland before. 3. The girls are making lists of what to take with them. 4. Susan needs to check her camera batteries. 5. Gillian has to get a new film for her camera. 6. Miss Anderson said they should take a raincoat with them. 7. They have to take a good pair of shoes for walking. 8. Susan has not decided yet which CDs to take.
3. 1. Between 6.30 am and 9 am. 2. You can eat cornflakes, toast, or the traditional English breakfast. 3. It's very cheap. 4. You must order it the day before. 5. Yes, there's a small kitchen which you can use.
4. 1. wrong 2. right 3. right 4. wrong 5. right 6. wrong 7. wrong
5. yours, Mine, Hers, hers, his, mine, his, ours, theirs
6. Individuelle Lösungen.

Mögliche Erweiterungen:
- TB PP als Lückentext (Überprüfung landeskundlichen Wissens)
- What do you know about English as a world language?
- Tell the story of Scotland's thistle. (vgl. TB B4)
- Folie 16: *Our next school trip*
- Which *Theme* in **Bayswater 3** did you like best? Say why.

1 ⭐ A telephone conversation

Listen to the telephone conversation and tick (✔) the right answers.

1. Who calls who?
   - ☐ David calls Karim.
   - ☐ Karim calls David.
   - ☐ Karim calls Charlie.

2. Karim saw the poster …
   - ☐ at school.
   - ☐ in Camden High Street.
   - ☐ at the youth club.

3. YHA stands for …
   - ☐ Young Holiday Association.
   - ☐ Youth Hostel Association.
   - ☐ Your Hotel Association.

4. They can go …
   - ☐ surfing.
   - ☐ walking.
   - ☐ climbing.

5. They will go from …
   - ☐ Friday afternoon until Sunday afternoon.
   - ☐ Friday morning until Saturday afternoon.
   - ☐ Saturday morning until Monday morning.

6. It costs …
   - ☐ £40.
   - ☐ £30.
   - ☐ £45.

2 ⭐ A school trip to Scotland

Find the correct order for these jumbled sentences and write them down.

1. Gillian • are • school trip • to • Vera • going • Susan • and • a • Scotland • on

_____

2. The • excited • to • have • are • girls • do • things • lots • and • of • they

_____

3. Susan • needs • her • batteries • camera • to • check

_____

4. Gillian • her • a • camera • needs • for • to • new • get • film

_____

5. Miss • they • raincoat • said • Anderson • should • a • take

_____

6. They • pair • take • have • shoes • walking • good • a • to • of • for

_____

7. Gillian • going • her • to • Discman • is • take

_____

8. Susan • which • take • to • decided • yet • hasn't • CDs

_____

ISBN 3-425-09103-4

Diesterweg

3 ★ Meals at the youth hostel

Read and answer the questions:

1. When can you eat breakfast?

_____

2. What can you eat for breakfast?

_____

_____

3. Why is a packed lunch a good idea?

_____

4. What must you do if you want a packed lunch?

_____

5. Can you cook your own meals?

_____

_____

> All meals are freshly cooked at the Youth Hostel and we try to give you a good choice of meals including a vegetarian option every day. Breakfast is between 6.30 am and 9 am and you can choose between different things like cornflakes and toast and the traditional English breakfast. For people who have plans for the day and get up early, a packed breakfast is perhaps the best idea. You can also have a very cheap packed lunch to take with you. All you have to do is order packed breakfasts and lunches the day before. In the evening there is a delicious three-course meal. For those who want to cook their own meals, the Youth Hostel also has a small kitchen which you can use.

4 ★ My holidays

Read the letter and tick (✔) the correct boxes.

> Hi Brenda,
>
> I must tell you about my holidays. I went sailing with my family in Greece. First my parents spent a week at the sailing club. That was a great time for me. The weather was hot and I could swim, lie on the beach or windsurf. I met a lot of nice boys and girls. We had fun together and went to many parties. Then the second week was sailing on a boat. It was boring! The only thing you can do is read or eat. I would never like to stay on a boat again for more than a day. Life in the little village was much nicer.
>
> Love, Lisa

1. Lisa's family went to South America.	☐ right	☐ wrong
2. The weather was hot.	☐ right	☐ wrong
3. She enjoyed swimming and windsurfing.	☐ right	☐ wrong
4. There weren't any young people around at the sailing club.	☐ right	☐ wrong
5. The young people went to many parties.	☐ right	☐ wrong
6. Sailing for a week was fun.	☐ right	☐ wrong
7. She would like to learn sailing next summer.	☐ right	☐ wrong

5 ⭐ Whose is it?

Complete the girls' conversation.

theirs　　mine　　yours　　hers　　his　　ours

Gillian: Is this T-shirt _____ , Susan?

Susan: No, it isn't. _____ is the yellow one over there. I think it's Vera's, isn't it?

Gillian: No, it isn't. _____ has got her name on it. But this one hasn't got a name on it.

Susan: Let's ask Miss Anderson later. – Listen, where is Vera? I haven't seen her for a while.

Gillian: I don't know. Is her jacket here? Isn't that blue one _____ ?

Susan: No, it isn't. That's Karim's jacket.

Gillian: What? Karim's? What's _____ doing in our room?

Susan: Well, we swapped jackets yesterday. He's got _____ and I've got _____ .

Gillian: Hey, that sounds like a great idea. Did you see those two cute German boys who came in

while we were checking in yesterday? How about swapping jackets with them? They could wear

_____ and we could wear _____ .

Susan: Gillian! But hmm, I like your idea!

6 ⭐ Scotland

Which words come to your mind when you think of Scotland? Write down 15 words.
(Think of geography, history, sights, …)

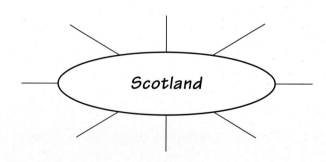

ISBN 3-425-09103-4

1 ★ ★ A telephone conversation

Listen to Karim and David on the phone and tick (✔) the right answers.

1. Karim saw the poster …
   - ☐ at school.
   - ☐ in Camden High Street.
   - ☐ at the youth club.

2. YHA stands for …
   - ☐ Young Holiday Association.
   - ☐ Youth Hostel Association.
   - ☐ Your Hotel Association.

3. They can go …
   - ☐ surfing.
   - ☐ bird-watching.
   - ☐ climbing.

4. They will go from …
   - ☐ Friday afternoon until Sunday afternoon.
   - ☐ Friday afternoon until Saturday afternoon.
   - ☐ Friday morning until Sunday afternoon.

5. It costs …
   - ☐ £40.
   - ☐ £30.
   - ☐ £45.

6. How will they earn the money for the trip?
   - ☐ Help in the garden.
   - ☐ Do a paper round.
   - ☐ Help in David's dad's supermarket.

2 ★ ★ A school trip to Scotland

Find the correct order for these jumbled sentences and write them down.

1. are • school trip • to • Vera • going • Susan • and • a • Scotland • Gillian • on

_____

2. Scotland • been • of • none • them • to • before • have

_____

3. what • them • making • to • with • of • girls • lists • are • the • take

_____

4. needs • her • batteries • Susan • camera • to • check

_____

5. her • a • camera • has • Gillian • for • to • new • get • film

_____

6. they • raincoat • said • Anderson • them • should • a • with • take • Miss

_____

7. pair • take • have • shoes • walking • good • they • a • to • of • for

_____

8. has • which • take • to • decided • Susan • yet • not • CDs

_____

3 ★★ Meals at the youth hostel

Read and answer the questions:

1. When can you eat breakfast?

_____

2. What can you eat for breakfast?

_____

_____

3. Why is a packed lunch a good idea?

_____

4. What must you do if you want a packed lunch?

_____

5. Can you cook your own meals?

_____

_____

> All meals are freshly cooked at the Youth Hostel and we try to give you a good choice of meals including a vegetarian option every day. Breakfast is between 6.30 am and 9 am and you can choose between different things like cornflakes and toast and the traditional English breakfast. For people who have plans for the day and get up early, a packed breakfast is perhaps the best idea. You can also have a very cheap packed lunch to take with you. All you have to do is order packed breakfasts and lunches the day before. In the evening there is a delicious three-course meal. For those who want to cook their own meals, the Youth Hostel also has a small kitchen which you can use.

4 ★★ My holidays

Read the letter and tick (✔) the correct boxes.

> Hi Brenda,
>
> I must tell you about my holidays. I went sailing with my family in Greece. First my parents spent a week at the sailing club. That was a great time for me. The weather was hot and I could swim, lie on the beach or windsurf. I met a lot of nice boys and girls. We had fun together and went to many parties. Then the second week was sailing on a boat. It was boring! The only thing you can do is read or eat. I would never like to stay on a boat again for more than a day. Life in the little village was much nicer.
>
> Love, Lisa

		right		wrong
1.	Lisa's family went to South America.	☐		☐
2.	The weather was hot.	☐		☐
3.	She enjoyed swimming and windsurfing.	☐		☐
4.	There weren't any young people around at the sailing club.	☐		☐
5.	The young people went to many parties.	☐		☐
6.	Sailing for a week was fun.	☐		☐
7.	She would like to learn sailing next summer.	☐		☐

ISBN 3-425-09103-4

Diesterweg

5 ⭐ ⭐ Yours or mine?

Complete the girls' conversation with the correct possessive pronouns.

Gillian: Is this T-shirt _____ , Susan?

Susan: No, it isn't. _____ is the yellow one over there. I think it's Vera's, isn't it?

Gillian: No, it isn't. _____ has got her name on it. But this one hasn't got a name on it.

Susan: Let's ask Miss Anderson later. – Listen, where is Vera? I haven't seen her for a while.

Gillian: I don't know. Is her jacket here? Isn't that blue one _____ ?

Susan: No, it isn't. That's Karim's jacket.

Gillian: What? Karim's? What's _____ doing in our room?

Susan: Well, we swapped jackets yesterday. He's got _____ and I've got _____ .

Gillian: Hey, that sounds like a great idea. Did you see those two cute German boys who came in

while we were checking in yesterday? How about swapping jackets with them? They could wear

_____ and we could wear _____ .

Susan: Gillian! But hmm, I like your idea!

6 ⭐ ⭐ Scotland

What do you know about Scotland? (Think of geography, history, sights, …)

_____

_____

_____

_____

_____

_____

_____